The Birth and Death of Companies

The Birth and Death of Companies

An Historical Perspective

Edited by
Philippe Jobert and Michael Moss

The Parthenon Publishing Group
International Publishers in Science, Technology & Education

Casterton Hall, Carnforth,
Lancs, LA6 2LA, UK

120 Mill Road, Park Ridge,
New Jersey, USA

Published in the UK and Europe by
The Parthenon Publishing Group Limited.
Casterton Hall, Carnforth,
Lancs, LA6 2LA

Published in the USA by
The Parthenon Publishing Group Inc.
120 Mill Road,
Park Ridge,
New Jersey 07656, USA

Copyright © 1990 Philippe Jobert, Michael Moss et al

No part of this publication may be reproduced, stored in a retrieval system or transmitted in any form or by any means, electronic, mechanical, photocopying, recording or otherwise, without prior permission from the publishers.

ISBN 1-85070-332-9

Typesetting by MG Photoset Ltd, Glasgow.

Printed and bound in Great Britain
at The Camelot Press, Trowbridge, Wiltshire.

Contents

	List of contributors .... page	v
	Preface	vii
1	Prologue	1
	Philippe Jobert and Michael Moss	
	Part 1	
	Global studies and methods	17
2	Firm creations and failures in nineteenth century France: regional differences	19
	Jean-Claude Chevailler	
3	The 1856 Companies Act and the birth and death of firms	33
	James Foreman-Peck	
4	The Land Registry: a source of demography for business – The Example of Basse-Normandie in the 19th century	47
	Alain Leménorel	
5	The managerial labour market in fast growth small firms	67
	David J Storey	

	Part 2	
	Local Studies	87
6	Parisian industries and national capitalism in the first half of the nineteenth century (1830-1850)	89
	André Straus and Patrick Verley	
7	Companies and manufacturers of the first period of industrialisation in Marseilles, 1810-1860	105
	Michel Lescure	
8	A demography of firms in Toulouse – a case study in delayed industrialisation – 1868-1940	121
	Jean-Pierre Allinne	
9	Industrialisation and financial networks: regional disparities in nineteenth century France	137
	Jean-Luc Mayaud	
10	Birth, growth and death of firms in a proto-industrial economy – the experience of the Ahmedabad textile industry, 1858-1929	157
	Dwijendra Tripathi	
	Part 3	
	Sectors	179
11	The life-cycle of firms in late nineteenth century Britain	181
	Stana Nenadic	
12	Building by numbers: the lifecycle of Scottish building firms, 1793-1913	197
	James Carroll, Nicholas J Morgan, Michael S Moss	
13	Formation and Transformation of Sociétés: The case of the French public works industry 1914-1939	215
	Dominique Barjot	
14	Bouchayer-Viallet of Grenoble: the rise and fall of a French metal working firm, 1870-1972	227
	Robert J Smith	

List of Contributors

Jean-Peirre Allinne, Université Paul-Sabatier, Toulouse, France.

Dominique Barjot, Université de Caen, France.

James Carroll, University Archives, Glasgow, Scotland.

Jean-Claude Chevailler, Université de Franche-Comté, Besançon, France.

James Foreman-Peck, University of Hull, England.

Philippe Jobert, Université de Bourgogne, Dijon, France.

Alain Leménorel, Université de Rouen, France.

Michel Lescure, Université de Paris X, Paris, France.

Jean-Luc Mayaud, Université de Paris-Nord, Villetaneuse, France.

Nicholas J Morgan, United Distillers, Edinburgh and University of Glasgow, Scotland.

Michael Moss, University of Glasgow, Scotland.

Stana Nenadic, University of Edinburgh, Scotland.

David Storey, University of Warwick, England.

Robert Smith, State University of New York at Brockport, New York, USA.

André Straus, Centre national de la recherche scientifique, Paris, France.

Dwijendra Tripathi, Indian Institute of Management, Vastrapur, Ahmedabad.

Patrick Verley, UFR d'histoire, Université de Paris I, Paris, France.

Preface

The Executive Committee of the International Economic History Association has willingly agreed to enter in the programme of its 10th *Congrès*, which is to be held at Leuven in Belgium in August 1990, a theme C 34 entitled *Life Cycle of Firms in the 19th and 20th Centuries*. We thank them sincerely, nevertheless adding an expression of regret that the most faithful rendering of the title of the contents of the project (in French *La démographie des entreprises*) has been set aside because of its bizarre connotation to English and American ears, it has not, therefore, been retained as the title of this present book.

However that may be, this book brings together papers delivered on the subject to a colloquium which was organized in Glasgow in September 1989, thanks to the warm hospitality of Michael Moss, Archivist of the University, as well as the recently established Centre for Business History in Scotland and its director Professor Anthony Slaven, and with participation of Dr David Jeremy of Manchester Polytechnic. This anticipation of the work which will be revealed at Leuven proved doubly useful. On the one hand the time allowed of one short morning for this theme C 34 at the *Congrès*, will allow neither an extensive presentation of each contribution or a thorough discussion, nor the possibility of any synthesis or of drawing any partial conclusions: our pre-session in Scotland has gone some way to remedying these difficulties. On the other hand, and most importantly, it seemed essential to consolidate the outline of the demography of enterprise in the nineteenth and twentieth centuries by investigating and collating in a preliminary stage, the relative knowledge of a limited number of national case studies from France, Great Britain and India.

This volume comprises all the contributions made to the meeting in Glasgow, with a prologue written by ourselves. *Malheurerusement,* to the *chagrin* of the French contributors, it proved impossible to find a publisher in Britain who was prepared to produce a multi-lingual volume. The French papers have, accordingly, been translated with the exception of the footnotes. We would like to thank Rita Hemphill for so cheerfully unscrabbling our scrappy notes in English and French and Bill McGuigan for efficiently typesetting the volume.

Philippe Jobert
Université de Bourgogne

Michael Moss
University of Glasgow

1
Prologue

1. Towards a demography of enterprises

The subject is certainly not new. On the French side, for example, as early as 1980, Francois Caron, in opening an important gathering devoted to the study of business and businessmen during the last two centuries, posed the question: *'une démographie des entreprises est-elle possible?'* In Britain, in the same year, Peter Payne published his study of the population of early Scottish limited liability companies established between 1856 and 1895, building on the seminal work of H A Shannon undertaken nearly fifty years before. Similar research was being undertaken in other countries with equivalent publications. The appeal made by François Caron and the work of Peter Payne suggested simultaneously several valid avenues of approach, probably applicable to the life-cycle of enterprise.[1]

As far as the *birth* of companies is concerned, historical analysis is constrained by the enormous difficulty of tracing the establishment of purely individual enterprises because of the lack of satisfactory sources with the possible exception of the *cadastre* (at least for industrial companies) in France and Post Office directories in the United Kingdom. In the majority of studies, births are taken to mean the establishment of enterprises, which result from the adoption of the different legal forms of industrial and commercial *sociétés* or companies – admittedly a very small fraction of all births. In French births, there is a close and direct statistical correlation between the annual totals of the creation of *sociétés* and the annual amount of investments. The closeness of these two sets of data tends to demonstrate the major role (if not the exact weight) of new *sociétés* in capital formation and in the finance of business in France.[2] Although hampered by similar difficulties of interpretation, the research in the United Kingdom tends to support this conclusion.

The importance of such an observation at once encourages explanation of the global totals, particularly to discover in what degree the great swings in the formation of *sociétés*/companies follows the general movement of the economy, or has on the contrary pursued a different path. Beyond the examination of the principal statistical series available for this first approach, the analysis of creations of *sociétés*/companies makes it possible also to address the methods used to finance enterprises during the Nineteenth and Twentieth centuries. All *sociétés*/companies are born, by definition, to gather funds, an objective so abstract that it yields little of significance to the eyes of an historian. It is sensible then to particularize the economic reasons which underline the data, the composition, legal type and objectives of each creation, and then to identify national or local trends over a coherent period. One corollary or complementary approach is the study of the partners themselves as investors and as directors of businesses pursued particularly in the United Kingdom. The ambition has been eventually to reconstruct the tangled web from which were recruited the personalities, both the bold and the reluctant, who joined together, at least in a material sense to form *sociétés*/companies. Such investigation also sheds light on the informal financial networks which provided the capital for *sociétés* at birth.[3]

As far as the study of *disparitions*/disappearances of enterprises is concerned, their history has largely been approached in both France and Britain by an analysis of *faillites* or bankruptcy proceedings.[4] The use of these obvious deaths poses various and serious difficulties for the historian from the outset. In the first place, there is a misleading symmetry between the birth of enterprises that have usually been limited to *sociétés* in France and companies in Great Britain and the decease which included (or rather has the potential to include) the whole population of enterprises, without distinguishing between individual enterprises and *sociétés* – at least in France.

Despite this methodological impediment, the use of *faillites* and bankruptcy proceedings presents evident advantages to the historian. From this source it is possible to examine: the fragility of investment after peaks in *faillites* or bankruptcies, their direct relationship with variations in prices, their behaviour in times of crisis. These investigations in turn allow preliminary answers to be formulated to the question as to how representative are *faillites* or bankruptcies as a cause of the death of firms. And on this basis strengthens the case for an examination devoted to *faillites* and bankruptcies, considered individually or in carefully selected groups, which should provide a detailed picture of the structure and function of enterprise, as through distorting spectacles.

This outline of the definition, that we have tentatively proposed, for the birth and death of firms provides the basis for extending the research and establishing more securely the general outlines of the methodology to be pursued. How is it possible to make comparisons in this area between historical researches undertaken in different countries? The nature of the surviving sources, which have been explained by the authors of the contributions to this volume, has evidently conditioned the homogeneity of the methods they have followed and consequently impedes reconciliation between the findings of each contribution even from the same country. What conditions are imposed and what weight should be accorded to the interpretation of such data? What are, in answer to this last question, the essential characteristics of the institutions which laid the foundations of the demography of enterprise in the nineteenth and twentieth centuries? In answer to this question, a brief account of the legal system of the two principal states represented at Glasgow and at Leuven, France and Great Britain, seems essential.

2. In France

There exist in France the legal records of the formalities imposed on enterprises marking the important stages in their existence from birth until death, which constitute the historian's primary source. These formalities or rules follow the legislative arrangements that have been elaborated since the Napoleonic period. In this way the *Code de Commerce* of 1808 – still in force, which has for long remained the central legislation, has been either amended profoundly or abandoned completely, in the case of *faillites* after 1838 and for *sociétés*, notably in 1867, and especially in 1925. Despite the English and then the German influence on the two last reforms, French law has preserved from the time of the Code a commercial statute especially designed to regulate the professional relations between commerce and industry and, as a result, other activities have been excluded in principle.[5] The persistence and vitality of this particular detail until our day has been traditionally explained by the necessity of facilitating the quick and accurate reporting of business profits, and of preventing the infringements of the rights of private individuals that the much respected *Civil Code* has provided for since 1804. In any case, and this is important for our purpose, merchants (and industrialists) have constantly and tenaciously expressed the wish of maintaining the *tribunaux de commerce* (commercial courts, around 200 in 1815) composed of judges elected from amongst them, expert in the courts of original jurisdiction in commercial litigation. These *tribunaux* played a considerable role in the nineteenth and twentieth centuries in shaping the law relating to the various forms of *sociétés* and bankruptcy proceedings that we will successively refer to.

The Sociétés. As in most other countries, the French *sociétés* must comply, at least since the introduction of the *Code de Commerce*, with rules of publicity which make known to third parties and interested partners forecasts of profits, how they are to be divided amongst the partners, and precisely the respective rights of the registered creditors (or individuals) in the capital of the *société* and eventually on the personal property of the partners. Completion of the required publicity provides the 'mark' of 'moral personality', which gives a *société* its own separate existence and legal autonomy which in time has a number of concrete advantages. Reciprocally, the only *société* which can without fraud remain 'secret', is deprived of moral personality (C.Com art.48-50) and therefore totally escapes the historian's attention. For all the others, which must publish details of their creation, there has traditionally been a distinction between five different types of *sociétés* (which appeared either in the *Code* or after) divided into three categories.[6]

A first category designated the *sociétés* called *'de personnes'* or again *'par intérêt'*, in which each *associé* (partner) enters and pledges himself in consideration of the personal value and property of his co-partners, that is to say, by bonds of mutual confidence. This *intuitus personae* entails important consequences for the individuals concerned because the personal property of each partner supports the final 'weight' of the 'moral personality' of the *société* itself. Thus in the relations between partners, the capital shares or 'intérêts' were in principle not transferable except by the unanimous agreement of the partners. And *vis-à-vis* third parties, the *société* conducted its activities under a *'raison sociale'* (business name) formed from the name(s) of the partner who was responsible for managing the enterprise or from amongst them all. But these *sociétés par intérêt*, which were the oldest and longest-lived form of *société*, were in reality divided into two different kinds (C.Com. art.20-28):

– *la société en nom collectif* (SNC) – general partnership, already known in the

Middle Ages, remained predominant for a long time by number if not by size: 65 per cent of French *sociétés* established in 1903 still adopted this formula notwithstanding the grave dangers it posed for the partners. In effect, all the partners were considered as *commerçants* (merchants) in the legal sense, with the inevitable consequence that the *faillite* (bankruptcy) of a *société* resulted in the personal bankruptcy of each of them, all were personally responsible, jointly and indefinitely for all the debts of the *société*. But this was the price of locating and maintaining credit.

– *la société en commandite simple* (SCS) – simple limited partnerships is distinguished from the SNC by the co-existence of two groups of partners. The *commandités* (active partners), who generally managed the *société* and who alone appear in the business name, being also *commerçants* with unlimited liability in an analogous position to members of an SNC. By comparison, the *commanditaires* (sleeping partners) uniquely invested cash or goods, but were not allowed to become involved in the direction of business. Their personal property was legally protected: not being *commerçants* they were only responsible for the debts of the *société* to the limit of their investment. These *sociétés* were supposed to be convenient for enterprises of middle size, controlled by professional men who devoted their technical or financial skill to the business, but were compelled to have recourse to outside capital, discreet and without excessive risk. This type of *société* enjoyed a relative yet constant popularity throughout the nineteenth century; when it oscillated at around 15 per cent of creations of *sociétés* in France each year.

The second category of *société* according to the classic doctrine covers the *sociétés* called '*de capitaux*' or '*par actions*', whose essential feature is the division of capital into *actions* (shares), that is to say, in shares of legally stated and equal nominal amounts which represent the right of the partner and does away with or attenuates considerably *intuitus personae*. These *sociétés* are divided in their turn into two types of which the respective importance has been completely reversed since the *Code de Commerce*.[7]

– *la société en commandite par actions* (SCA) – joint stock limited partnership was a novel hybrid in 1808, seeing that it also allowed for the co-existence of two groups of partners. On the one side were *commandites* active partners to whom the rules of *commandite simple* applied without alteration. For the *commanditaires* – sleeping partners by contrast, not only were their responsibilities limited by the amount of their investment, but (thanks to the existence of *actions*) their shares were freely negotiable, and the *société* was not obliged to be dissolved following the decease or bankruptcy of one of them. This institution occupied the middle ground between a *société de personnes*, inspired by the worth as much as by the credit of the managers, and a *société de capitaux*, capable of the difficult task of raising funds of sufficient size. The founders received theoretically a double guarantee, the joint responsibility of the managers and capital *en actions*, which provided the legal justification for forming a *commandite par actions* with complete freedom. But this facility caused several *commandites*, which were purely speculative or even fraudulent in character, to catch cold and collapse with great damage to investors. These scandals compelled Napoleon III to introduce in 1856 a legal requirement seeking to assure investors of the seriousness and honesty of enterprise. This dealt a fatal blow to the progress of the SCA, which represented around 10 per cent of creations in 1850, falling rapidly thereafter to below 1 per cent.

– *la société anonyme* (SA) – limited company, the second type of the *société par actions*, pursued an opposite numerical path: with a minute percentage of the creations of *sociétés* until after the great liberalising law of 1867. They reached a peak of more than 26 per cent in 1925, the year when the SARL was introduced into French law, which quickly became a victorious rival.

The success of the SA rests principally on the advantages of a merger of internal capital with outside capital to the exclusion of all *intuitus personae*. The *associés* (partners) were all holders of negotiable shares and only incurred liability to the amount of shares they held. At their general meetings they elected the *administrateurs* (directors) of the *société* who then became their temporary and removable trustees, holding office only on the terms of the mandate given at the meeting. Attracted by this ability to control (or so it seemed) the management, savers and investors desirous of contributing to a massive raising of capital have therefore chosen the *société anonyme*. Besides, the absence of *associés* personally liable and trading under their own business name, which explains the qualification 'anonyme', was an important motive for the choice of this form for the creation and operation of large enterprises. In the face of a considerable capital commitment, the guarantees provided by the fortune of even the most imposing directors would have proved to be perfectly illusory. The difficult problem always remained of instilling in the minds of *associés* the seriousness of the legal power of such guarantees.

The third and last category of *société* – *la société à responsabilité limitée* (SARL) was unknown under the *Code de commerce* and derives from a reform put into effect in 1925 on the German model. Its popularity was already striking even by 1927, nearly 60 per cent of creations of *sociétés* adopted this novel form. Its brilliant trump card was to include little enterprises which could now be run according to the wishes of merchants and industrialists themselves rather than outside shareholders. As in a *société par interêt* the minimum number of partners was fixed at only two and capital was divided into shares that were difficult to transfer. As in a *société de capitaux* the directors were provided with permanent positions and with extensive powers to conduct the *société's* economic activities without incurring any personal liability.

The convenient distinction used till now for describing the central features of the various types of *sociétés* in existence in France in the nineteenth and twentieth centuries does not correspond precisely to the general directions for publicity essential for giving birth to these *sociétés*, or for subsequently changing clauses likely to interest third parties. The SA was subject to a separate regime until consolidating legislation in 1867.

Before that date, the two types of *sociétés de personnes*, but also the *commandite par actions*, were free to choose at formation the legal procedure which served to support the publicity: *acte sous seing privé* (simple contract), or *acte authentique* (certified act) drafted by a notary, compulsory in certain limited cases such as those where premises or patents for inventions formed part of the capital. The publicity itself was based on a simple *extrait* (extract) of the *acte de société* and had to take the form of a triple publication within fourteen days of the *acte constitutif:* 1) transcription from the register of the *tribunal de commerce* providing the registered address of the *société* and of the names of all the tribunals in whose jurisdiction the *société* possessed branches: 2) a bill posted for three months in the audience room of the tribunals: 3) insertion of a notice in the one or more newspapers authorised to carry legal announcements in the same jurisdictions.

During the same period, the absence of responsible *associés* (partners) as has been explained for *société anonyme*, necessitated authorisation from the government provided by a rigorous inquiry which verified in particular the reality of the registered capital as well as the degree of supervision granted to the shareholders. The meeting of these conditions was confirmed by further publicity in an *acte constitutif*, which had to be drawn up in the *authentique* form, deposit of the entire document and note of an extract, and insertion of notices in various official newspapers or gazettes like the *Bulletin des Lois* and the *Moniteur*. In fact, this procedure lasted between twelve and eighteen months which tended to act as a deterrent to the formation of *société anonyme* in preference to *commandite par actions*.[8]

The well-known law of 1867, introduced under English influence and which remained in force for exactly a century, effected a twin reform. In the first place it freed SAs from all previous authorisation, substituting for it a liberal regulation which was intended to prevent frauds and to preserve the rights of shareholders in regard to the appointment of the managing director and the board of directors. In second place the law of 1867 consolidated the publicity measures which from then on had to be made within one month of

a *société* being validly constituted. These innovations, which concerned the formation of *sociétés* but also subsequent amendments to the statutes, was as follows:
 – abolition of bill posting
 – deposit of the *acte* in its entirety, private or public, and for *SA*s of annexes such as the list of subscribers. The deposit was from now effected not only through the *tribunaux de commerce* but also through the justices of the peace courts to improve their dissemination. It should be pointed out that the clerks of these two *tribunaux* had a purely passive role, to receive the deposit of the documents required by the law and not to appraise their legal validity
 – extension to the *SA*s of the rules previously applicable to other *sociétés* relating to the insertion of legal notices in the newspapers. The list of necessary references was simply extended: clauses allowing a *société* to be individualised, limiting financial guarantees provided to creditors, spelling out any other conditions and setting its duration.

The method of disseminating the 'publicity' of the relative *actes* throughout the commercial world was improved belatedly by the introduction of the register of commerce (law of 1919 amended in 1935). Its modest objective was not to replace the legal publication which remained fragmented, but uniquely to centralise the information to facilitate more thorough research in the future. Acting as a sort of administrative repository for the scrupulous use of historians, it refers to the registration of all French *sociétés* collecting information constantly despite the great increase in the population. In the same manner, information about the dissolution (voluntary liquidation) of a *société*, and the disappearance of an enterprise following a bankruptcy, was also included in the register.[9]

Les faillites (bankruptcies) – The *faillite* was and still is in France a procedure uniquely applicable to merchants and to industrialists who are unable to pay their debts as they fall due. The *tribunaux de commerce* are alone competent to determine the active and passive bankrupt and to share out dividend instalments amongst the creditors. The details collected under the *commercial law* in this matter are evidently vital for economic historians, since the definition of *faillites* determines in reality the field of economic activity in difficulty, without any possible confusion with the insolvency of private individuals or those engaged in agriculture who were dealt with under the *Code Civil*. But to succeed in using *faillites* to analyse the death of firms, it is important to be aware of certain constant features to be found in a pattern of changing legislation. These always relate to the fraught relationship between the opposing interests, on the one side the bankrupts protesting at the assassination of their firm and on the other of the creditors complaining at loss of their interest amounting almost to robbery.[10]

Since the introduction of the *Code de Commerce*, a *faillite* could only be triggered by the 'cessation of payments' which disclosed a defalcation in funds and presumed the insolvency of the *commerçant* without it having to be formally substantiated. This particularly rigorous stipulation has been traditionally explained by practical considerations relating to the multiple pledges and acceptances of the *commerçants*. Confidence in the credit world neither tolerates partial payments nor delayed payments and was maintained by the threat or the use of the severe punishments available in this area. Where the cessation of payments was made worse by serious mistakes or by fraud, it qualified as a 'banqueroute', a penal offence dealt with by the *tribunaux criminels*.[11]

The procedure could be initiated by the debtor himself, by the creditors, or by the *tribunal de commerce*, but in all cases the opening of the *faillite* must be declared by a judgement which verifies the cessation of payments and dates the death of the firm. The methods of initiating and opening a *faillite* were common to individual firms undertaken by the patrimony of the entrepreneur and to *sociétés*, embodying the notion of the firm as an autonomous legal entity. The subsequent development of the procedure was adapted to both these two situations. This understanding is perpetuated moreover in the statistics of the Ministry of Justice, which enumerates openings of *faillites* without distinguishing the legal status of the failed firms.

The application of the *Code* has constantly encountered one important obstacle, that is of the numerous failed firms which sought to avoid so long, so heavy and so costly a procedure. How many amicable arrangements have been made between the hard-pressed debtor and some wily creditor at the expense of the others? How many *sociétés* have been dissolved in haste before the stipulated term? Two lenient laws (1838 and 1889) sought in particular to encourage *commerçants* to prefer judicial intervention. Clearly the increase in judgements opening *faillites* during the few years following each of these laws has no direct bearing on the development of the economy as a whole. Inversely, measures of clemency have been taken in order to mitigate the effects of political or military troubles on merchants and industrialists as in 1848, in 1870-72, and during the two world wars. As a consequence the ascending graph of opening of *faillites* is slowed down or interrupted.[12]

The judgement, which opened *faillites* and came into immediate effect in all cases, was subject to special publicity comparable slightly to that for the formation of *sociétés* before 1867 – bill posting and insertion of notices in newspapers (C.Com art.442), to which was added in 1919 mention in the register of commerce and in 1926 insertion of a notice in the *Journal officiel*.

This cumulative publicity furnishes a point of departure for research, but the archives left in the courts by the progress of the procedure until its conclusion contains a rich treasure store for the historian.

3. The United Kingdom

In the United Kingdom there are far fewer generally used corporate forms than in France.[13] As in that country the largest number of enterprises are conducted by sole traders. The only record of their creation is to be found in sources like Post Office directories, trade directories, and local rating records which provide similar information to the *cadastre* in France. All these sources are difficult to interpret. In some cases an entry in a directory could only be secured by payment, and the quality of Post Office directories, used for the delivery of mail, varies from place to place and from year to year. However, as in France, the names of sole traders and descriptions of their business activities are to be found in bankruptcy records (see below).

Partnerships

Where one or more people were involved in forming a business, a contract of co-partnery was often drawn up by a lawyer or a member of the firm. Unlike France there has never been any legal requirement in the United Kingdom for the publication or deposit of such documents with the courts. In England copies of contracts can occasionally be found amongst the voluminous records lodged with the Court of Chancery in London, similarly in Scotland (where the legal system was different) contracts were sometimes enrolled in the Register of Deeds maintained in the Register House. Formal notification of changes in partnerships were published in the official gazette, *London Gazette, Edinburgh Gazette,* and *Irish Gazette,* along with certain local newspapers, from the seventeenth century as a way of protecting the partner who had withdrawn from the business from legal proceedings in the event of a bankruptcy. Although advisable, such notification was not mandatory. Since even very large firms (except for commercial banks) continued to be organised as partnerships into the twentieth century, the lack of any formal notification of formation and even disappearance (except in the case of bankruptcy) makes it impossible to investigate the demography of enterprise in the United Kingdom from legal records as in France.[14]

Limited Companies

The 1844 Joint Stock Companies Act allowed for the formation of companies with unlimited liability by 25 or more members (shareholders with freely transferrable shares), which were to be registered with the newly formed Register of Joint Stock Companies. Limited liability was introduced in the 1855 Companies Act. The 1856 Companies Act required existing companies to re-register, reduced the minimum number of person who could form themselves into a limited liability company to seven and established additional registers of companies in Edinburgh and Dublin. Legislation affecting limited liability companies was consolidated in the 1862 Companies Act, which remained in force for the rest of the nineteenth century until further consolidating legislation was passed in 1908. Initially very few firms took advantage of the protection offered by limited liability. Indeed, informed contemporary opinion regarded the Act of 1856 as a dead letter; even the obligation that companies originally registered under the Act of 1844 must re-register under the Act of 1856, failed significantly to swell the number incorporated. Not until the early 1870s did annual registration exceed 1,000, explained in part by the impact of the 1872 Ballot Act which led to numerous registrations of local political clubs. After the collapse of the City of Glasgow Bank in 1878 with catastrophic calls on its members who were unprotected by limited liability (in effect *commanditaires*), many partnerships converted themselves into limited liability companies. It also became illegal for banks to be organized in this way. Over the next thirty years limited liability was heavily used as a form of corporate organisation for small family concerns, for large public utilities, and for large-scale international businesses. The trend accelerated in the mid-1890s after the introduction of death duties in 1894. In 1900 4,000 companies registered compared with just 230 in 1856. Even though numbers expanded, the majority of companies registered between 1880 and 1906 used their articles of association to limit the transfer of shares to the families of the original members. This private status was not legally recognised until the Companies Act of 1907. Although there were various amendments to the reporting requirements of companies after 1907, no further changes were made to their legal definition until after the Second World War.

Unfortunately for the historian the title Register of Companies is misleading, because it does not imply the maintenance of a register in the strict sense of the word. There have never been continuous registers recording individual company registration numbers, names, dates of incorporation, or changes of names and dates of dissolution as in France. The nearest there is to a register is the Joint Stock Company Return which were published in the British Parliamentary Papers from 1857 to 1900. Thereafter these were published in the *Investors' Guardian* (formerly *The Investors' Guardian Limited Liability Review*). These provide the company's name, objects of business, date of registration, country of operation, number of shareholders, and registered and paid-up capital. The Registers proper consist of the companies incorporated and, in a technical sense, alive and are, therefore, constantly changing as new companies are added and dissolved ones removed.

Since 1844, all companies have been required to lodge certain documents with the Registrar in London or his Assistants in Edinburgh and Dublin (prior to 1922) on incorporation, to make annual returns, and lodge notices relating to liquidation. From the beginning these papers have been stored in separate files for each company arranged by registration numbers. They are an invaluable source of information for historians and other researchers. As long as the company is on the Register, even if it has changed its name or become the subsidiary of another company, the file remains open from the date of its inception and is retained in its entirety. As public documents they can be consulted at Companies' House. After a company has been dissolved, either compulsorily by the courts or voluntarily, it is removed from the Register and placed in a separate register of defunct companies. Files are held at Companies' House for twenty years after a company's dissolution and are then either destroyed or transferred to the Public Record Office, London; the Scottish Record Office, Edinburgh; the Public Record Office of Northern Ireland, Belfast; or the National Archives of Ireland, Dublin. Retention policy for these files differs in each country. In practise by far the largest bulk of files are held at the Public Record Office in London. Until 1907 when private limited companies were legally recognised for the first time, the majority of files have survived. Thereafter there has been a policy of ruthless weeding of files relating to private limited companies, which accounted for over 90 per cent of all company registrations in the United Kingdom.[15]

Failures – Bankruptcies

As in France bankruptcy proceedings make no distinction between sole traders and partnerships, as partners with a limited liability were liable jointly with other partners and in Scotland severally also, for all debts and obligations that a firm incurred. Formal bankruptcy, administered through the law courts, was a procedure that most individuals and firms sought to avoid by making compositions with their creditors. Nevertheless, trends in formal bankruptcies do mirror the trade cycle.[16] Throughout the United Kingdom bankruptcy proceedings could be initiated in the courts by either individuals, firms, creditors, or the courts themselves, although the methods of supervising the process varied from country to country and over time. The principal difference between Scotland and the rest of the United Kingdom was that in

PROLOGUE 13

Scotland the process has always been administered directly by the courts. As a result, in the majority of cases very full details of the examination of the bankrupt, along with lists of creditors and debtors, and information regarding the winding up of estates is available amongst the papers of the Court of Sessions in Edinburgh.[17] The processes that are to be found in the records of the Court of Bankruptcy in London contain far less information.[18] However, from the seventeenth century there was a legal obligation for notices of bankruptcies of either individuals or firms to be published in the three official gazettes and relevant local newspapers. Although the notices in the three official gazetts should in theory contain a comprehensive list of all bankruptcies, there seems to be some omissions, in Scotland accounting for some 5 per cent of cases. Bankruptcy records have been used by historians for a variety of studies relating to the demography of enterprise, from national enquiries to local and particular studies.[19]

Winding-up of Limited Liability Companies

Limited Liability companies could be wound up either compulsorily by the courts (because they had acted fraudulently or failed to meet their creditors) or, and this was far more commonly the case, voluntarily by the shareholders. As with bankruptcies, formal notification had to be published in the official gazettes and relevant local newspapers so that creditors could lodge claims. There was also a requirement to notify the Registrar of Companies so that the company could be removed to the register of defunct companies. When the final process of winding up was completed, formal notification had to be made to the Registrar; but this could sometimes be many years after the firm had ceased to trade. Except in those cases where the process was compulsory, winding up was supervised by an individual (known as a liquidator – normally an accountant) elected by the creditors and responsible to them. There was no legal requirement for the liquidator to deposit records of his activities or the distribution of funds to the creditors with the courts or the Registrar of Companies until 1890. In many cases the winding up of a limited liability company cannot be taken as a surrogate for the death of an enterprise. Sometimes a company was wound up and a new company formed to carry on the business by the same shareholders. This could be for a variety of reasons unconnected with failure, like changes in the fiscal environment. On other occasions businesses were wound up because they had fulfilled their objectives and the shareholders wished to recover their investments, as in the case of companies formed to own buildings or operate single ships. Although it is therefore difficult to use statistics of company formation and dissolution for the study of the life cycle of firms, company files, as in France, do provide invaluable information about the occupations of shareholders and sources of capital. Like bankruptcy proceedings, files of dissolved companies have, therefore, been widely used by historians.[20]

4. The Demography of Enterprises – A Research Agenda

The essays in this volume investigate the demography of enterprise nationally, locally and by sector, using different approaches and different sources. However, they all share problems of definition. What is a firm? Does the legal status of a firm tell the historian anything about the size or relative importance? If it does not, can size be measured in other ways, for example, by using data drawn from the *cadastre* in France or rating records in the United Kingdom? What is the life expectancy of firms? Do firms with different legal status live longer than others? What constitues a death? Are legal bankruptcies a typical or untypical cause of death? If individuals continue in the same business with different partners or if physical assets continue to be employed by others, has death occurred or would a better analogy be a sudden serious illness – a thrombosis? These are important questions which must be common to the study of firms throughout the world.

Is it worth undertaking the arduous and difficult task of finding solutions nationally and then attempting international comparisons? Since firms are by necessity the engines of economic growth in capitalist economies, then seeking to understand more about their behaviour in different legal, social and geographical contexts should shed light on such complex issues as comparative economic behaviour, the rôle of the entrepreneur and the structure of capital formation. How then is work to proceed?

A preliminary and essential practical step is to compile a second volume in this series, laying out the development of the legal framework for business creation and failure in different countries – expanding and extending the information provided in this chapter. This would help to establish the definitions vital for comparative study. In parallel, historians from different countries represented in the Demography of Enterprises Group need to agree on one or two questions to be addressed over the four years from 1990 to 1994 before the Congrès of the International Economic History Association meets again. These should be simple and conducive to international comparison, like do enterprises in different countries have different life expectancies? or what is the population of large firms in different countries, localities or sectors? what contribution, if any, do they make to economic development? and what implications do they have for the creation of small firms? These are only suggestions. One of the principal tasks of the meeting at Leuven in 1990 is to agree this research agenda.

Footnotes

1. F Caron, 'Présentation' in *Entreprises et entrepreneurs, XIXe-XXe siècles, Congrès de l'Association française des historiens économistes mars 1980,* Paris, 1983, pp.1-4; Peter L Payne, *The Early Scottish Limited Companies 1856-1895* (Edinburgh, 1980); H A Shannon, 'The First Five Thousand Limited Companies and their Duration', *Economic History Review II,* 1932; and H A Shannon, 'The Limited Companies of 1866-83', *Economic History Review IV,* 1932-33.

2. Tentative de croisement des deux séries statistiques: P Jobert et J C Chevailler, 'La démographie des entreprises en France au XIXe siécle. Quelques pistes', *Histoire, Economie et Société,* 1986, pp.233-264.

3. D Jeremy (ed.), *Dictionary of Business Biography,* 5 vols. (London, 1986 –1987 , and S G Checkland and A Slaven (eds.), *Scottish Dictionary of Business Biography,* 2 vols., (Aberdeen, 1986 and 1990).

4. See, for example, Julien Hoppit, *Risk and Failure in English Business 1700-1800,* (Cambridge, 1980); Michael S Moss and John R Hume, 'Business Failure in Scotland, 1839-1913: A Research Note', *Business History,* 25, 1983; and Richard G Rodger, 'Business failure in Scotland 1839-1913', *Business History,* 27, 1985.

5. J Hilaire, *Introduction historique au droit commercial,* Paris, 1986.

6. A Lefebvre-Teillard, 'Les sociétés', in *Les entreprises,* dir. P Jobert, coll. Annuaire statistique de l'économie française aux XIXe et XXe siècles, à paraître, Paris, 1990: présentation juridique, sources statistiques, bibliographie.

7. A Lefebvre-Teillard, 'Le développement des sociétés par actions en France' in *Industrial Age and the Law,* coll. Comparative Studies in Continental and Anglo-American Legal History, dir. H Coing and K W Nörr, vol. 8, Berlin, 1990; J Hilaire *et al, La commandite entre son passé et son avenir,* Paris, 1983.

8. C E Freedman, *Joint Stock Enterprise in France, 1807-1867. From Privileged Company to Modern Corporation,* Chapel Hill, 1979; A Lefebvre-Teillard, *La société anonyme au XIXe siècle. Du Code de Commerce à la loi de 1867. Histoire d'un instrument juridique du développement capitaliste,* Paris, 1985.

9. P Pic et J Kreher, *Des sociétés commerciales,* t. 1, 3e éd, Paris, 1940.

10. P Jobert, 'Introduction' et 'Faillites' in *Les entreprises,* déjà cité; J Percerou, *Des faillites et banqueroutes et des liquidations judiciaires,* 2e éd, Paris, 1935-1938, 3 vols.

11. P Lascoumes, 'Banqueroutes' in *Les entreprises,* déja cité.

12. Description statistique dans L Marco, *La montée des faillites en France. XIXe-XXe siècles,* Paris, 1989.

13. An outline of the different legal forms of enterprise can be found in L M

Richmond, 'Corporate Records' in Alison M Turton, *Business Archive Administration* (London, 1990).

14. John Orbell, *A Guide to Tracing the History of a Business* (Aldershot, 1987), pp.6-7.

15. Lesley Richmond and Bridget Stockford, *Company Archives – The Survey of the Records of 1000 of the First Registered Companies in England and Wales* (Aldershot, 1986), 'Introduction' by P L Payne, pp.ix-xiii, and T A Lee and R H Parker, *The Evolution of Corporate Financial Reporting* (London, 1979), pp.197-207.

16. See Moss and Hume, op.cit., and Rodger, *op.cit.*

17. John McLintock, *A Guide to Scottish Sequestrations 1839-1913,* available from the Scottish Record Office, HM General Register House, Edinburgh EH1 3YY.

18. Sheila Marriner, 'English Bankruptcy Records and Statistics Before 1850', *Economic History Review,* 33, 1980.

19. See Keith Brooker, 'Some Approaches to the Study of Small Scale Industries prior to 1914', *Business Archives,* No.47, 1981.

20. See, for example, P L Cottrell, 'The Steamship on the Mersey, 1815-80: investment and ownership' in P L Cottrell and D H Aldcroft, *Shipping Trade and Commerce,* Leicester, 1981.

Part 1
Global studies and methods

2
Firm creations and failures in nineteenth century France: regional differences

Jean-Claude Chevailler

What features characterise the demography of firms in the different regions of France in the nineteenth century? This important question regarding the structure and economic geography of the country can be approached by analyzing two series of statistics: the creation of companies and the initiation of proceedings for winding up firms for every year from 1840 to 1913. These are to be found in the *Compte général de la justice civile et commerciale*. In two previous studies, we have discussed the problems associated with the use of this source[1], setting out a method of approach and presenting our first results for the country as a whole and by departements. This essay examines the behaviour of the regional statistics. The results we have arrived at seem interesting to us, perhaps surprising at first sight. We leave to historians the task of making sense of them.

1. The data

The *Compte général de la justice civile et commerciale* provides the relevant data for the ninety departments into which France was divided after the First World War. Those series, however, are not entirely complete because the Dukedom of Savoy and the Earldom of Nice did not re-unite with France until 1860, and also, because following the Franco-Prussian war of 1870, Alsace and part of Lorraine was annexed and the Territory of Belfort created. The reconstitution of these missing series was not considered to be within the scope of this paper. The analysis which follows is based on the aggregation of departmental data by present day regions. The sole exception is Corse where the data have been grouped with that for the region of Provence-Alpes-Côte d'Azur.[2] The two Alsatian departments remain a problem because together they constitute the region of Alsace. They have, therefore, been excluded from a significant part of the analysis.

Naturally, the actual administrative divisions of the country are not impartial and consequently the individual entities are of very different sizes. Table 2.1 is revealing in this respect. Because of the imperfections in the statistics, the figures only show the total number of formations and failures and are imprecise for Alsace. For this region the proportion of formations and failures during the period it was all part of France is given in parenthesis.

The most remarkable feature of the Table is the predominant position of the Parisian region: Ile-de-France accounts for 40 per cent of all formations and 26 per cent of all failures in the whole country, and the department of the Seine 37.9 per cent and 23.3 per cent of these totals. Now, in the first pioneering study on the subject, we highlight the distinctive behaviour of this departments' statistics, the steady fall in the number of failures after 1885.[3] The same phenomena cannot be observed in any other department until the end of the century, when the same decline in failures occurs in the departments of the Nord and of the Rhône. This being so, we have placed all the other 89 departments in a category called Province.

The table also shows that in the majority of regions the number of failures is higher than the number of formations. Only Ile-de-France, the Nord-Pas-de-Calais, and Rhône-Alpes, are exceptions to this rule; that is to say, the regions comprising the three principal urban industrial centres in France. Together they represent nearly 60 per cent of all formations and 40 per cent of all failures. These totals suggest a great concentration of economic development, concentration which appears at first sight greater for formation of firms than for failures.

Table 2.1

Créations et faillites by regions between 1840 and 1913.

Region	Créations Total	%	Faillites Total	%
IDF	127485	39·6	118481	26·1
dont Seine	121899	37·9	105708	23·3
CHA	8720	2·7	16188	3·6
PIC	8761	2·7	18306	4·0
HNO	13305	4·1	19658	4·3
CEN	6147	1·9	14564	3·2
BNO	3977	1·2	13202	2·9
BOU	5576	1·7	15739	3·5
NPC	21029	6·5	26176	5·8
LOR	5996	1·9	8681	1·9
ALS	1816	0·6 (1·9)	2895	0·6 (2·5)
FOO	4474	1·4	7744	1·7
PLO	9572	3·0	15213	3·4
BRE	4101	1·3	8230	1·8
POI	6156	1·9	14423	3·2
AQU	16919	5·3	32639	7·2
MPY	7513	2·3	16691	3·7
LIM	2981	0·9	4763	1·1
RHA	36381	11·3	39368	8·7
AUV	3502	1·1	9464	2·1
LAN	8871	2·8	15984	3·5
PACA	18459	5·7	36211	8·0
Total Province	199842	62·1	348912	76·8
Total France	321741	100·0	454620	100·0

II. Growth of Regional Differences?

Regional growth in formation and dissolution of firms have been broken down by calculating averages for sub-periods of ten years and by constructing indices affecting changes over time and disparities between the different regions.[4] The formation and the dissolutions are first examined separately; the two series are next brought together to identify a regional typology.

(i) The formation of companies:

The growth in formation of *sociétés* is investigated by comparing the figure for the ten years at either end of the period 1840-1913. It is a matter then of calculating for the period 1900-13 a simple index, taking the period 1840-49 as a reference. The most striking fact to emerge is further evidence relating to the behaviour of the Parisian region. With an index of 100 based in 1840-49, it advances to 282 for the whole country (Alsace excepted), it is equal to 371 for the Ile-de-France and to 368 for the department of the Seine. The Ile-de-France, which represents 32.8 per cent of formations in 1840-49 increases its dominant role decisively, reaching 43.2 per cent in 1900-13. In these circumstances, the relative position of the majority of the regions decreased. Those regions with an index above the national average, and which therefore do not follow trend, are Nord-Pas-de-Calais (460), Bretagne (372), Provence et Corse (325), Auvergne (294) and Midi-Pyrénées (288).

The most spectacular example is Nord-Pas-de-Calais which in 1849 was only sixth in order of importance for formations behind Ile-de-France and Rhône-Alpes, but also behind Haute-Normandie, Aquitaine, and Provence et Corse. By 1900-13 Nord-Pas-de-Calais had climbed to third place immediately behind Rhône-Alpes. Amongst the remaining fourteen regions, only three record increases in formation rates above that of Province where the index reached 242; Limousin (267), Aquitaine (256) and Franche Comté (254). Finally, formations in eleven regions increased but at a lower rate than Province: Rhône-Alpes (236), Bourgogne (229), Languedoc-Roussillon (222), Champagne-Ardenne (211), Centre (204), Lorraine (202), Poitou-Charentes (197), Pays de la Loire et Picardie (181), Basse-Normandie (169) and Haute-Normandie (148).

The example of Haute-Normandie is interesting: placed third in 1840-49 with 5.7 per cent of formations in all France, its share is almost halved to 3 per cent in 1900-13 when its position dropped to sixth place. Does the fact that its experience is shared by its neighbour Basse-Normandie reflect the difficulties encountered during the late nineteenth century by traditional industries in that part of France? Without being exactly on the same scale, the example of Rhône-Alpes has a similar statistical profile; its relative weighting diminished slightly from 12.2 per cent to 10.2 per cent. At the beginning of the period studied there are practically two and a half times more creations in Rhône-Alpes than in the Nord-Pas-de-Calais, while by 1900-13 the divergence is no more than 30 per cent.

Figure 2.1 is obtained by dividing the regions into four classes constructed by calculating the mean[5] and the standard deviation of the index, the thresholds being respectively equal to 215, 292 and 369. To the north of a line from Bordeaux to Belfort would appear to be the regions that experienced the weakest growth, with, nevertheless, three notable exceptions: Ile-de-France, Nord-Pas-de-Calais and Bretagne which have the strongest rate

Figure 2.1

Geography of the evolution of créations (dispersion around the area).

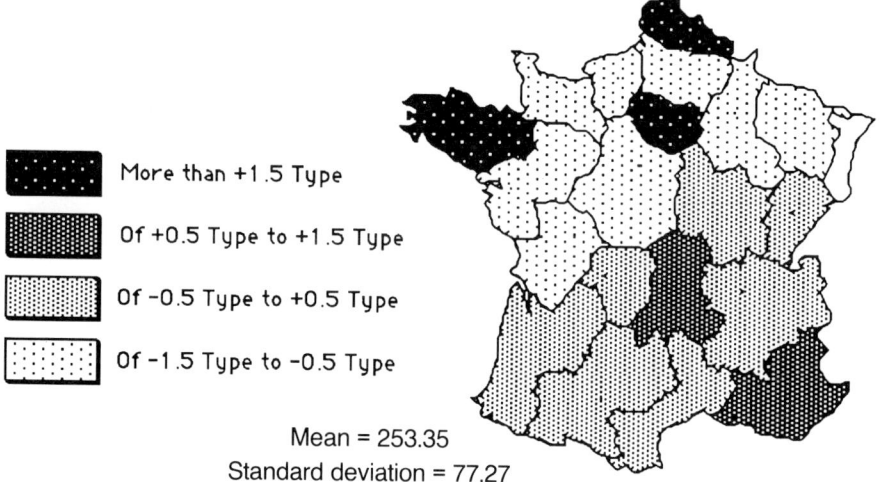

Mean = 253.35
Standard deviation = 77.27

of increase in the formation of companies of any part of France.

Table 2.2, elaborated for three sub periods, brings into focus the increasing concentration which characterise the formation of *sociétés* in France between 1840 and 1913. Not only does the weighting of the ten smallest regions diminish, but also that of the intermediary group. The spectacular growth of the relative weighting of Ile-de-France in great measure explains this phenomena, but the good performance of Nord-Pas-de-Calais and of Provence et Corse must equally be taken into account.

The Theil indicator,[6] constructed on the idea of entropy, has been used to measure the evolution of concentration in the formation and failure of enterprises over the entire period. To do this, the indicator was calculated for each of the seven sub-periods.

For the sake of homogeneity, Alsace has been left out of the calculation. Figure 2.2 confirms the trend for the growing concentration in the formation of companies. It would be tempting to link the decline revealed in the third and fourth quarter to the recession in the economy after 1860. Nevertheless an increase in concentration takes place by the time of the great economic crisis of the nineteenth century in France towards 1896. It seems thus hazardous, without a more profound analysis, to link in the medium term the growth of regional concentration in the formation of enterprises to the rate of expansion of production.

Table 2.2

Overview of the concentration of créations de sociétés.

In percentages		1840-49		1870-79		1900-13
The 5 most important regions	IDF	32·84	IDF	36·36	IDF	43·24
	RHA	12·17	RHA	11.56	RHA	10·19
	HNO	5·70	NPC	6·87	NPC	7·75
	AQU	5·23	PACA	5·86	PACA	5·96
	PACA	5·16	AQU	5·71	AQU	4·76
Total		61·10		66·36		71·90
The 5 following	NPC	4·75	HNO	4·78	HNO	3·00
	PLO	3·92	CHA	3·39	PLO	2·52
	PIC	3·59	PLO	3·16	LAN	2·50
	LAN	3·17	LAN	3·13	CHA	2·35
	CHA	3·14	PIC	3·11	PIC	2·31
Total		18·57		17·57		12·68
The 10 régions		18·30		16·07		15·42
(Alsace)		(2·30)		-		-

Figure 2.2
Evolution of the concentration of créations and of faillites.

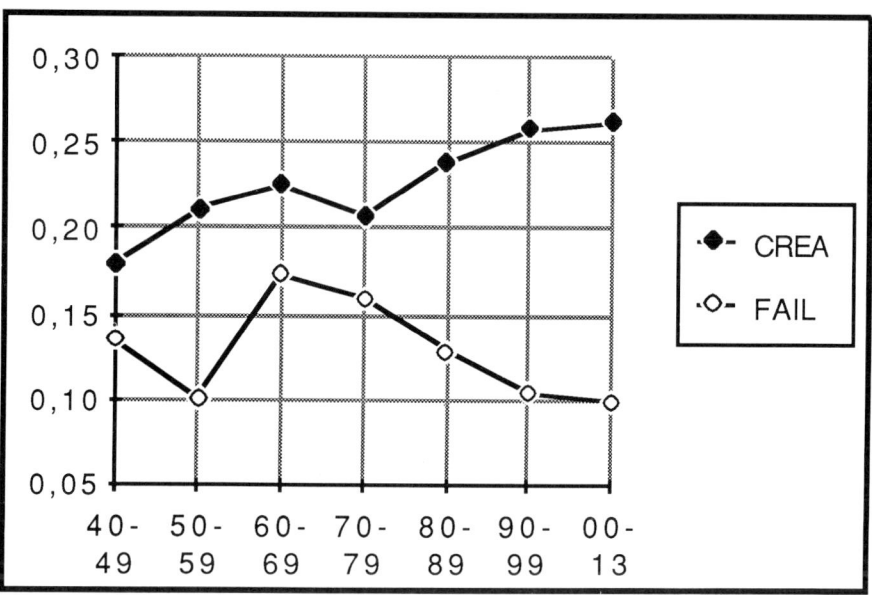

2. The failure of enterprises

As far as failures are concerned, the profile is practically inverse to that for creations. Consequently a heavy decrease is recorded in the region of Ile-de-France in the number of failures for the whole of France. From 28.1 per cent in 1840-49, its share drops to 20.8 per cent in 1900-13. Once again it is the department of the Seine which dominates the region's performances representing more than 90 per cent of the region's failures in 1840-49, and nearly 84 per cent in 1900-13. As a result a majority of regions (eleven out of twenty) experienced an increase in their relative weighting as a proportion of all failures in the country as a whole. Amongst these, it is worth examining those whose index, reflecting the development between 1840-49 and 1900-13, is above the index for Province (296): Provence et Corse (1009), Languedoc-Roussillon (593), Nord-Pas-de-Calais (587), Auvergne (435), Aquitaine (435), Rhône-Alpes (371), Bretagne (364) and Poitou-Charentes (336).

Beyond the remarkable rise in failures recorded in Provence et Corse, it is possible to identify in this group four regions which appear equally at the top of the classification for the least growth in the number of formations for the same period (Provence et Corse, Nord-Pas-de-Calais, Auvergne, and Bretagne). In these cases where failures and creations are on equal footing, the higher level of the index could reflect a strong dynamism associated with the concepts of restructuring enterprises, of changing the appearance of a firm, or of economic growth. The region of Poitou-Charentes provides a different illustration in the statistics. It features amongst the regions with the worst record for growth in the number of enterprises. In this case a marked rise in failures corresponding to a poor rate of formation can be attributed to a collapse of the regional economy, untypical of the country as a whole. Only the regions of Languedoc-Roussillon and Rhône-Alpes come near this pattern of statistical behaviour. Thereafter three regions are associated with an index value which reflects intermediate behaviour between the Province and the whole of France (267): Limousin (291), Midi-Pyrénées (286) and Pays-de-la-Loire (284).

Finally, with index values lower than the national average and therefore with a declining rate of failures compared to the country as a whole, are the following regions: Centre (263), Bourgogne (257), Franche-Comté (220), Ile-de-France (197), Picardie (195), Champagne-Ardenne (186), Lorraine (171), Basse-Normandie (131) and Haute-Normandie (99). Here again it is advisable to draw distinctions between the relative positions of the different regions. The case of Ile de France, for which the gradual increase in the number of failures is associated with very strong growth in the number of formations, is in no way comparable to those of the two regions in Normandie which occupy the last two places in both the failure and formation tables. Figure 2.3, constructed in the same manner as for formations on the distribution on either side of the mean of the index, confirms the constant factor in the pattern. If Provence et Corse are treated as an isolated region with a pattern of development comparable to no other region, then the north east zone stands clearly apart with the exception of Nord-Pas-de-Calais.

As in formations, it is possible to examine the spatial concentration of the failures of enterprises over time. Table 2.3 records two salient features. To begin with, failures are less concentrated than formations: the proportion in the five largest regions never rises above 60 per cent of all failures, whereas it is never lower than this percentage for all formations. The second noticeable characteristic is that concentration of failures does not develop in any uniform fashion until placed in the context of the three sub periods. The rapid advance of Provence et Corse to second place in 1870-79 is striking as it did not feature in the top ten in 1840-49. In contrast the experience of Haute-Normandie is equally remarkably ranked second in 1840-49, tenth in 1900-13.

FIRM CREATIONS AND FAILURES IN FRANCE

Figure 2.3

Geograpy of the evolution of faillites (dispersed around the area).

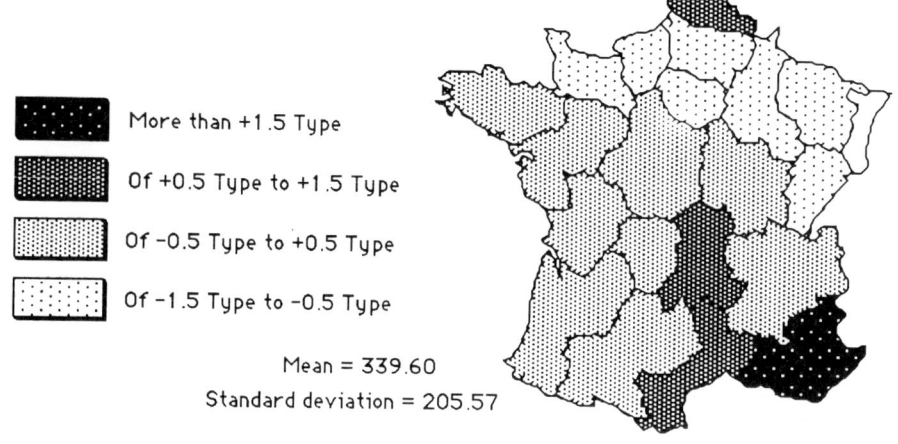

More than +1.5 Type
Of +0.5 Type to +1.5 Type
Of -0.5 Type to +0.5 Type
Of -1.5 Type to -0.5 Type

Mean = 339.60
Standard deviation = 205.57

Table 2.3

Overview of the concentration of faillites of firms.

In percentages	1840-49		1870-79		1900-13	
The five most important regions	IDF	28·13	IDF	33·21	IDF	20·79
	HNO	9·55	PACA	7·58	PACA	11·11
	RHA	7·20	RHA	7·52	RHA	10·01
	PIC	5·58	AQU	6·73	NPC	7·61
	BNO	5·02	NPC	4·43	AQU	7·12
Total		55·48		59·47		56·64
The 5 following	AQU	4·37	PIC	3·75	LAN	4·44
	CHA	4·26	BOU	3·73	PIC	4·08
	CEN	3·49	HNO	3·72	PLO	3·65
	NPC	3·46	CHA	3·53	MPY	3·59
	PLO	3·43	MPY	3·39	HNO	3·55
Total		19.10		18·12		19·31
The ten remaning regions		22·53		22·41		24·05
(Alsace)		(2·98)		-		-

Scrutiny of Figure 2.2 shows that the growth in concentration of failures over time, measured by the Theil indicator, has greater contrasts than the concentration of formations. The maximum concentration is achieved from 1860-69, then it continues to decrease until the period 1900-13. Analysis of the profile of failures, independent of formations, is nevertheless inadequate. A slight increment in the number of failures has different significance depending on whether it is linked to a poor or strong growth in the number of formations. Consequently it is important to compare the two series.

3. Sample of regional typologies

Figure 2.4 is obtained by plotting once again the relative proportions of each region's failures and creations to the national totals between the periods 1840-49 and 1900-13. This summary typology illustrates the very particular behaviour of Ile-de-France which is the only region where the share of formation grows (% C<0) and where that for failure decrease (% F>0). With the exception of this region and of Nord-Pas-de-Calais, all the rest, which see their relative importance decline in the two series, are situated to the north east of a line drawn from Mont Saint-Michel to Genève.

Figure 2.4

Typology the development of the regions (créations and faillites) between 1840-49 and 1900-13.

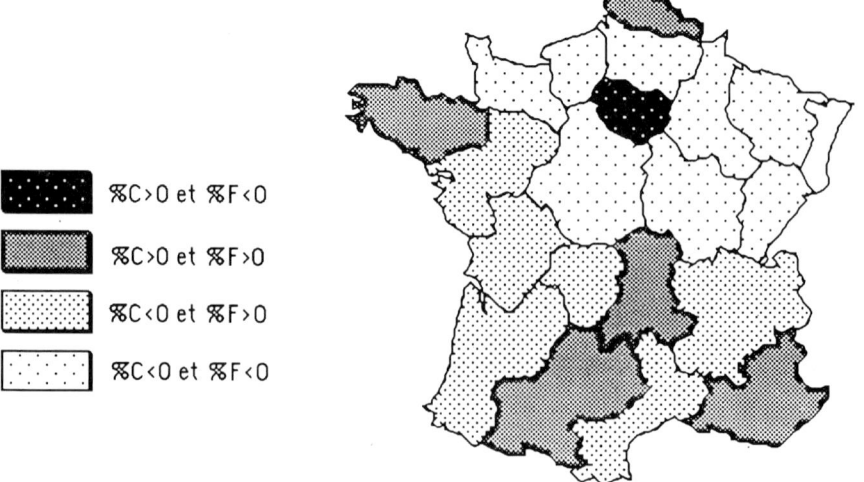

However, it is possible to construct a more meaningful typology by using the geographical distributions represented in Figures 2.1 and 2.3 (on pages 23 and 27). From these, shown in Figure 2.5, it becomes evident that there are three distinct groups and seven isolated individual regions. The first group, corresponding to the weakest values in the indices, contains other than the two Normandie regions: Picardie, Lorraine, and Champagne-Ardenne. This confirms the view of the economic inertia in these regions associated with long established traditional industries.

Table 2.4

Typology established on the dispersal around the mean.

	class of créations	class of faillites	regions
group 1	1	1	BNO HNO PIC CHA LOR
group 3	1	2	PLO POI CEN
	2	1	FOO
group 2	2	2	BOU RHA MPY AQU LIM
	2	3	LAN
	3	3	AUV
	3	4	PACA
	4	1	IDF
	4	2	BRE
	4	3	NPC

The second group is composed of regions where behaviour is nearest the mean of the two criteria.[7] It is less geographically homogeneous than the previous group, including on the east Rhône-Alpes and Bourgogne, and in the west Limousin, Midi-Pyrénées, and Aquitaine. The third and last group is made up of the central regions, Pays de la Loire and Poitou-Charentes, which behave in line with the mean from the perspective of failures, but beneath the mean for creations, which is not considered to be a favourable combination.

Amongst the isolated regions, the growth in formations is more significant than that of failures for four of them. Of course, Ile-de-France is numbered in this category along with Bretagne and Nord-Pas-de-Calais where, as has already been shown, there was a spectacular increase in formations. To a lesser degree, also figures Franche-Comté where the behaviour corresponds to the mean for formations but is beneath the mean of failures.

Figure 2.5

Geography of the typologie.

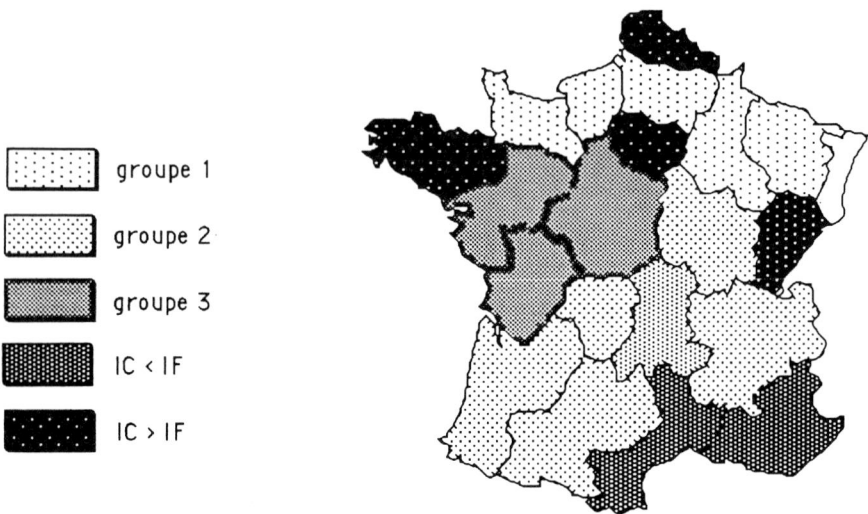

groupe 1

groupe 2

groupe 3

IC < IF

IC > IF

In the final category, as well as the region of Languedoc-Roussillon, is to be found Provence et Corse, which is diametrically opposed to the region of Nord-Pas-de-Calais. In these last two regions, like Auvergne, the values of the two indices are very high, suggesting that profound changes occur. But contrary to Nord-Pas-de-Calais, the profile of failures in Provence gets the better of creations, reflecting a different structure in the regional economy.[8]

Conclusion

At the end of this study, it is possible to assert that stable elements exist. Apart from the very distinctive manner in which the Paris region behaves, the differences revealed in the concentration of creations and failures and in their respective development is essential to the understanding of the birth and death of firms. Geographically, the typologies which are presented show the sharp contrast which exists between the demography of industry in the north east of France and that of the south west.

Nevertheless, this analysis has obvious limitations of which the author is only too well aware, deriving in part from the statistical sources which are available. The sectoral data only exists for failures and then only since 1874.[9] Moreover, the series for formations and failures do not relate to the same populations of firms: the formations registered by the Ministry of Justice concern only *sociétés*, whereas failures relate to every type of firm. Since it is evident that all firms do not assume the status of *sociétés*, it is impossible to be certain whether the proportion of firms with *sociétés* status remain stable throughout the period in the whole country let alone different regions.

The second limitation derives from the regional divisions chosen for this study. In the first place one can question the relevance of the actual regional division in a study of nineteenth century France. If in the calculations it seems that the formations and failures are concentrated in certain parts of the regions, it is possible to confirm these doubts by recourses to an analysis by department. However, even if one abstracts the more important departments (partly investigated in our first article) the majority represent less than one per cent of total creations and failures in the whole country which renders the results of any quantitative analysis by departments extremely precarious.

In these circumstances, the choices that have been made appear to be the only possible choices. This, however, does not detract from the interest of this kind of analysis, which must be considered as the outline of a more extensive work, which, by studying the statistics retracing the development of company creations and firm failures, complemented by sector-based studies, makes it possible to identify and describe the functioning of different regions within the general economic development of nineteenth century France.

Footnotes

1. Ph. Jobert et J-Cl. Chevailler, La démographie des entreprises en France au XIXe siécle. Quelques pistes, *Histoire, économie et société*, 1986, n°2, p.233-264. J-Cl Chevailler, En passant par la Franche-Comté. La démographie des entreprises françaises au XIXe siécle in *Les agents de l'industrialisation et de l'innovation dans une région française: la Franche-Comté*, Université de Franche-Comté, 1988, 49 p.

    Pour les sources, se reporter à *Les entreprises*, sous la direction de Ph. Jobert, coll. 'Annuaire statisque de la France aux XIXe et XXe siècles', dir. F. Caron, Presses de l'Ecole Normale Supérieure, Paris, à paraître 1990.

2. Alsace, Aquitainme (AQU), Auvergne (AUV), Basse-Normandie (BNO), Bourgogne (BOU), Bretagne (BRE), Centre (CEN), Champagne-Ardenne (CHA), Franche-Comté (FCO), Haute-Normandie (HNO), Ile-de-France (IDF), Languedoc-Roussillon (LAN), Limousin (LIM), Lorraine (LOR) Midi-Pyrénées (MPY), Nord-Pas-de-Calais (NPC), Pays de la Loire (PLO), Picardie (PIC), Poitou-Charentes (POI), Provence-Alpes-Côte d'Azur et Corse (PACA), Rhône-Alpes (RHA).

3. Ph. Jobert et J-Cl. Chevailler, op.cit., p.259 à 262.
4. Pour plus de détail J-Cl. Chevailler, *Naissance et mort des entreprises en France au XIXe siècle. Disparités régionales,* document CETAP, Université de Franche-Comté, 39 p. +XXVII p., juin 1989. Papier présenté à la pré-session de Glasgow, septembre 1989, et résumé ici.
5. Il ne faut pas perdre de vue qu'il s'agit ici de la moyenne des indices qui ne saurait être confondue avec l'indice national.
6. L'indice varie entre O (concentration nulle) et 1 (concentration maximale). Pour la définition de l'indicateur de Theil, se reporter à l'annexe 1 du document cité en (3).
7. Le comportement moyen, tant pour les créations que pour les faillites, est représenté par la classe 2.
8. M. Lescure, *Companies and manufacturers of the first industrialization at Marseilles,* communication à la pré-session de Glasgow, septembre 1989.
9. On trouvera les données sectorielles disponibles dans L. Marco, 'Faillites et crises économiques en France au XIXe siècle', *Annales ESC,* 1989, n°2, p.372.

3

The 1856 Companies Act and the birth and death of firms

James Foreman-Peck

As suppliers of goods and services, originators of new technology, employers of labour and investors in productive capital, firms are at the centre of the economic growth process. Their births, growth and deaths must therefore play a major role in any explanation of economic development. Businesses are not all easily identified however because of their variety of legal forms. Most apparent are publicly quoted joint stock and limited liability companies; less obvious in historical records are unlimited sole proprietorships and partnerships.

With the introduction of Value Added Tax (VAT) registration, all but the smallest enterprises are recorded. Before then, and after 1917, the Registry of Business Names probably provided the most comprehensive national coverage (Foreman-Peck 1985). Otherwise studies of business demography must have recourse to local or trade directories for data on the formation, stock and liquidation of businesses.

What all this implies is that official statistics on the birth and death of firms have different meanings depending upon the legal category considered. A partnership may 'die' because it has 'gone public'; a limited liability firm is 'born', but in fact an already existing economic unit has merely changed legal status. The 'death' of a limited liability firm may be recorded because of a merger or takeover, but again the assets live on. By contrast, the opening for business of a sole proprietorship trading from under a railway arch is unlikely to be announced in official statistics, even though it is an economic 'birth'. Nineteenth century official statistics of firm formation and closure must therefore be interpreted with care. But recognition that these numbers are generated by a legal process can be made to yield information. That different legal forms were available for enterprise may have influenced the behaviour of the business. In one version, this proposition has been long discussed in economic history under the heading of the family firm; would British (and French) business have performed better with professionally managed joint stock companies? The present paper approaches a similar problem; how did the legal framework impinge upon the birth of firms and therefore upon the performance of the business sector in nineteenth century Britain? The following section outlines some theoretical issues raised by the introduction of general limited liability under the 1856 Act. Section II explores the evidence of accounting information, stock exchange new issues, the more tightly regulated and varied French regime and the incentive created by bankruptcy legislation. The third section estimates investment and production functions, testing whether limited liability 'births' raised investment and estimating how productive that investment was.

I

From 1856 to 1948 British legislation governing the formation and operation of limited liability companies imposed among the least requirement of information disclosure to shareholders or outsiders of any major economy in the world, with the exception of the United States of America. The dominant view of the mid-century was that of classical and neo-classical economics; that resources are best managed by those who own them. Others have less incentive to exert themselves, to evaluate risk correctly or to be honest. On the other hand, an increasing number of businesses needed a great deal of capital (especially railways and banks) which could not be provided by partnerships nor could it be accumulated from retained profits. On the supply side there was alleged to be a need to mobilise the savings of widows and orphans who could not be expected to evaluate the risk of investments accurately and for whom the minimalist state provided an insufficient supply of government bonds to buy. Implicit was presumably that fixed interest company bonds could not remedy the deficiency because there was a low limit to the safe debt/equity ratio of the firm.

In is simplest form the problem is one of risk-shifting. Innovative business is essentially a risky activity, which can be shared by the issue of equity. A sole proprietor may take his rewards from the sale of shares and work less hard as a salaried manager, or merely retire. But each shareholder is still liable for a portion of the downside risk over which they can have little control in a large enterprise. When the Bank of Glasgow failed in 1878 with 1,200 proprietors, £8 million deposits and losses of around £6 million, the unlimited liability of the proprietors involved calls amounting to £2,750 on each £100 share. Here the problem was mismanagement and fraud which unlimited liability had not prevented.

That is not to deny that with limited liability the problem could have been more widespread. Under limited liability, some risk is shifted to the company's suppliers, creditors and customers, away from shareholders, who only risk the capital they have subscribed or are committed to subscribing (uncalled capital). On the one hand, the supply of capital therefore becomes more abundant. On the other, trade creditors and suppliers, realising they may not be paid in the event of failure, should have demanded premia for dealing with a limited liability company, thereby reducing the benefits from, and the formation rates of such companies.

Since managers typically have better access to information about the firm than either shareholders or outsiders, the lack of legal obligation to reveal the state of the company in these years may have given rise to general moral hazard and a misallocation of investment (Cottrell 1980, p.54, Hannah 1983, p.19). The moral hazard arises because the supply of capital is increased but the opportunity to use it productively is not necessarily enhanced. There are thus incentives to take the capital and run, to establish fraudulent companies with no genuine assets or earnings prospects, as the distribution of early company failures under the 1856 Act implies. Finance, insurance and banking showed very high failure rates while coal, iron and engineering were much more likely to be genuine enterprises (Thomas 1973, p.117).

In a market where information flowed fairly freely, the response of genuine entrepreneurs and businesses to the asymmetries of information between managers and shareholders would be either to remain family firms, and not involve shareholders, the criticism often made of nineteenth century Britain, or to provide full and effective information as to how the company was performing. For shareholders would recognise they were in danger of losing their money in limited liability companies as well, unless they were provided with sufficient information to satisfy themselves that the risk was acceptable. Then limited liability would actually limit genuine risk, not encourage fraud. This process is unlikely to occur instantaneously; learning by promoters and shareholders would take place over perhaps quite a considerable period of time.

Even genuine risk could be shifted by issuing small enough denominations of shares and diversifying holdings, although the ability to appreciate the quality of investment in a diversified portfolio would require more formal methods of assessing company performance than were in widespread use in the nineteenth century. Average share denominations did fall as the century progressed, suggesting an increasing appreciation of risk shifting.

Incentive effects are not the only matters of relevance to the appropriate company form. Managerial competence, or comparative advantage, must also be taken into consideration. Those who own capital are not necessarily those best suited to manager it. Moreover, the leisure preference of rich capitalists may be higher than of poorer managers so that if suitable contracts can be designed, both parties could gain from trade. The simplest form of contract is one in which the manager is awarded a share of the (uncertain) return achieved for shareholders. Atkinson and Stiglitz (1980 pp.119-120) outline a model in which the manager's optimum share increases with managerial effectiveness, and decreases with managerial risk aversion and the elasticity of managerial effort. A smaller share requires managers to achieve a higher return to attain a given income. The lazier are managers, the lower their optimum share to give an incentive to exert themselves and raise the firm's income above what they would otherwise choose. Shareholders are assumed risk neutral; managers need a greater incentive to take risks on their behalf the more risk averse they are. Where managerial effectiveness is concerned, interests of shareholders and management converge in encouraging management to raise income. The practical significance of this type of model is limited by the unobservable nature of the key parameters. Moreover, a greater nineteenth century problem was the unobservable real return, thanks to the primitive nature of accounting and secrecy which legislation did not discourage.

II

One form of accounting, auditing, eventually became accepted in Britain thanks in part to the needs of the public sector and of a substantial export trade to the US and other English speaking countries (Jones 1981, Watts and Zimmerman 1983). In cost accounting Jones' (1981) far more pessimistic assessment is now being questioned (Edwards and Newell 1990). Even before

1850 a number of firms operated advanced 'total' cost accounting systems, and cost estimates were widely used to guide management decisions. However sophisticated costing methods are likely to have been no more widespread than comprehensive voluntary disclosure, which, even after the turn of the century varied widely between firms in the same industry (Edwards 1981).

Stock exchange quotation imposed additional reporting requirements but these were still minimal. The provincial exchanges may have been better informed of the real value of the assets they traded because of their smaller size relative to London. The active markets in insurance shares, in steel and coal, in shipbuilding, cycles, gas, and telecommunications were in the provinces for that is where the major shareholders in these sectors lived. But the claim that provincial stock exchanges supplied any shortfall of funds to domestic industry left by London is hardly supported by the estimate that before 1914 all stock exchanges provided only one-fifth of net home investment and in the Edwardian period perhaps only one-sixth of this came from the provinces on average. Nor did the provincial exchanges' disclosure requirements and their speculative booms suggest the use made of the funds was necessarily efficient. When share prices rose in 1872-3, dozens of Yorkshire ironmasters seized the opportunity to convert into public companies at inflated prices on the Sheffield exchange. The cycle boom, beginning on the Dublin exchange in 1893, culminated in 1896 with the formation of 312 companies, most of which were overcapitalised even when they survived (Thomas 1972, p.123, 130-1).

The foregoing implies that the efficient market solution would have been, not limited liability, but a reduction of the assymmetry of information between the seller of new issues and the buyers, which high transactions costs supported. More rigorous reporting obligations that encouraged the spread of best practice accounting techniques would have been a move in this direction and smaller share denominations would have helped pure risk shifting.

Naturally the first proposal would have been resisted by business interests, in part for fear of takeover fever which could not emerge on any scale until after the disclosure requirements of the 1948 Companies Act. The best that could behoped for was they would be prepared to be certified honest, by accepting auditing (a requirement of an Act of 1900). Even that was less than fully effective, as the Royal Mail case of 1931 revealed. The secret creation and use of reserves by companies was widespread until then (Jones 1981).

In continental Europe, where business was politically less powerful, more onerous obligations could be imposed upon companies. France offers a marked contrast to Britain. Partly by accident, company law was more liberal in one sense until 1856. British firms like the London General Omnibus Company crossed the Channel in 1855 and paid substantially for the benefit of being a French company. By an oversight the Code of 1807 had permitted a form of joint stock which apparently offered a solution to the moral hazard problem. The *société en commandite par actions* subjected the manager of the company *(gerant)* to unlimited liability but partners who merely supplied capital *(commanditaires)* possessed limited liability. *Gerants* had a substantial stake in ensuring their companies were run well. *Commanditaires* could not participate in management and were therefore at the mercy of *gerants*, if they chose to be arbitrary. Alledgedly *gerants* were likely to disappear in event of insolvency. (Freedman 1965, 1967, BPP, 1899). Legislation in 1856, intended to improve matters by establishing permanent shareholder committees of surveillance, reduced the demand for this type of company by imposing the penalty that committee members would lose their limited liability if they failed in their duties. Whatever the inadequacies of the *en commandite*, and the *société anonyme*[1], investment in new joint stock enterprise exceeded that of other forms by more than 9 to 1 in the Paris area between 1842 and 1847.

Eventually in response to pressure to emulate Britain and Belgium, liberalized limited liability legislation was introduced in France during 1867. Even so more information was required than in Britain. Joint stock companies were obliged to furnish a half-yearly balance sheet, an inventory and a profit and loss account to a committee of shareholders forty days before the general meeting, and the documents were to be available to all shareholders free of charge fourteen days before the meeting. A compulsory reserve fund was required. Five 5 per cent of net profits were to be transferred to the reserve until the total amounted to ten per cent of nominal capital. Penalties were to be imposed upon company officers for false statements. After 1867, the *société en commandite* fell into disuse, because of relatively free access to the *anonyme* form. (Table 3.1)

The consequences of the managerial incentive imposed by lack of limited liability in the *société en commandite* then failed to compensate for the advantage of full limited liability of the *société anonyme*. Since the *anonyme* was more tightly regulated than the British limited liability company, the implication that British limited liability must have been equally or more desirable cannot be drawn. A wide range of legal forms might be expected to encourage more economic activity so long as businesses are free to choose. But in general numbers of new registrations were lower in France than in Britain, perhaps because there were fewer fraudulent or ill-conceived French enterprises thanks to the tighter controls and because the economic potential

Table 3.1

Annual Average French Company Formations 1880-1913.

	société par actions			en nom collectif	Total *
en commandite		anonyme	à capital variable		
1880-90	102	483	56	3431	4615
1891-1900	73	595	127	3406	5091
1901-10	79	868	275	3935	6183
1911-13	90	1270	323	4592	7308

Note * *Sociétés en commandite simple* (undivided share capital) are included in the Total figure.

Source *Annuaire Statistique de la France 1936*, Revue Retrospectif.

was lower in France.

Unlimited liability offers an incentive to managers and shareholders to run their businesses efficiently; an incentive that is greater the more astringent are the bankruptcy laws. The higher the penalties of bankruptcy, the greater the attraction of limited liability, and the lower the level of bankruptcy, both because of the shift to limited liability and because of any deterrent effect encouraging better management.

On these counts the 1883 Act in England and Wales should have boosted company registrations. Liquidation by arrangement was abolished by the 1883 Act and bankruptcy increased. At the same time, becoming bankrupt was made more unpleasant. The bankrupt was unable to hold civil office. Whereas under the 1869 Act an undischarged bankrupt was protected for three years from the close of bankruptcy proceedings, under the 1883 Act the Court could requisition any property acquired since the proceedings until the bankrupt was discharged (which depended upon conduct). The undischarged bankrupt was required to inform any creditor or seller with whom he transacted for more than £20 of his status (BPP 1883). There was in consequence a strong incentive to acquire limited liability.

Seven years later the anodyne Winding Up Act attempted to tighten up the penalties for misconduct in the limited liability sector. The 1890 Act laid down that company officials guilty of misconduct, misinformation or trading while insolvent could be required to pay full compensation to those affected (BPP 1890). The report of the Comptroller General for bankruptcies for 1895 indicates that this provision was not in general implemented. Many liquidations still occurred solely because joint stock companies provided the opportunity to defraud creditors, the report complained. The Comptroller General referred to 'the temptation afforded to ingenious persons by the state of the law relating to joint stock companies for the formation of companies which do not meet and are frequently not intended to meet any real public requirements' and to 'the numerous breaches of trust which frequently accompany failure of this class (Board of Trade 1895, p.6). And 'It is to be regretted that the lack of adequate information with regard to the large class of limited companies which annually go into voluntary liquidation and many of which involve trading liabilities of large amounts, still leaves an important gap in the general statistics of insolvency which on public grounds it is desirable should be filled' (Board of Trade 1895, p.5) By far the bulk of the capital was involved in voluntary liquidations; between 1898 and 1907 93 per cent, the remainder being compulsory and supervised liquidations (Companies, 17th Annual Report of the Board of Trade 1908 in Webb (1911)). Matters were little different in 1926 when it could be said that 'under the present law there is no statutory obligation on a company to keep proper accounts . . . particularly with private companies on liquidation, books are so defective that it is impossible to find what has happened to goods and money belonging to them.. This was often deliberate, it was claimed (BPP 1926, para.67). Enterprises which were not going concerns acquired limited liability status merely for that purpose.

Both numbers of bankruptcies, liquidations and compositions and the excess of liabilities over assets declined from high levels. In 1879 the excess was over £19 million in England and Wales. Eventually, in the mid-1880s, because of the 1883 Bankruptcy Act, a break came in the early high mortality rate. In 1885 the excess of liabilities was just under £6 million. The liquidation risk continued to decline thereafter, falling by one-half between 1883 and 1913. These changes are likely to have been a mirror image of the increasing popularity of limited liability companies in these years. Tigher bankruptcy legislation encouraged more firms to adopt limited liability and wider adoption of limited liability reduced bankruptcy.

III

How did increasing popular limited liability affect investment? If not as many companies registered as was desirable and possible because of deficiencies in the 1856 Act and successors, then numbers of registrations will be positively associated with investment and it will be possible to calculate how much more investment would have taken place with more registrations. An investment function is therefore estimated with the form:

$I = f(y, r, w, p, B)$

Table 3.2

OLS Investment Equations

Period	1858-88	1858-88	1858-83	1858-83
New Registrations (−1)	0·1250	0·0923	− − − −	− − − −
	(1·3229)	(1·0818)		
(−2)	0·1987	0·0179	− − − −	− − − −
	(2·1313)	(2·0352)		
Effective Public Registrations (−1)	− − − −	− − − −	0·1254	− − − −
			(1·4369)	
(−2)	− − − −	− − − −	0·2012	− − − −
			(2·6108)	
All Effective Registrations (−1)	− − − −	− − − −	− − − −	0·1532
				(2·0559)
(−2)	− − − −	− − − −	− − − −	0·2214
				(3·31372)
interest rate (−1)	− 0·0273	− 0·0024	− 0·0224	− 0·0270
	(1·8778)	(1·6963)	(1·7311)	(2·4903)
interest rate (−2)	0·0425	− 0·0381	− 0·0403	− 0·0418
	(2·8801)	(2·8008)	(2·9783)	(3·5677)
wages (−1)	0·4207	0·3383	− 0·0122	0·4787
	(0·4617)	(0·3834)	(0·0117)	(0·5813)
wages (−2)	0·5963	0·2989	1·9629	1·9135
	(0·6867)	(0·3856)	(2·0369)	(2·4687)
GDP (−1)	− 0·2592	− − − −	− 0·3905	− 0·6784
	(0·3993)		(0·6723)	(1·3837)
GDP (−2)	− 0·1429	− − − −	− 0·1514	− 0·4476
	(0·2151)		(0·2352)	(0·8254)
Prices (−1)	2·3619	2·4580	1·5622	1·6932
	(3·3487)	(3·7027)	(1·4965)	(1·9220)
Prices (−2)	− 1·6953	− 1·5930	− 2·8815	− 3·2146
	(2·2509)	(2·2112)	(3.·1159)	(4·1657)
constant	− 4·8147	− 5·7584	5·5750	6·9780
	(2·5490)	(3·6733)	(7·5566)	(2·3008)
DW	1·5339	1·4520	1·2443	1·5865
R2	0·9026	0·9074	0·9378	0·9572

Note: t statistics in parentheses. All variables except the interest rate are in natural logarithms. (–1), (–2) indicate one and two year lags respectively.
Sources: New Registrations; Payne (1986), Shannon (1932) Interest; (3 mos bills) Mitchell (1988) p.683 Wages; Real GDP, Prices (plant and machinery) Feinstein (1972) T24. Investment; Feinstein and Pollard (1988).

where y is gross domestic product, r is a rate of interest, w is the wage rate, p, a price index, and B, numbers of new registrations, each with two (annual) lags.

Greater investment does not necessarily raise output. Both Shannon (1932, 1933) and Cottrell (1980) emphasized waste through fraudulence and short lives of new limited liability companies. Fraudulence might be merely a transfer or it may have reduced investment and switched resources to consumption. The principal effect though was likely to have been that ill-conceived projects and short business lives could have lowered the long term productivity of capital. To test this possibility a production function is estimated in error correction form:

$$dy = g(dk, dl, y, k, B, i)$$

where d indicates a first difference, k, net capital, l employment and y l and k are lagged. To avoid simultaneous equation bias, instrumental variable estimation is necessary.

A similar pattern emerges from all investment equations (Table 3.2 on page 41). Two year lags are necessary to eliminate the specification error suggested by autocorrelation. The two year elasticity of company registrations implies that a 100 per cent increase in company formation raises investment by 30 per cent. The best equation is for all effective registrations (i.e. excluding those companies that could not raise the capital from shareholders after registration). The statistically significant registration elasticity in this equation is 0.37. Higher interest rates reduce investment, but although the coefficients are significant, the elasticity is small, at 0.06-0.7. Given the range of variation of the rate on three month bills, interest impacts on investment must have been minimal.

The wage coefficients have the correct signs in most cases, becoming large and significant when ineffective registrations are excluded. Rises in wages, holding interest rates and prices constant, cause much more than proportionate increases in investment, as capital is substituted for labour. Greater labour scarcity in Victorian Britain might have thereby promoted the American system of manufacture'. Gdp is insignificant and persistently has the wrong sign, suggesting perhaps that it is acting as a proxy for a capital stock adjustment term.

Table 3.3

Production Functions.
Dependent variable: proportionate change in real GDP.

Period Method	1859-88 ols	1857-83 ols	1857-88 tsls	1857-88 ols	1857-83 ols	1857-88 tsls
propn. change employment	0·8042 (6·4770)	0·8406 (8·1052)	0·6947 (2·9700)	0·6765 (6·7273)	0·7296 (6·1133)	0·4658 (1·8307)
propn. change net capital	−0·1821 (0·4141)	−0·3624 (0·6922)	1·5836 (0·9505)	1·2464 (1·4323)	1·1970 (1·2492)	3·9930 (1·8307)
net capital (−1)	0·5021 (4·3457)	0·5341 (4·7915)	0·5226 (3·4498)	0·5613 (5·5225)	0·6063 (5·2078)	0·6930 (4·2048)
employment (−1)	1·0500 (4·8083)	1·0331 (4·5183)	0·6923 (1·74860)	1·0062 (5·6890)	1·0449 (4·8028)	0·8865 (3·7818)
gdp (−1)	−1·02007 (5·1498)	−1·0915 (5·3078)	−0·8974 (3·3345)	−1·0964 (6·3302)	−1·1891 (5·7805)	−1·1216 (5·2175)
All new registr. (−1)	−0·0010 (0·0607)	− − − −	−0·0040 (0·2754)	0·0095 (1·0311)	− − − −	0·0183 (1·3241)
(−2)	0·0055 (0·2736)	− − − −	− − − −	− − − −	− − − −	− − − −
(−3)	−0·0050 (0·3510)	− − − −	− − − −	− − − −	− − − −	− − − −
Effective public registr. (−1)	− − − −	0·0100 (0·8846)	− − − −	− − − −	− − − −	− − − −
All new reg. x incr. in net cap.	− − − −	− − − −	− − −	−0·2369 (1·9692)	− − −	−0·5886 (1·8854)
All effective reg. x incr. in net cap.					−0·2754 (1·8030)	
constant	−9·8680 (4·9998)	−9·7358 (4·7504)	−7·1060 (2·1851)	−9·6695 (6·0083)	−10·0631 (5·0957)	−9·1375 (4·6165)
R2	0·7910	0·800	n.a.	0·8291	0·8167	n.a.
DW	2·303	2·251	1·315	2·4910	2·3334	2·3467

Note: All variables in natural logarithms. t statistics in parentheses. Instruments in (3) and (6) wages, Plant and Machinery Prices (Feinsten 1972 T) and interest rates (Mitchell 1988 as in investment). (−1), (−2) and (−3) indicate respectively one, two and three year lags.

Sources: real net capital Feinstein and Pollard (1988), employment Feinstein (1972) T126. Other variables as in investment.

Limited liability encouraged investment and the more effective registrations, the higher the investment. The small number of registrations in the early period, probably due to information deficiencies, therefore reduced investment relative to what might have been attained. That higher investment was not necessarily likely to increase output though. More new firm formation has no significant effect on output in the production function, holding constant the effects of capital and labour (Table 3.3 on page 43). But there does seem to be a just detectable negative effect of company registrations on marginal capital productivity. Higher investment was less productive. At the end of the period the point estimates imply that in the TSLS equation (6) the marginal productivity of capital was negative when taking company registrations into account. The legislation's net effect must have been then to reduce output.

IV

A higher proportion of British investment went overseas than in other European countries because better information was available about overseas issues. It was not available about manufacturing (Kennedy 1976). By implication, if it had been, not only would the distribution of investment have been different, but the volume would have been greater and therefore so would the size and number of firms and the volume of British national product. Inverse swings between home and foreign investment during the nineteenth century supports the case by implying that they were substitutes. The 1856 Companies Act and subsequent companies legislation before 1948 missed an opportunity to encourage productive investment by failing to require the optimum mix of information provision and incentives to efficient management. An inadequate regulatory framework at first reduced the popularity of the limited liability form. Then changes in bankruptcy law and learning in the 1880s provided compensation, but productivity of limited liability investment may still have been low because of minimal company reporting obligations.

Comparison with the more tightly regulated French company sector shows the popularity of limited liability over the mixed *en commandite* company which theoretically gave stronger incentives to efficient management. That implies regulation of limited liability companies could reduce managerial moral hazard to acceptable levels.

Econometric evidence shows that investment increased with limited liability registrations but is consistent with a reduction in productivity of that investment as well. Possibly then the seeds of British relative economic decline in the later nineteenth century and beyond were planted by the 1856 Act.

Footnotes

1. Limited liability joint stock companies *(Société Anonyme)* could be formed before 1867 but the process was long, with departmental prefects being required to give opinions on the prospects of the enterprise and the character of the principals. Then the request was considered by the Minister of the Interior before being placed before the *Conseil d'Etat*. If these hurdles were cleared, the public accepted the prospects for the business were bright and typically the subsequent sale of shares at a premium was facilitated.

References

A B Atkinson and J E Stiglitz, *Lectures on Public Economics*, 1980.

Board of Trade, *12th Annual Report of the BoT into s131 of the Bankruptcy Act of 1883*, 1895.

BPP 1883 c85 LV 59 *Memo Showing the General Effect of the Change in the Law Proposed by the Bankruptcy Bill.*

BPP 1889 c5627 LXXVII.I *Report from HM Representatives Abroad Respecting the Formation, Regulation and Dissolution of Public Companies in Foreign Countries.*

BPP 1890 c133 XIII 31 *Standing Committee on Winding Up Act.*

BPP 1926 *Report of the Company Law Amendment Committee 1925-26* Cmnd 2657.

P L Cottrell, *Industrial Finance 1830-1914*, Methuen, 1980.

J R Edwards, *Company Legislation and Changing Patterns of Disclosure in British Company Accounts 1900-1940*, I C A, 1981.

J R Edwards and E Newell, 'The Development of Industrial Cost and Management Accounting before 1850: a Survey of the Evidence', *Business History* (forthcoming).

C H Feinstein, *National Income, Expenditure and Output 1855-1962*, Cambridge University Press, 1972.

C H Feinstein and S Pollard (eds), *Studies in Capital Formation in the United Kingdom 1750-1920*, Clarendon, 1988.

J S Foreman-Peck, 'Seedcorn or Chaff? New Firm Formation and the Performance of the Interwar Economy', *Economic History Review*, XXXVIII, 1985.

C E Freedman, 'Joint-Stock Business Organization in France 1807-1867', *Business History Review*, XXXIX, 1965.

C E Freedeman, 'The Coming of Free Incorporation in France 1850-1867', *Exploration in Entrepreneurial History*, 4, 1967.

L Hannah, *The Rise of the Corporate Economy*, Second Edition, Methuen, 1983.

E Jones, *Accountancy and the British Economy*, 1981.

W Kennedy, 'Institutional Response to Economic Growth: Capital Markets in Britain to 1914' in L Hannah (ed), *Management Strategy and Business Development*, Macmillan, 1976.

B R Mitchell, *British Historical Statistics*, 1988.

P L Payne, 'Introduction' to L Richmond and B Stockford, *Company Archives – the Survey of the Records of the First Registered Companies in England and Wales*, Gower, 1986.

H A Shannon, 'The First 50,000 Limited Companies and their Duration', *Economic History*, 4, 1932.

H A Shannon, 'The Limited Liability Companies of 1866-1883', *Economic History Review*, 1933.

W A Thomas, *The Provincial Stock Exchanges*, 1972.

R L Watts and J L Zimmerman, 'Agency Problems, Auditing and the Theory of the Firm: Some Evidence, *Journal of Law and Economics* XXVI, 1983.

H L Webb, *New Dictionary of Statistics*, 1911.

4
The Land Registry: a source of demography for business

The example of Basse-Normandie in the 19th century

Alain Leménorel

The historian is always in search of the perfect source. To be such a source for the study of the demography of businesses, it must at the same time provide information on the changing pattern and total number of establishments, and be reliable enough to allow for the well-known instability in the population of firms. Time series sources hardly match such criteria. The great industrial surveys of the nineteenth century can be dismissed straight away: certainly irreplaceable – but only for specific periods and even these are incomplete. Again, recently, M Lévy-Leboyer has rightly challenged the estimates of the ISEA[1] either for a superficial examination of the industrial fabric of the country or for an analyses of the structure of production which can anyway only be achieved after rigorous investigation. Consequently the available surveys, 1839-1845 and 1861-1865, are too exceptional to use in a study of economic demography.

Although available over a longer period, monthly returns and quarterly reports by the prefects and under-prefects to central government[2] are speculatively more use for analyses of the overall economic situation but they do not always have the expected quality of information. More attractive, *a priori*, are the statistics of creations of *sociétés* and failures kept since 1840 by the *Compte général de la justice civile et commerciale en France*.[3] From experience we can appreciate their regularity and their coverage, but, as Philippe Jobert[4] has shown, regret on the one hand at the impossibility of determining the total stock of enterprises – whatever the year, and on the other hand at the 'false symmetry' between the rise and fall of firms – only those firms which were established using the *sociétaire* form were registered, while the series for *faillites* (failures) comprises individual enterprises and *sociétés*. The last major drawback of this source is that the assets and liabilities shown relate to bankruptcy processes completed during the year, which, given the delays in the courts, introduces a disparity in the chronology between the observation of changes in the rate of bankruptcy proceedings and assessments of their severity. Certainly, archives of notaries and the registries of the *tribunaux de commerce* have been used to produce some remarkable investigations and local studies at the expense of time consuming abstraction of information and with unequal success depending on the region: deprived of judicial archives, because they were destroyed in 1944, Basse-Normandie, for example, cannot be hoped to be scrutinized in the same way that le Nord has been.[5]

The Register of Patents (licences) might be a perfect source for such research: the tax dates back a long time, continuous and covering all productive activities. P Lévêque has proved this tax is a good indicator of differential economic growth.[6] In fact this source is entirely suited to our objective as it makes it possible to reconstitute the total population of enterprises from the end of the eighteenth century and make annual corrections. For all that, it is not without faults, both in conception and in the way in which the records were kept. There is a lack of homogeneity over time, owing to reforms in 1844 and 1880, and in its content – the professional classes are included but mining is excluded! It is not always accessible and can only really be exploited at a national level and at best at a department level from the beginning of the annual publications by the Ministry of Finance.[7] For more precise investigations, the historian can only deplore the too numerous destruction of fiscal archives and put his faith in the chance preservation of papers or of local directories, but at best it will be only possible to isolate particular instances and not arrive at a true demography of business activity. Really fruitful endeavours are only possible in the urban setting, thanks to the richness of municipal archives.

Despite their respective limitations, all these archives have been put to good use in notable studies of the industrial history of France, but have only provided approximate estimates of the population of enterprises – the method of counting varies with each source, with a natural bias towards the more important establishments. When used to determine the rise and fall in the population in different sectors, it becomes very difficult to determine precisely the peaks and troughs of the cycles. Can one hope to do better, by going further?

It is with this ambition that the Association *Histoire et Patrimoine industriels de Basse Normandie* in 1980 took the initiative in exploiting another source: the *cadastre* or land registry. On the basis of a convincing pilot study, limited to three industrial valleys,[8] the association has with equal success extended the exercise to inventory the industrial heritage of Basse Normandie and to master the technicalities of the source.[9] This work has demonstrated the vibrancy and concentration of industry in the valleys in the nineteenth century, adapting itself to the contingencies of successive inter-connected business cycles. It is only recently, with the obsolescence of hydraulic power, that the valleys have lost their predominance. From this perspective the *cadastre* is shown to be an effectual source for the historian, providing details that other sources failed to capture. A *priori* then the *cadastre* provides access to information that would otherwise be elusive, the minute details of the industrial structure, which is so unobtrusive that only with difficulty can it be discerned in an economy dominated by huge units, but which contributed to the vitality of the concentration of enterprise in the valleys. By providing testimony to the diversity and the comings and goings of artisan and industrial businesses, can the *cadastre* ensure that economic reality will no longer be deformed by the inadequacy of sources? Is this to say it is a perfect source?

We have already, on the basis of a systematic card index of the units of production recorded by the *cadastre*, enlarged the field of study to the whole of Basse-Normandie, with the intention of improving, by repeated tests, the history of the industrial fabric of the region.[10] In this article we wish to demonstrate the interest of these documents for the investigation of industrial demography both in plotting craft/industrial enterprises and in interpreting the micro-economy of a region.

The Cadastre, perfect source?

The historian, if he refers to the basic principles of the *cadastre*, can expect to extract from it an exhaustive and continuous coverage of the structure of production. In the first place, because the *cadastre*, introduced by Napoleon in 1807, was intended to identify small plots, it enumerates both landed and developed property.[11] Buildings, excluded at first because revenues were variable, were finally included on the understanding that as soon as the building was demolished it ceased to be liable for property tax. The historian can only rejoice at this extension, which is essential as the land tax was then divided between contributions from undeveloped property with only superficial buildings, and developed property. Another advantage of the source is the regular record of the actual day a new building was completed, demolished or converted to other purposes: frequently a mill was converted into a spinning factory – consequently it also records rises and falls in cadastral revenue from developed property. The historian thus can be certain in principle of finding in the *cadastre* information from which to make an assessment of the productive heritage, at the beginning of the study, of an area based on the number of establishments and the free value of the cadastral revenue. Moreover it is possible to adjust this assessment year after year. Total populations and changing patterns, the essential elements in any demography of enterprises at a local level are brought together.

Before the source can be used there is the tedious task of collating the information in the registers and overcoming problems of interpretation – The *cadastre* is in effect composed of three basic documents: *l'état de section, la matrice,* and *l'atlas.*[12] The historian will at first need to locate the industrial and artisan establishments in *l'état de section,* which gives the number and content of each plot, the name of the proprietor or life tenant, the cadastral revenue, the precise character of the property, with a summary at the end of each section. Next it is necessary to consult the alphabetic list of proprietors in *la matrice cadastrale,* to find a folio reference in the same *matrice* to the plot of developed property which he is researching. The *matrice* being in general contemporaneous with the *états de section,* the entry date of a plot is, therefore, that of the beginning of the *cadastre.* All further changes in character, in proprietor, or even of cadastral revenue, are, as a rule, inscribed in the registers of increases and decreases. As a result it is possible to trace a plot from folio to folio reconstructing its entire history.[13] Finally *l'atlas,* very accurate and organized by sections, allows maps to be drawn of all the identified sites.

Very technical and immensely time-consuming to use – and for that reason, certainly, abandoned by historians to the benefit of notaries and lawyers, the *cadastre* as a source is not in all respects faultless, despite its intrinsic quality. For example, the *cadastre* of Calvados begun in 1808 was only completed in 1837, and the director of direct taxation recalled 'without a doubt the operation was open to error and imperfections'. Such an experience makes it impossible to identify certain plots and difficult to study their chronology because of the repeated absence of registers of changes, which is the case for Calvados. The demographer of enterprise, always anxious for continuity, will be equally troubled by the delay in registering changes, sometimes for several years. The oversight in reporting makes it hard to examine metal working, a sector of great irregularity, alternating between extinguishing and rekindling furnaces. Finally, the cadastral revenue charged on the face value of each plot must not be confused with the rental values recorded by the inquiry of 1839-45.

Even if there are complexities, these are fat outweighed by the quality of detail recorded which, unlike other sources, allows for analysis of the pattern and value of business activity. The complexity should not discourage the historian from using cadastral revenue or rentals of licences as we have shown in an examination of the industrial geography of a department such as Orne in the middle of the nineteenth century which presents the same features.[14] As for the delay in registering changes to property, the problem is entirely comparable to that of bankruptcies. Nothing prevents the historian, aware of the imperfections of the documentation, from using the graphs of the number of establishments and of cadastral revenue to provide a moving average of the rate of industrialisation, ironing out annual peaks and troughs, particularly at times of economic crisis.

Likewise, despite the apparently exhaustive principles on which the *cadastre* was compiled, it has been established that it is the best source to elucidate the fine detail of the fabric of production, but the greatest drawback is the omission in the *cadastre* of the fundamental infrastructure of proto-industrialisation. Insufficient reference to handloom weavers makes proto-industrialisation decidedly difficult to find out about. The documentation is more reliable when it concerns large establishments – as the mechanical weavers after 1863-65 in the neighbourhood of Flers and La Ferté-Macé. On the whole, the source stands up well to tests. Not without its differences in interpretation, particularly when it comes to the precise definition of chronology, the *cadastre* shows itself to be a completely effective and usable source from the series of archives available for the most sensitive study possible of the natural progression of enterprises.

Demography of enterprises: the example of Orne

In commenting on the results of our study relating to the department of Orne, chosen for the quality of its *cadastre*, we have eliminated the cases less than 30 francs, numerous but insignificant, and often the most ephemeral.

Orne XIXe Siècle

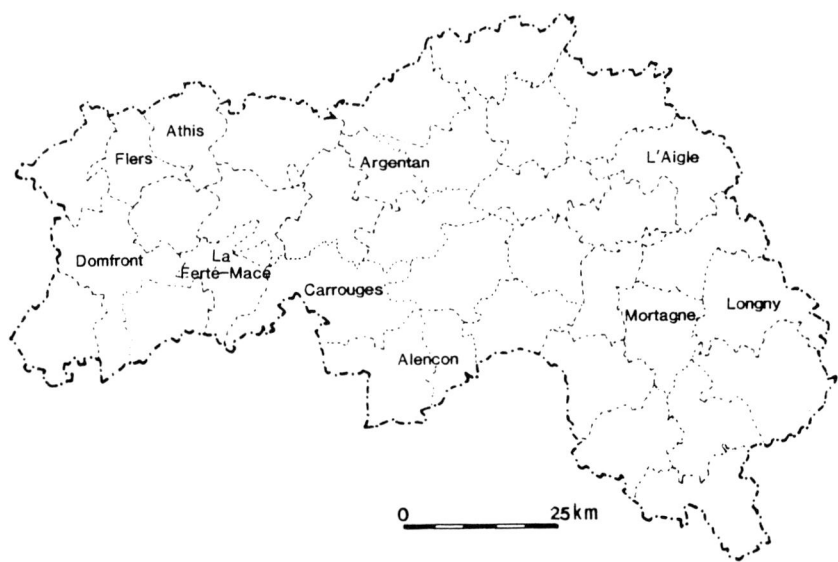

Even so, the industrial network of the department of Orne is one of pronounced density, only 22.6 per cent of communes have no artisan/industrial sites in 1830-35, against 45.2 per cent in Calvados. The number remains constant in the long term with 1,040 establishments in 1830/35 and still 1,036 in 1881. This stability is, however, only the result of two contradictory movements before and after 1859-60 (Figure 4.1, graph 1). The graph of cases above 30 francs exhibits dynamic growth until 1859 – it falls away gently during the economic crisis of the mid-nineteenth century and collapses markedly thereafter. Is this the effect of concentration? Not at all, since the graph of cases greater than 200 francs (Figure 4.1, graph 2) climbs steadily until 1868, and then falls away rapidly over the following ten years. In effect the average size of a case (Figure 4.1, graph 3) rose to a maximum of 222 francs in 1849 before returning in 1881 to its level in 1830 (212.99

francs against 212.89 francs). Can one believe that such an experience suggests that an industrial revolution has occurred?

Table 4.1

	Number cases > 30 francs	Number of cases > 200 francs
1830-1881 −0·4 %		−1·5 %
1830-1859 +5·8 %	1830-1844 +2·4 %	+3·9 %
	1844-1852 −1·7 %	
		+1·2 %
	1852-1859 +3·8 %	
1859-1881 −5·8 %	1859-1869 −1·4 %	+2·3 %
	1869-1881 −4·5 %	−8·4 %

If the profile of the graph of cadastral revenues (Figure 4.2, graph Orne) differs to a slight extent, the general impression is confirmed: positive growth during the July Monarch (+ 5 per cent from 1836 to 1847) succeeded by a period of real stagnation under the Second Empire (0.5 per cent from 1850 to 1869) which reflects the difficulties of the west of France in adapting to the acceleration at this time of the industrial revolution. The conclusion to be drawn from all these graphs is that there is net decline even before the change of fortunes in 1870, which accelerates after 1860 with the attack on archaic and modest business structures. There is quite a retraction in the number and value of enterprises making up the productive fabric of the department, the history of which is very unsettled. Out of an initial stock of 1,040 establishments at the beginning of the period, we have counted from 1830 to 1881 468 creations and 472 disappearances – proof of healthy regeneration in the economic structure. Figure 4.3 can be summarised in this way.

Alternatively, size does not play a positive role in the increasing density of the fabric in the periods 1830-44 and 1853-59 or its thinning out. The marked weakening after 1870 mostly affected larger enterprises which had enjoyed their greatest success in the July Monarchy (+ 6 per cent from 1830 to 1847), with a brief recovery from 1860 to 1868 (+ 3.3 per cent). There is indeed a crisis in both the fabric and composition of the regional economy. The stark

Figure 4.1

Orne

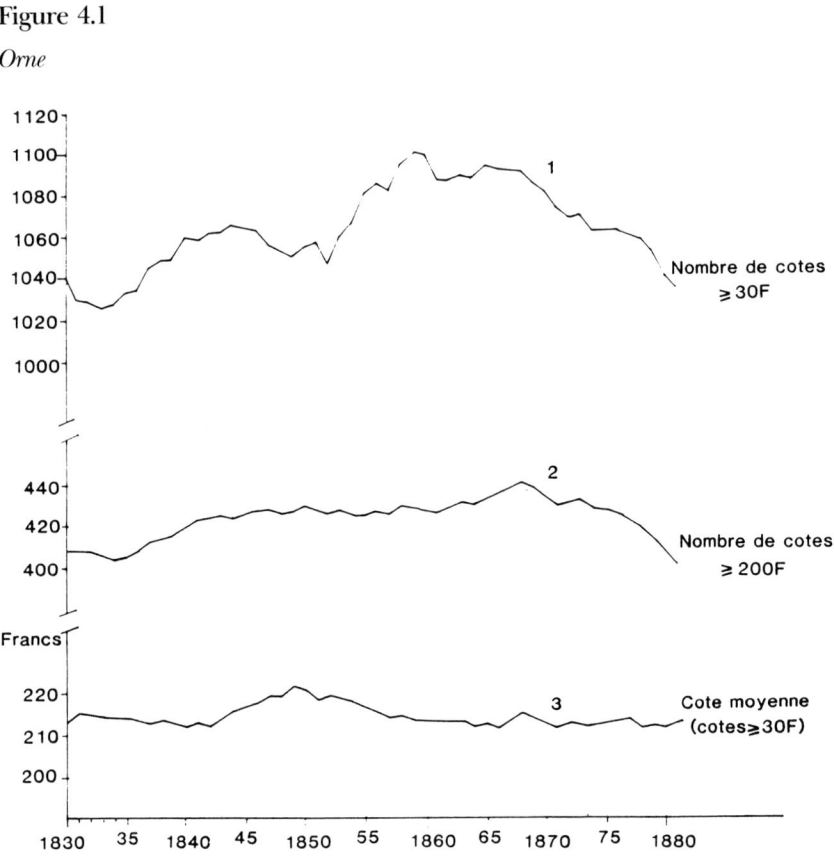

profile of movements in the cadastral revenues (Figure 4.3), is influenced by high values, when in most cases values are very low, nevertheless, it confirms the cycle already observed. Creations more than compensate for disappearances up to 1845 (30,598 francs against 21,371 francs), reaching a peak in 1858 (1846-1858: 33,770 francs against 29,566 francs). Thereafter the position is reversed (1859-1869: 22,038 francs against 24,569 francs: 1870-1881: 21,114 francs against 32,816 francs).

The cause should not so much be attributed to the mortality rate but to the birth rate. The mortality rate averages 8.9 a year in 1853-59, rises to 9.1 in 1860-69 and 10.3 in 1870-81, an unremarkable progression to be expected in a more and more competitive economy. The birth rate on the other hand collapses from an average of 15.9 a year in 1853-59 to 7.7, and finally to 6.4.

THE LAND REGISTRY – BASSE-NORMANDIE IN THE 19th CENTURY

Figure 4.2

Cadastral revenue (cases > 30F).

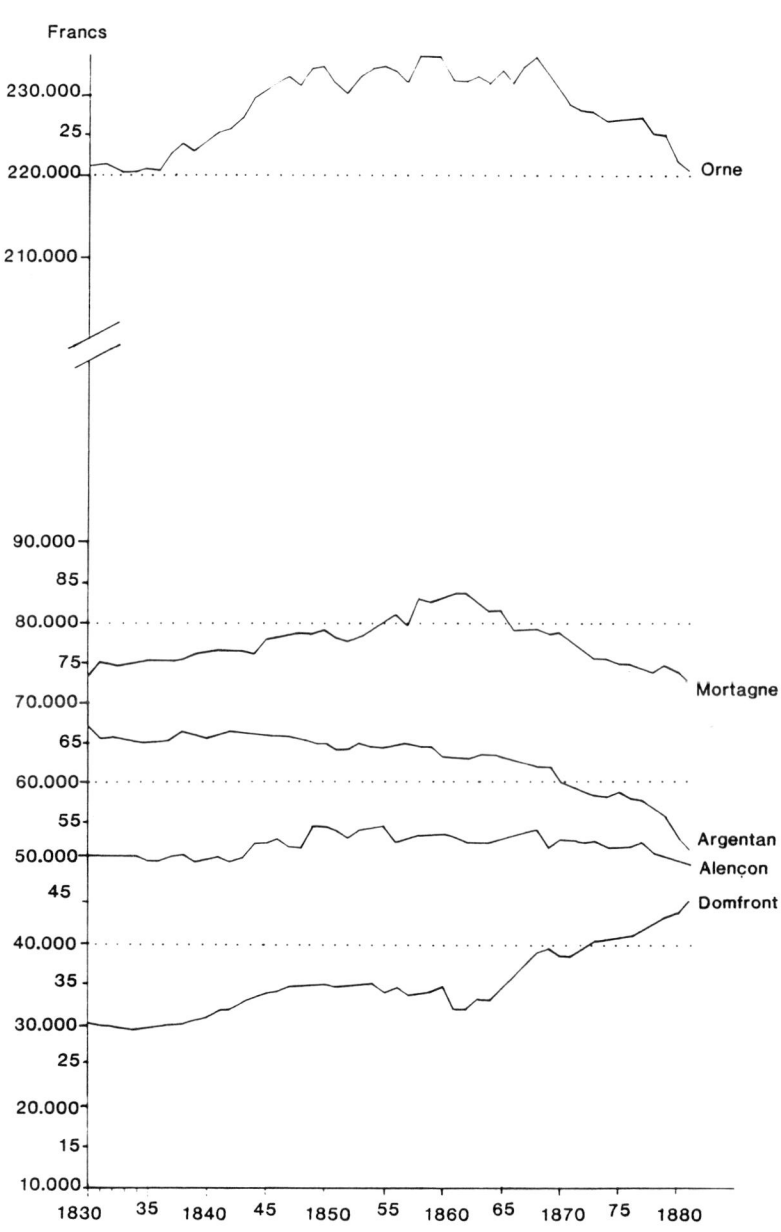

Table 4.2

	cases > 30 francs			cases > 200 francs
	créations (C)	disparitions (D)	C/D	C/D
1830-1831	468	472	0·99	0·96
1830-1859	302	242	1·25	1·34
1860-1881	166	230	0·72	0·65
1830-1844	119	94	1·27	1·67
1845-1852	63	81	0·78	1·10
1853-1859	120	67	1·79	1·17
1860-1869	84	99	0·85	1·59
1870-1881	82	131	0·63	0·38

From 1860 the natural movement is in deficit, and the reproduction of productive sites can no longer be assured. Now, as F Caron has noted, 'a system in which the birth of enterprises is high tends constantly to find a point of equilibrium'.[15]

The result of contingency or the lack of creative spirit, it suffices to say that the entrepreneurial Malthusianism of the department threatened its economic prospects. Hope for the future would have been provided by an increase in the average value of a case, but from this perspective its stagnation was very serious because the dwindling numbers of new creations was not even compensated for by their greater size or by a growth of existing firms.[16] On the contrary the bigger units (<200 francs) are more harshly affected by the economic circumstances after 1870, with a mortality rate averaging 12 a year (1870-1881, against 10.3 for all cases above 30 francs), and a birth rate averaging 4.6. These levels suggest an economic catastrophe, and not only an opposition to progress.

To validate our source, we next compared the ratio of creations/disappearances in the *cadastre* with the ratio of formations/failures found in the *Compte général de la justice commerciale*. The two series correspond loosely because the differences in scope of the two sources, the *cadastre* indicates all new creations, including 'sole traders', whereas the *Compte* is restricted to

THE LAND REGISTRY – BASSE-NORMANDIE IN THE 19th CENTURY

Figure 4.3

Orne.

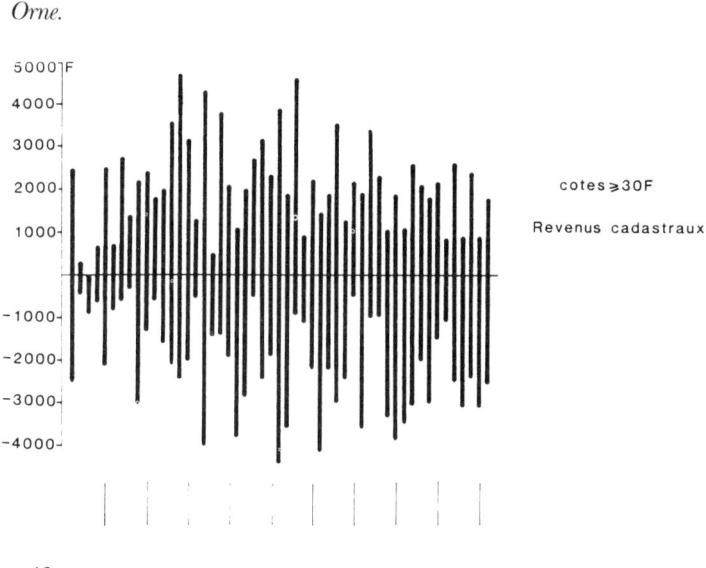

cotes ⩾30F
Revenus cadastraux

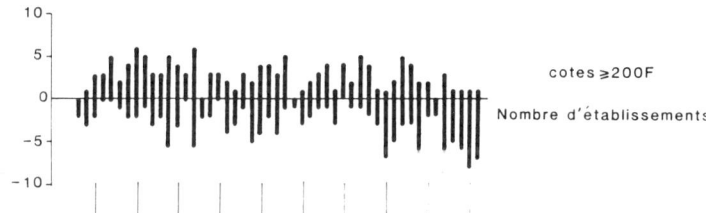

cotes ⩾200F
Nombre d'établissements

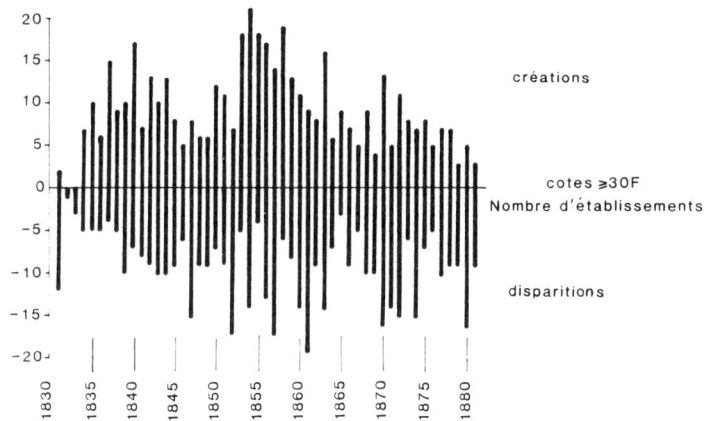

créations

cotes ⩾30F
Nombre d'établissements

disparitions

sociétés. Equally disappearances from the *cadastre* are not always the result of bankruptcies recorded in the *Compte*. However, taken as a whole, the ratio of C/D are more homogeneous in their composition than those of C/F which, comparing two strikingly different movements by their definition, present at times surprising cycles in the light of classical economic history.

The retreat in cases greater than 200 francs after 1868 gives rise to even greater concern when it is considered that they represent such an essential ingredient in the total stock of enterprises formed at the beginning of the period: 73.2 per cent in 1830-35. In fact their proportion remains stable until the end of the period under review: 73.7 per cent in 1860, and still 72.5 per cent in 1880, despite a slight regression in their average value (397 francs in 1830-35, 396 francs in 1860, and 388 francs in 1880). However, these averages are sustained by varied pressures, narrowly confined both geographically and sectorally. The greatest influences were definitely the recession in milling, the shift away from the iron and steel industry towards textiles, which was promoted to the leading industry in the department after 1870, symbolised by the rise of Domfront area.

The structural development of the principal units of productions (cases greater than 200 francs) effectively benefited textile mills:

Table 4.3

	1830-35		*1860*		*1880*	
moulins (mills)	342	83·8%	332	77·2%	284	71·4%
tuileries/verreries (tile/glassworks)	14	3·4 %	19	4·4 %	19	4·8 %
textile	12	2·9 %	25	5·8 %	46	11·6%
métalurgie	16	3·9 %	24	5·6 %	24	6·0 %
sidérurgie (metal working)	21	5·1 %	22	5·1 %	7	1·8 %
tannerie	2		3		2	
divers	1		5		16	
	408	100	430	100	398	100

Twenty-one establishments strong in 1830, of which eleven were in the *arrondissement* of Mortagne and of an average cadastral revenue of 902 francs the iron and steel working dominated industry properly speaking, the mills can be considered as the vestiges of a pre-industrial economy. But it had already reached its peak and, closure following closure, just ten establishments were still active in 1880. By then it was based on modest sites, with an average cadastral revenue of 323 francs, and enterprises had practically all been transformed into foundries re-working metal smelted elsewhere. Nevertheless, the *arrondissement* of Mortagne had switched rapidly to wire-drawing, nail and needle making, giving life back to the valley of the Risle. The nine establishments in 1830 had grown to 17 by 1881 and their average revenue had climbed from 656 francs to 742 francs. But in these trades, as in others, the essential fabric was created before 1860, from 16 factories in the department in 1830 the number reached 20 in 1850 and a maximum of 25 by 1861, and then stagnated until 1881 when 23 remained.

From 1860 the textile trades were in the ascendant to the benefit of Domfrontais, at that time a region removed from the map of metal working and metallurgy since at least 1857. The history of textiles in the Orne department is itself at once identified with the development of spinning, which was most creatively dynamic between 1835 and 1840 (Figure 4.4) with ten foundations all in the valley of the Vère and of the Noireau. But on the whole this industry remained very modest at a point where the graph of revenue raised followed that of the natural progression of the number of cases, and the average value clearly declined, falling from 210 francs around 1830 to 169 francs in 1858 (Figure 4.4, graphs 2,3 and 4). In fact the vital ingredient in the textile industry was not the spinning, which represented only 32 per cent of the total, but fulling mills, dye-works and bleach fields.

Changing in pace after 1860, all the graphs of the textile trades are on the increase, contrasting with the noticeable dullness or even decline in other graphs. Reflecting then this rise from 1860 to 1881, eight new spinning businesses were established, and more significantly 25 mechanical weaving enterprises, of which seven were set up in 1863/65 at the very beginning of the new cycle. These are essentially the establishments which, thanks to their high cadastral valuations, reinflate the average for the sector, bringing it back to 213 francs in 1881.[17] And it is the textile sector which prevents the departmental graphs of global and average revenue from plunging any further (Figures 4.2 and 4.1).

The demography of the textile industry then largely compensates for the loss of iron and steel working, which the renewal in metallurgical trades had not been able alone to make up for:

Table 4.4

Revenus Cadastraux.

	sidérurgie metal working	métallurgie	textile
1830	18 942 f	8 030 f	9 823 f
1881	3 235 f	14 700 f	29 868 f

The success of textiles is strictly confined to the Domfront area; that *arrondissement* accounts for 115 of the 140 sites counted in 1881, some 82 per cent against 47 per cent in 1830 – with even higher proportions for weaving (85 per cent), spinning (92 per cent) and bleachfields (100 per cent). Does this graph subtend with that of the whole of the department (Figure 4.4, graphs 1 and 3)? Without the impact of mechanical weaving, the region would, after 1860, have shared the experience of its neighbours since, despite a growth in numbers of enterprises from 1847 to 1862, the cadastral values had fallen:

Table 4.5

Revenus Cadastraux.

	creations + increases	disparitions + decreases	balances
1830-46	6 237 f	2 340 f	+ 3 897 f
1847-62	6 162 f	8 448 f	− 2 286 f
1863-81	19 112 f	5 571 f	+ 13 541 f

Weaving alone represents more than half of the surplus in the final period and textiles accounts for a total of 86 per cent.[18]

Unlike the department as a whole, the birth rate of firms in Domfront was always in excess of the mortality rate, particularly for units greater than 200 francs of which the stock improved to 69 per cent between 1830 and 1881, compared with 27 per cent for establishments valued at between 30 and 200 francs. This demographic vitality of the *arrondissement* of Domfront was unusual as it was the only one to record a positive relationship between creations and disappearances over the whole period under review, with a

Figure 4.4

Orne: Textile industries, 1830-1880.

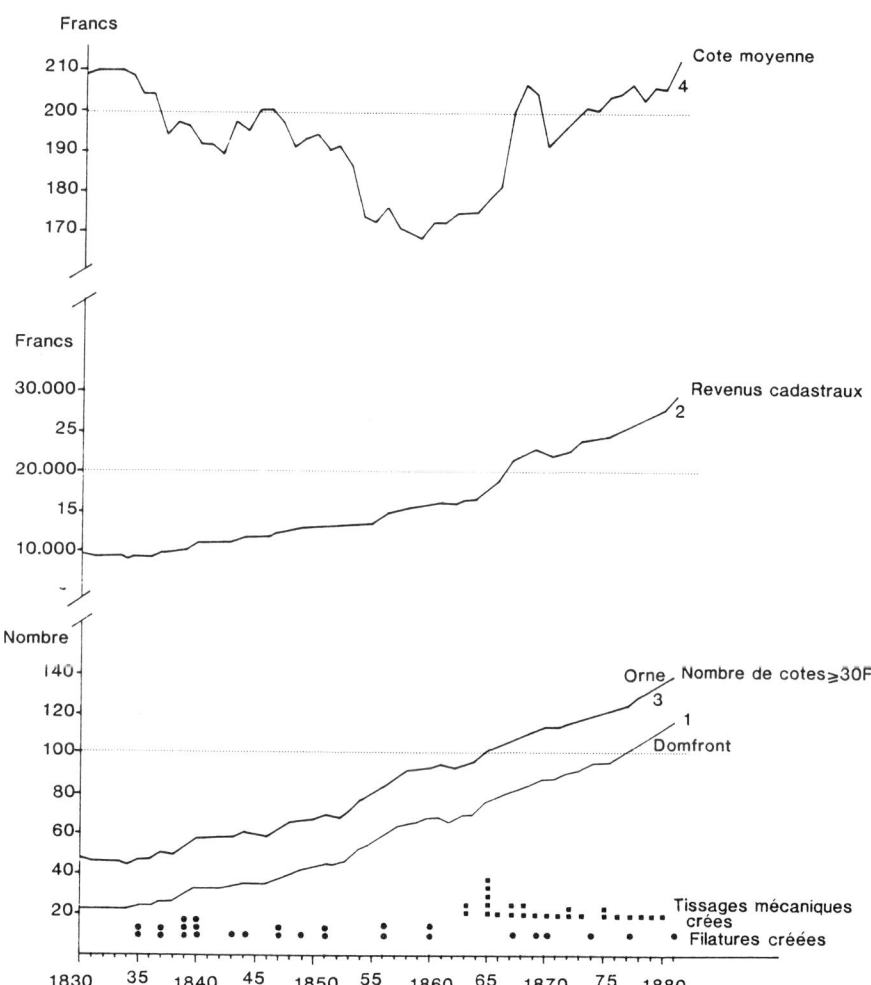

notable performance from 1853 to 1859 – it is true more in number than in worth – and from 1870 to 1881:

Table 4.6

Relationships of créations/disparitions.

	Argentan	Mortagne	Alençon	Domfront	Orne
			(cases > than 30 f)		
1830-1881	0·65	0·87	0·98	1·99	0·99
1830-1859	0·88	1·20	1·39	2·02	1·25
1860-1881	0·40	0·55	0·57	1·95	0·72
1830-1844	0·84	1·26	1·24	2·67	1·27
1845-1852	0·55	0·75	0·85	1·18	0·78
1853-1859	1·36	1·57	2·40	2·64	1·79
1860-1869	0·55	0·92	0·58	1·71	0·85
1870-1881	0·31	0·31	0·55	2·15	0·63

Comparisons of the birth and mortality rates always favours the *arrondissement* of Domfront:

Table 4.7

	Birth rates		Mortality rates	
	Orne	Domfront	Orne	Domfront
1853-1859	15·9 %	17·1 %	8·9 %	6·5 %
1860-1869	7·7 %	11·3 %	9·1 %	6·6 %
1870-1881	6·4 %	13·0 %	10·3 %	6·0 %

In this way a new industrial geography was gradually built up in the department of Orne, stemming from the replacement around about 1860 of iron and steel working by textiles, which especially in weaving initiated concentration and mechanisation. In this geographical redistribution, which depended on sectoral changes, the *arrondissement* of Domfront alone really advanced in the long term, allowing its economy to come back into equilibrium to the benefit of the west of the department which was singularly depressed before[19]:

Table 4.8

Cases 30 f > (1 = by number; 2 = by value).

Arrondissements	1830-35		1860		1880	
	1	2	1	2	1	2
Mortagne	32·9 %	33·2 %	32·4 %	35·5 %	31·2 %	32·9 %
Argentan	29·2 %	30·1 %	26·5 %	27·8 %	23·8 %	24·0 %
Alençon	17·8 %	23·0 %	18·2 %	21·7 %	17·6 %	22·0 %
Domfront	20·1 %	13·7 %	22·9 %	15·0 %	27·4 %	21·1 %

The noticeable improvement of western Orne at the end of the period merits comment. The redressing of the economic balance was too recent to have overturned traditional hierarchies until the end of the century and was anyway confined to three cartons and at that only the three chief places, Flers, La Ferté-Macé and Athis experienced a real improvement. This was a very transitory upturn as this first industrial revolution in urban mechanical weaving, which literally robbed the countryside of its domestic systems of manufacture and its population, ran out of steam after 1890. Even the rise in spinning predominantly urban after 1896 counts for nothing: hardly had the twentieth century opened than the development of the textile industry in Orne was definitely checked.

Stopping as it does in 1881, our study cannot represent in its totality that short-lived geographic and economic composition of a department adversely affected by the circumstances of the first half of the twentieth century. The choice of that date is simply the result of a decline in the quality of the *cadastre* as a source. A document of quality, despite its faults, for a great part of the nineteenth century, it must be approached with caution after 1880 because, on the one hand of a failure to record changes, and on the other because of a break in the statistical continuity.[20] As for the revision of the Napoleonic *cadastre* initiated by the law of 16 April 1939, this was only completed for our department in 1977!

A very technical source full of 'traps for the unwary', the *cadastre* nevertheless reveals a demography of enterprise in two dimensions, spacially and over time, with the possibility of a very precise analysis of cycles in the overall economy and by sector in the short term, as well as in the commercial heart of the department – the industrial valley. Its other major utility is in the homogeneity of the information it provides about the flow of entries and departures, and those of the natural movement of enterprises, unlike the *Compte général* of failures and creations of *sociétés*. Certainly the ambition will be to try to cross tabulate the information from the *cadastre* with that of *patentes*.

Footnotes

1. M. Lévy-Leboyer, F. Bourguignon: *L'économie française au XIXeme siècle. Analyse macro-économique*, 1985, pp.254-257.
2. Arch. Nat. F 12-4475 à 4450 (de 1825 à 1888), et Arch.dép.
3. 1er volume 1830-31, puis volumes pluri-annuels et annuels. Complément pour les années 1820-1840 avec Arch. nat. F 20-722.
4. Ph. Jobert, J.Cl. Chevailler: 'La démographie des entreprises en France au XIXème siècle'; *Histoire, économie, société*, 1986, 2.
5. P. Deyon, J.P. Hirsch: 'Entreprise et association dans l'arrondissement de Lille, 1830-1862'; dans: *Entreprises et entrepreneurs, XIX-XIXemes siècles*, 1983, pp.5-21.
6. P. Lévêque: 'La patente, indicateur de croissance économique différentielle au XIXème siècle' dans: Entreprises et entrepreneurs, XIX-XXèmes siècles, 1983, pp.46-73.
7. *Compte général de l'administration des Finances 1825-1840*, 1 volume par an. Puis: *Compte définitif des recettes*, 1 volume par an à partir de 1841. Renseignements récapitulatifs également dans *l'Annuaire statistique* (ex. 1966). Statistiques sur l'année 1827 dans: Arch. Nat. F 20-743.
8. 'Patrimoine industriel en Normandie', n° spécial des *Annales de Normandie* 1982, n°3.
9. 'Vère, Noireau, Saire: trois vallées industrielles'; *Le Pays Bas-Normand* 1984 n°2.
10. A. Leménorel: Le cadastre, source d'histoire industrielle; 23ème Congrès des Soc. hist. et archéol. de Normandie, L'Aigle oct. 1988.
11. Sur l'histoire du cadastre et son mode d'emploi, voir l'introduction *de S. de Poorter au: Répertoire numérique de la sous-série* 3P *Cadastre 1800-1940*, Arch.

dép. Calvados 1980, pp.11-97.
12. Pour s'initier aux règles juridiques de leur conception: R. Lemercier de Jauvelle: *Répertoire généralé des contributions directes*, 1877 (états de sections; pp.330-334; matrices: p.432-434; atlas: pp.552-556).
13. A partir de 1881 sont tenus des registres séparés pour les propriétés non-bâties et les propriétés bâties, ces dernières étant alors 'sorties' des matrices foncières; dès lors le folio devient la 'case'.
14. Voir notre étude citée, oct. 1988.
15. F. Caron, présentation du Colloque des historiens économistes de mars 1980, dans: *Entreprises et entrepreneurs XIX-XXe siècles*, 1983, p.2.
16. Valeur moyenne des créations et augmentations: 1830-1844: 230 f 65
　　　　　　　　　　　　　　　　　　　　　　　　1870-1881: 257 f 49

　　Il n'y a pas de 'révolution' notable!
17. 1880: revenu cadastral moyen des tissages mécaniques: 530 f à Flers (filatures: 247 f), 473 f à La Ferté-Macé (filatures: 330 f), 660 f à Athis (filatures: 463 f).
18. Sur 153 établissements nouveaux de 1830 à 1881 dans cet arrondissement, 105 appartiennent au secteur textile.
19. revenu cadastral des cotes < 30 f, 1830-35 à 1880:
　　Argentan: -23.3%; Alençon: -8%; Mortagne: -4.6%; Domfront: +48.4%; Département: -3.8%.
20. En raison de la loi du 08.08.1890 sur les contributions foncières, qui substitue les valeurs locatives aux revenus cadastraux.

5

The managerial labour market in fast growth small firms[1]

David J Storey

1. Objectives

There is increasing interest amongst both public policy-makers and financial institutions in the characteristics of highly successful small firms. [Department of Employment, 1989, Turok and Richardson, 1989, Storey, Watson and Wynarczyk, 1989]. Whilst the criteria according to which growth is measured may, in some contexts, be employment whereas in other cases it may be measured in financial terms, it remains almost a truism to say that the quality of the management is central to the performance of a fast growing small firm. It therefore remains something of a surprise that improving our understanding of the management of small firms is an inadequately researched area. Our current purpose, which forms part of a long term programme of work [Storey, 1985, Storey, Keasey, Watson and Wynarczyk, 1987], is to investigate the extent to which it is possible to relate the skills and practices of management to the performance of the small business.

In the research reported in this paper we distinguish between two sources of supply of managerial expertise in small firms. The first is the owner(s) of the business who, in a very small firm, will provide all of the managerial resources. Even as the firm grows the owner is likely to continue to make all the key decisions, and many of the minor ones [Scott and Bruce, 1987]. Nevertheless firm growth is likely to lead to greater devolution of managerial responsibility to professional managers. These are individuals who exercise a managerial function, defined as the supervision of others and reporting back to the owners, but who are not themselves (significant) owners of the business.

For the owners of the business we are interested in matters such as their educational and employment background, the factors influencing their decision to start the business, the business skills which they (and possibly their co-owners) had at start up, how they developed their own expertise as well as that of others as the business grew. Scott and Bruce argue that the style and role of management in a small firm changes as the business grows and develops. New forms of managerial expertise are required as well as increasing numbers of managers. These individuals both serve to meet the current requirements of the firm, but also provide the opportunity for the firm to develop in possibly new directions. Hence the ability of the owner to ensure that 'round pegs are placed in round holes' is critical to ensuring the growth and development of the business. It is towards a better understanding of this process that this paper is directed.

2. The Fast Growth Small Businesses

Two groups of businesses are investigated. The first are those firms which are known to have to have grown exceptionally rapidly from start up. The definition of 'fast growth' which we have chosen is a company which reaches the Unlisted Securities Market (USM) within ten years of start up. The disadvantage of this definition is that it excludes at least two groups of companies which could quite reasonably claim to be regarded as fast growing. The first are those which have reached the USM but which are relatively old. For example, there are a number of old established companies which are on the USM, have experienced rapid growth in recent years, but were established either in the last or at the start of this century – the three Funeral Directors on the USM are illustrations.

The second is that there will be fast growing small companies that have no wish to sell equity and obtain a quotation on the USM. Such companies will also be excluded under this definition of fast growth. These disadvantages are, in our view, offset by the advantage of using the 'ten year USM' criteria.

These are that all companies satisfying the criteria are fast growers, and secondly that these companies are relatively easy to identify. Furthermore reasonably complete data on the performance of these companies are readily available, both for the years in which they have been on the USM, and for prior years. This enables the group itself to be subdivided according to performance, and also for direct comparisons to be made with other, longer established, USM customers. In short, it is not being suggested that the 'ten year USM' criteria is the only one possible for defining fast growth, or even that the businesses selected in this way are necessarily typical of fast growth firms. They are, nevertheless, a subgroup of fast growers which are amenable to analysis.

3. Fast Growing USM Companies: Comparisons with the Small Business Population

Preliminary analysis of these fast growth companies – Stoddart and Storey (1989) – shows them to be heavily concentrated in certain sectors, not typical of the UK small business population. USM companies as a whole are disproportionately concentrated in computing and related activities and in business services – the so-called people businesses of advertising, PR, and consultancy. In no way do they reflect the sectoral pattern of small businesses in the UK, where retail, distribution and construction are major components. [Gangulyu (1986)]. The sector in which a firm is located is therefore a major factor influencing the probability of reaching the USM. Stoddart and Storey show that even amongst USM companies, the younger firms are more heavily concentrated in the electronics, oil and business service sectors, than even older USM firms.

Our earlier work – Storey, Keasey, Watson and Wynarczyk (1987) – has shown that in comparing the performance of small firms, age is also a crucial element. In particular young small firms tend to grow faster than older firms, but also are more prone to failure. The fast growth companies tend to be those currently concentrated in the age range of 6 – 15 years. A random sample of UK small businesses might expect to show more than 30 per cent being six years old or less and just over 20 per cent being more than 15 years old. [Johnson (1989)]. In this crucial sense therefore the current collection of fast growth firms also differs markedly from the population of UK small firms.

A third area of difference between a random sample of small firms and the fast growth firms examined here is in terms of ownership patterns. In choosing the criteria of fast growth to be that of reaching the USM within ten years of start up, it would clearly be inappropriate to include companies which are subsidiaries of other firms. In the case of subsidiaries the parent companies may be able to provide resources normally unavailable to start-up independent companies. Thus the companies included in this study are legally independent when they reached the market, even though some may have subsequently been acquired.

Mason (1985) has shown that the South East of England has a disproportionately high number of USM companies, compared with other regions of the UK. There is also some evidence of regional variations in small firm performance in the UK – Harrison and Mason (1986), Fothergill and Gudgin (1982) – suggesting that small firms in the prosperous South East of England have performed rather better than those in the more 'peripheral' regions such as Northern England, Northern Ireland, Scotland and Wales. The present collection of fast growth companies is therefore likely to contain an under representation of firms from the less prosperous regions and more from the South East of England than would be the case if a random sample of UK small firms had been drawn.

In examining the contribution which management practices and characteristics have upon small firm performance it is therefore necessary to take explicitly into account the sector in which the business is located, the age of the business and the region in which the business is located. This is achieved through the following sampling process.

4. Sampling Method

There are three main ways in which the problem of identifying the managerial characteristics of fast growing small firms could be analysed. The first is to use existing commercial databases, such as 'UK Fastest growing Companies' in which those companies experiencing the fastest percent rate of profit over the previous year are ranked and identified. However, a one year change, particularly where this was based on only one single index of growth, was deemed to be inappropriate. A second way would have been to identify a random sample of small firms and then examine the sub-group of the sample which grew particularly quickly. [See for example Turok and Richardson (1989) and Solem and Steiner (1989) of Norway]. This procedure we excluded because it would have provided insufficient numbers of the type of fast growth firms which were our prime interest. Only by vastly increasing the sample size would it be possible to generate a sufficient number of exceptionally fast growth firms from a random sample of UK small firms.

It was our judgement that the research required face to face interviews with owners of exceptionally fast growth small firms. We would have been unhappy with using a case study type of approach because of the inevitable specificity of its findings. The sample had therefore to be of sufficient size to enable some rudimentary statistical analysis to be undertaken. We judged this to require a minimum of about fifty interviews. Making valid statements about those aspects of management of fast growth small firms, which distinguishes them from other small firms, required having some sort of 'norm' for comparative purposes. To achieve this we have chosen to use a matched sampling technique, involving several stages, which in some respects parallels that of Hitchens and O'Farrell (1989).[2]

Stage 1 required the identification of all USM companies which were independently UK owned and reached the market within ten years of start up. Out of the 603 companies which by the end of 1987 had ever been quoted on the market since its inception in 1980, we estimated there were about 125 which qualified on these grounds. Stage 2 involved an attempt to obtain a separate face to face interview of about one hour with both the key individual in the company – normally the chairman or chief executive – and a senior manager. These firms are however the subject of intense interest amongst researchers, journalists and the media generally. The owners and managers are extremely busy running rapidly expanding businesses, and are inundated with requests for information and co-operation, with this being particularly true for the key individual. Given the media interest in these individuals, many have become 'household names'. Because of the immense pressures on their time, key individuals in these businesses are extremely reluctant to devote themselves to a research study of this type. Nevertheless a total of sixty face to face interviews were conducted with key individuals in USM companies. This constitutes slightly less than one half of the eligible group.

Once an interview had been conducted with a fast growth USM company then Stage 3 involved the identification of a 'match' company. Matching took place according to the four criteria outlined above, notably age, sector, ownership and geography. Thus if the USM company is a London based PR firm about ten years old, then the 'match' firm would be expected to have similar characteristics. The correct term for the procedure employed is 'one for one matching'. By this we mean that each USM company is directly compared with a 'match', rather than ensuring that the two samples have broad comparability according to the four criteria of sector, age, ownership and geography. In our view it is this combination of characteristics which has to be held constant if valid comparisons are to take place. It is not acceptable to allow the 'trading off' of criteria which inevitably occurs when only broad comparisons are made according to individual criteria.

In some instances, of course, there may be particular problems over matching. For example it may be that the USM company was a management buy out, so this would have to be taken into account in the matching. It may present particular problems if there is no other MBO in that trade and region, or if the only 'match' firm satisfying the criteria refuses to collaborate. In all cases we have endeavoured to ensure the best possible matching has taken place, but in a number of instances it has not been possible to satisfy all four criteria for the match simultaneously. We have therefore chosen to exclude the USM company, even though the interview had taken place, from further analysis. In total eleven USM companies were not matched, so that the sample discussed is of 49 USM or 'fast growth' companies and 49 'match' companies.

It should be emphasised that performance is NOT one of the criteria for matching. The method chosen does not take performance into account in the matching process, except by assuming that the USM company outperforms its 'match' counterpart. However, it certainly does not assume that the match firms are poor performing companies. For example the typical 'match' company is about twelve years old, with a median employment of 24 workers. To have survived for this period and to have achieved this size is a considerable achievement. Our purpose is to only use the 'match' firm in order to make comparisons with the exceptional performers.

There are two implications of this methodology for the concept of firm performance. The first is that, in terms of the chosen measures of growth, the 'match' firm always performs less well than its 'fast growth' firm counterpart. The 'match' firm could still, however, be growing rapidly, in some absolute sense. The second is that match firm must be of sufficient size to warrant the employment of managers. The size at which this happens varies from one trade to another but, in most forms of manufacturing, it appears to happen when firms employ between eight and twelve workers, or achieve an annual sales turnover of about £300,000. In no sense can the 'match' firm be therefore considered as one which is not exhibiting growth.

The USM companies are regarded as being synonymous with 'fast growth', but the implications of this also have to be clearly understood. Within the sample no 'match' firm is larger, in terms of employment, than the equivalent USM company and, in this sense, the two distributions of firm performance will not overlap. Thus, on a 'one for one' matching basis, there is no overlap. However, some 'match' firms outperform some USM firms in the sense of having higher rates of profitability, or higher levels of employment. For example, a 'match' manufacturing company may have more employees than a 'fast growth' Advertising Agency, although the latter will always be larger than its 'match' counterpart. In the former sense the distribution of performance between the two groups of firms can overlap, but not in the latter sense of allowing for easier sector, age, ownership and geography.

Equating 'fast growth' and USM status in this way could cause an additional problem of comparison between the groups if quotation on the market imposed particular conditions upon company development which destroyed the validity of such comparisons. Two examples are appropriate. Firstly it could be argued that performance comparisons, using publicly available data, between quoted and unquoted companies are always difficult because of the differing objectives of the two groups of firms, as suggested by Hay and Morris (1984). They argue that the quoted company may be more keenly aware of the need to declare profitability, since it is this which ultimately determines the quoted share price and hence the company valuation. On the other hand it is more likely to be managed by professionals who are divorced from ownership, and who therefore have fewer incentives to follow a profit maximisation policy.

For the unquoted company the incentive to declare profits, which will be subject to taxation, is weaker. It may be more tax efficient to combine the operations of the business with the consumption patterns of the directors and their families, even though such individuals also benefit directly from increased profits within the company. Hay and Morris found that the Gross Operating Profit rate of unquoted companies was significantly greater than that of quoted companies. The extent to which this is a function of size, and the extent to which it reflects the simple difference between quotation and non-quotation is less clear. It is at least possible that some of these differences are due to the ownership dimension, and so this has to be borne in mind when interpreting the following findings.

A second example of how apparent performance differences between the two groups of firms may, at least in part, be a reflection of the choice to have shares quoted on the USM is seen in the requirement that the latter type of companies need to satisfy certain managerial targets. The clearest example of this is the requirement of the Market for all companies to have a Finance Director in post at the time of application for membership. For both these reasons it is necessary to examine the history and development of both the USM and the 'match' firms. This is particularly important for the USM companies to determine whether they were fast growers prior to joining the market.

5. The USM and 'Match' Companies

This paper discusses only a small segment of the overall project designed to examine empirically the managerial development of fast growth small companies. It reports some results of face to face interviews with the key actors – normally the chairman or chief executive – of both the USM and their 'match' companies. A total of 49 interviews with owners of USM companies, and 49 interviews with 'match' owners are reported. The present paper does not include material on the interviews with managers in these companies, this being the subject of separate analysis. Finally no attempt is made here to relate the results directly to the performance of the companies, other than the fact that a distinction is made between USM and 'match' companies.

(i) The size and growth of companies

Table 5.1 provides a comparison of the companies in both the USM and the 'match' group. It shows that at the time the interviews took place in 1988/89 the arithmetic mean employment size of the USM companies was 452.4 workers and 45.2 for the 'match' firms. Not shown in the table is that median employment of the USM companies is 250 workers and that of the 'match' firms is 24 workers.

The table also makes it clear that the USM companies, as a group, have experienced massive employment growth over the last two years. The USM companies have increased their mean employment from 170.6 to 452. The 'match' companies have also experienced considerable growth from 31.8 to 45.2 workers over the same period. This illustrates that several of the key objectives of the sampling methodology have been achieved – to identify a group of spectacularly growing firms and to enable comparisons to be made with a group of firms which, whilst not achieving such high rates, have also been achieving good rates of growth.

Finally the table shows that the USM companies expect their spectacular rates of growth to continue. Within two years almost one-third of the sample expect to have more than 500 employees, compared with about 8 per cent four years previously. The 'match' firms expect, over the next two years, to continue at about the same growth rate as they have achieved over the last two years.

(ii) Other characteristics of the companies

In this section we very briefly outline some of the other characteristics of the companies surveyed. It will be recalled that each of the matching of companies takes place according to four key characteristics on a 'one for one' basis. The two groups of firms should therefore be close to identical according to the criteria of age, sector, region and ownership.

Given that, in the above section, we have compared the size of the firms in the USM and 'match' groups it is important to demonstrate that the age of firms in each group is approximately equal. The median age of the USM

Table 5.1
Employment Change.

	100 Workers				100-499 Workers				500 + Workers				Total			
	USM		MATCH		USM		MATCH		USM		MATCH		USM		MATCH	
	n	Emp	n	Emp	n	Emp	n	Emp	n	Emp	n	Emp	n	Emp	n	Emp
1 Employment in 1986/87 X	22	18	46	949	23	4994	3	610	4	2,456	–	–	49	8,358 170.6	49	1,559 31.8
2 Employment in 1988/89 X	9	461	45	1200	24	5714	4	1015	15	15,504	–	–	48	21,715 452.4	49	2,215 45.2
3 Projected Employment in 1990/91 X	5	234	41	1233	25	6370	6	970	16	36,445	1	500	47	44,249 941.5	48	2,703 56.3

firms is 13 years for the USM and 12 years for the 'match'.

About two-thirds of the companies in both groups are in the service sector, with major concentrations being found in business services, notably advertising, design, PR, and finance. There are also significant concentrations in the Hire, Wholesale and Distribution sectors and also in Property and Leisure. Manufacturing is the second most important single grouping and within manufacturing almost half of the firms are in the electronic and electrical sectors. The geographical distribution of the companies shows a very heavy bias towards London and the South East with about three-quarters of companies in this area. Other regions represented are South West, West Midlands, Yorkshire and Wales. There are no companies in Scotland or Northern Ireland.

6. The Entrepreneur

In any discussion of management in a smaller company the role of the entrepreneur, or key founder, is of major importance. In this section we examine some of the characteristics of this individual in the hope that this may shed some light on managerial style which characterises the firm. Almost all the entrepreneurs are male. There are three key founders of 'match' firms who are female and one USM key founder. The median age of the key founder at the time of the interview was almost identical for both groups, being 47 years for the USM companies and 45 years for the 'match' firms. The likelihood of having educational qualifications did seem to vary between the two groups, with 42 per cent of USM key founders having a degree, compared with only 14 per cent of 'match' founders.

Thirty-nine per cent of both USM and 'match' key founders currently owned or part owned a business other than their main business. 26 per cent of all USM key founders owned more than two businesses, compared with 18 per cent of 'match' founders. In the case of both the USM and the 'match' key founders these businesses were almost always established after the main business. For the 'match' entrepreneur the business was much more likely to have been started on a part-time basis than is the case for the USM firms. Approximately one-quarter of 'match' firms start in this way compared with only 8 per cent of USM companies.

The unemployment motivation is more apparent amongst the 'match' than the USM grouping. 24 per cent of 'match' entrepreneurs claimed they either were unemployed, or were likely to become unemployed immediately prior to starting their business. Only 8 per cent of USM founders felt this way.

7. Expertise within the Managerial Team

A variety of different skills are required in the successful running of a growing small business. In some cases the skills are present within a single individual or key founder but, more commonly, groups of individuals come together to create a team. In the early days of the business the key founder is instrumental in developing that team, deciding when new expertise is required and often in ensuring appropriate people get appointed. In this section we examine the owners perception of the expertise of the managerial team when the business started, and how it is perceived to have developed as the business has grown.

Table 5.2

Expertise within the Business.

	START UP				NOW			
	USM	Per cent Con sid	MATCH	Per cent Con sid	USM	Per cent Con sid	MATCH	Per cent Con sid
Production	2.09	24	2.11	22	3.61	71	3.30	54
Finance	1.63	13	1.64	7	3.63	65	3.18	36
Marketing	1.84	16	1.95	27	3.33	56	2.89	42
Personnel	1.42	7	1.93	7	2.62	18	2.75	18
R & D	1.52 *	11	1.03	9	2.89 *	43	1.91	11
General Management	1.96	16	1.88	12	3.37	50	2.93	27

Note: * indicates significant difference at 5 per cent level.

Table 5.2 identifies six functional areas of business expertise – Production, Finance, Marketing, Personnel, R & D, and General Management. Each owner respondent was asked to identify the extent of that expertise both at the start of the business, and as it is today. Respondents were given five options: considerable, good, moderate, some and none. A scoring system was then used in which considerable scored four and none scored none. Under this system the greater the self assessed expertise the greater the score. The first and third columns of Table 5.2 show these scores at start up for the USM and the 'match' firms, whilst the second and fourth columns show the proportion of all respondents who felt that their expertise was considerable in the chosen functional area.

Taking columns one and three, the three highest scores or prime areas of perceived expertise within the firm were similar in both groups. For example, both USM and 'match' firms thought they were relatively good at Production and Marketing, placing them in a top three position. The USM companies thought they were also good at general management and the 'match' companies thought they were good at personnel at this time. Neither group of firms placed Finance or R & D in their top three.

In undertaking statistical significance tests, however the self assessed level of expertise in the business at start up in each of the areas of expertise is not significantly ($p < 0.05$) different between the two groups. The only exception is that the USM companies regard themselves as having greater expertise in the area of R & D than the 'match' companies. Nevertheless, as we have noted above, R & D is not an area in which either group felt there was much expertise at start-up. Broadly similar conclusions are apparent from an examination of only those areas which the owner regarded the firm at start-up as having considerable functional expertise.

The right hand side of the Table provides a comparable assessment for USM and 'match' firms of the perceived expertise of the business as it is today. There are some similarities but also some striking changes. First there has generally been an increase in the scores, indicating a perceived increase in expertise. It should be noted in passing that, of course, this was not the case for all respondents. Several felt that their businesses had grown so fast that, although there may have been some growth in expertise, this had been swamped by the increase in the problems which the business had to face.

The key similarity between 'start-up' and 'current' is the continuing relatively low levels of expertise in R & D and, to a lesser extent, personnel. Not only do these functions continue to occupy the two lowest positions but they show for the 'match' firms the lowest percentage improvement since start up. Nevertheless there continues to be a statistically significant difference in the level of perceived R & D expertise between the 'match' and the USM companies. The recognition of a relative lack of expertise in the personnel function, particularly in the 'match' companies, may appear to contrast with the number of owners who claim to see the firm as family businesses which place a considerable emphasis upon worker involvement and satisfaction. We interpret these apparent contradictions as a reflection of the fact that personnel expertise is assumed to be a formal function, and that the companies do not regard themselves as having this function unless they employ a Personnel professional. Only on rare occasions did firms express a fear that the absence of such a professional was likely to lead to an unacceptably low level of job satisfaction within the firm.

The key change since start-up for both USM and 'match' firms has clearly occurred in the area of Finance. When asked to score their current expertise, Finance was identified by both groups as the area where expertise was currently greatest. In fact Finance has experienced a 123 per cent improvement for USM firms and a 94 per cent increase for 'match' firms, which is higher than for any other functional areas.

8. Assembling the Managerial Team

This section examines the ways in which the increase, since start up, in managerial expertise noted above has actually occurred. Broadly we postulate there are three ways in which this can occur. The first is by the original owner or owners becoming more expert in these areas themselves. The second is where the firm recruits individuals from outside to supplement existing managerial resources. The third is where managerial skills are developed by individuals employed within the company but in a non-managerial role – in-house promotion. There are other possibilities, such as the use of 'outsiders' – consultants, friends, family or the use of non-executive directors, but these occurred so infrequently that they are not included here.

In some companies all three main ways were used, but even here the emphasis varies from one area of expertise to another. For example in areas such as finance, where there has been a major improvement since start-up, different methods may be favoured compared with an area such as personnel or general management where improvement has been more modest. The responses of both the USM and the 'match firms are shown in Table 5.3 The most striking aspect of the Table relates to Finance, which it will be recalled was the functional area perceived to have experienced the major increase in expertise since start-up. It appears that Finance expertise occurs almost exclusively through outside recruitment.

Several explanations of this finding are possible. It might simply reflect the fact that all USM companies are required to have a qualified Finance Director at the time of their application to the market. Yet, if that is the time at which such an individual is first appointed, and if that individual is the reason for the perceived increase in expertise, then two interesting points follow. Firstly, that individuals with finance expertise are rarely part of a start up team. Secondly, that the company will have grown very rapidly – to the stage of being considered for a USM flotation – without having had such an individual as part of the team.

However, since 'match' companies also regard themselves as having made a major leap in financial expertise since start-up, and have also achieved that through outside recruitment, it seems that the requirements of the Unlisted

Table 5.3
Assembling the Management Team.

EXPERTISE/ BACKGROUND	DEVELOPED BY START UP TEAM				RECRUITMENT OF OUTSIDERS				PROMOTED IN-HOUSE			
	USM No	Per cent	Match No	Per cent	USM No	Per cent	Match No	Per cent	USM No	Per cent	Match No	Per cent
Production	3	8	10	15	2	3	4	10	8	26	4	14
Finance	4	10	10	15	26	39	19	45	1	3	3	11
Marketing	9	22	14	21	15	23	7	17	4	13	5	18
Personnel	11	28	16	24	11	17	5	12	9	29	6	21
R & D	4	10	8	12	6	9	3	7	5	16	3	11
General Management	9	22	10	15	6	9	4	10	4	13	7	25
	40	100	68	100	66	100	42	100	31	100	28	100

ns Market are not the key explanation for this finding. Instead it seems to be more generally true that financial expertise is rarely on board at start-up, but is added at an appropriate point in the development of the firm. Unfortunately from the results of this survey we are unable to pinpoint exactly when that takes place, and whether it differs from one type of firm to another.

An examination of the other areas of functional expertise in Table 5.3 shows that outside recruitment is the prime way in which USM firms acquire new management expertise, although only in Finance is it dominant. For 'match' firms there is much more evidence of new sources of expertise being developed by the start-up team, in all functional areas except for finance. There are some important differences between the other functional areas. For example, responsibility for, and expertise in, Personnel is acquired by the start-up team – normally the founder – and by in-house promotion. In this sense it is the exact opposite to Finance. A broadly similar result is found for General Management, with the 'match' firms relying more heavily than their USM counterparts on internal promotions. It will be recalled from Table 5.2 on page 77 that Personnel and General Management were the two areas, other than the special case of R & D, in which firms perceived there had been least improvement since start up. They are also the areas in which outside recruitment was least. Conversely, Finance is the area in which firms feel the greatest strides have been made and where external recruitment has been most apparent. This suggests that firms seem to equate the external recruitment of managers with perceived increases in corporate expertise. Of course the extent to which there is a causative link between these elements cannot be determined from the Table.

9. The Requirements of Management

In our discussions with key founders we were interested in their perception of the required characteristics of their job, as it is today, and the personal qualities which they bring to this task. The responses are shown in Table 5.4. All respondents were asked, for each characteristic, whether they felt their job required none, some or a lot. When the question was posed each of the characteristics was given a single sentence definition which is not shown in the Table. Each key founder was also asked whether they felt there was a need to improve in this particular aspect of their job.

Table 5.4

Job Characteristics and the Abilities of Key Owners/Founders.

	Percentage replying that their job required a lot		Percentage replying that they needed to improve	
	USM	MATCH	USM	MATCH
LEADERSHIP				
Persuasion	89	79	59	47
Quick Thinking	90	85	37	40
Decision Making	83	77	54	53
Originality	52	63	67	60
Entrepreneuarial Initiative	59	68	33	41
Rapport	75	81	65	41
$\bar{X}$	74·7	75·5	52·5	47·0
LOGICAL				
Memory	51	68	44	56
Perception	45	77	44	47
Methodological	55	66	56	62
Reasoning	83	81	52	47
Logical	62	73	52	53
Numeracy	59	62	50	60
Finance	59	66	82	69
$\bar{X}$	59·1	70·4	54·3	56·3
COMMUICATIONS				
Verbal Communications	72	77	48	48
Speech Fluency	69	87	67	49
Written Fluency	63	79	56	51
$\bar{X}$	68·0	81	57	49·3
PRACTICAL				
Spatial	25	43	26	40
Manual Competence	7	21	32	28
$\bar{X}$	16·0	32·0	29·0	34·0

The results are presented so as to again highlight any distinction between the responses of the USM key founders and those of the 'match' founders. Taking first the six characteristics grouped under the category of Leadership there is a fairly strong consensus between the USM and 'match' key founders on the qualities required to do their job. Both groups of respondents feel their jobs require a lot of persuasion and decision making, and to a slightly lesser extent decision making and rapport.

We were surprised that significantly fewer respondents from either the USM or the 'match' group felt their job required a lot of originality or entrepreneurial initiative. This result is, if anything, even more surprising since even fewer USM key founders placed emphasis upon these characteristics than was the case for 'match' firms. Amongst the functions in the Logical group there appears to be less unanimity between the key founders of USM and 'match' firms upon their relative importance than was the case for Leadership functions. For example, whilst both USM and 'match' key founders place considerable emphasis upon the importance of Reasoning, there appears to be a greater divergence of opinion on the importance of Memory, Perception and Methodology. It is also the case that the scores were generally lower for the Logical group which average 59 and 70 respectively for the USM and the 'match' firms than for the Leadership group, where scores average 75. This suggests a lower emphasis placed by key founders upon Logical than on Leadership functions.

Both USM and 'match' key founders place considerable emphasis upon Communications, with average scores of 68 and 81 respectively, this being consistent across all three forms of communications. However, neither USM nor 'match' key founders have much requirement for practical skills, although this perceived need is somewhat greater amongst the 'match' key founders. This presumably reflects the greater need for this group to 'get their hands dirty' in practical matters from time to time. The final two columns of the Table indicate the extent to which respondents indicated that they needed to improve their own performance in certain aspects of their job. The areas most frequently singled out by USM key founders for a need to improve their own performance was in Finance, Originality, Speech Fluency and Rapport.

Of all the eighteen job characteristics identified, the one which 'match' founders felt they most needed to improve was in Finance. In this they are identical to the USM founders, although a lower proportion of 'match' founders felt this way. Three other areas in which more than 60 per cent of 'match' founders expressed a need to improve was in the areas of methodology, originality and numeracy.

To summarise, the table demonstrates that the managerial task today of a key founder of a growing small business relies heavily upon the ability to communicate and to exercise leadership. Within the Leadership grouping, perhaps surprisingly, relatively little emphasis is now placed by founders upon originality and on entrepreneurial initiative. Both groups placed particular emphasis upon a need to improve in the area of finance.

10. Conclusions

This paper has examined several aspects of the managerial task and development of managerial teams in fast growth smaller firms. It has employed a sophisticated sampling technique using 'one for one match matching', the purpose of which is to ensure that any differences in the characteristics of the fast growth firms are not attributable to age, sector, ownership or the location of the firm. It has to be emphasised that whilst the 'match' firms have grown, and are likely to continue growing, the USM firms have experienced spectacular growth and many are no longer small firms.

It is shown that when key founders of both USM and 'match' firms were asked to estimate the functional areas where managerial expertise was greatest at start up they both highlighted the areas of production and marketing. Neither group identified Finance as a key strength at start up. The only functional area where the USM founders consistently regarded their expertise as higher than their 'match' counterparts was in Research and Development. The interesting result is that, when both USM and 'match' firms are asked to identify current expertise, they now pick Finance as the prime area. It is in this area that the greatest perceived increase in expertise has occurred. It also appears that this expertise is generated primarily through the appointment of an outsider – both in the case of the USM and the 'match' companies.

This all suggests that rarely is Financial expertise on board when the firm first starts in business. Instead the types of people who start both 'fast growth' and 'match' companies are those with marketing and production skills, and that as their companies grow they buy in the financial skills. Once in the company, however, Financial expertise is required as being of paramount importance.

The paper has also considered the characteristics of top management of small and medium sized companies. It shows that in many ways the qualities required in both cases were fairly similar, with both placing considerable emphasis upon quick thinking and decision making. Nevertheless, we were certainly surprised about the relatively low emphasis, in both groups, placed upon originality or entrepreneurial initiative. Finally it was noteworthy that USM key founders were much more likely to indicate, throughout a range of functions, a need to improve than was the case for the 'match' founders.

Footnotes

1. This paper is the initial output from research funded by the UK Economic and Social Research Council on Managerial Labour Markets, funded under the Competitiveness and Regeneration of British Industry Programme. The research is directed by the author, and by Kevin Keasey and Robert Watson, whose comments on an earlier draft of this paper are much appreciated. My thanks are also extended to Pooran Wynarczyk and Sue Marlow for their analyses, but the responsibility for the paper lies with the author alone. It is envisaged that the full results of the study will be published in *The People Gap: The Managerial Labour Market in Small Firms*, to be published by Basil Blackwell, Oxford, 1991.

2. The major difference is that we use 'one for one' matching, whereas Hitchens and O'Farrell merely try to achieve broad similarity, according to the chosen criteria, between the groups of firms. The basic purpose of the matching procedure, i.e. that of obtaining a 'control' group is the same for both this study and those of Hitchens and O'Farrell.

References

1. Department of Employment, *Small Firms in Britain*, HMSO (London, 1989).
2. S Fothergill and G Gudgin, *Unequal Growth*, Heinemann (London, 1982).
3. P Ganguly, *UK Small Business Statistics and International Comparisons*, Harper and Row (London, 1985).
4. D A Hay and D J Morris, *Unquoted Companies*, MacMillan (London, 1984).
5. R Harrison and C M Mason, 'The Regional Impact of the Small Firms Loan Guarantee Scheme in the UK', *Regional Studies*, Vol.20, pp.535-550, 1986.
6. S Johnson, 'Employment Change in Small Businesses: Expectations and Reality', paper given at 12th National Policy & Research Conference, Thames Polytechnic, (London, 1989).
7. C Mason, 'The Geography of "Successful" Small Firms in the United Kingdom', *Environment & Planning A*, Vol.17, pp.1499-1513, 1985.
8. D M W N Hitchens and P O'Farrell, 'The Comparative Performance of Small Manufacturing Companies in South Wales and Northern Ireland: An Analysis of Matched Pairs', *Omega*, Vol.16, pp.429-438, 1989.
9. M Scott and R Bruce, 'Five Stages of Growth in Small Business', *Long Range Planning*, Vol.20, No.3, pp.45-51, 1987.
10. O Solem and M P Steiner, 'Factors for Success in Small Manufacturing Firms

– and with special emphasis on growth factors'. Paper presented at Conference on 'SMEs and the challenges of 1992', Mikkeli, (Finland, 1989).

11. H Stoddart and D J Storey, 'The Characteristics of Young Companies quoted on the Unlisted Securities Market', University of Warwick SME Centre, Working Paper No.1, 1989.

12. D J Storey (ed), *Small Firms in Regional Economic Development,* Cambridge University Press, (London, 1985).

13. D J Storey, K Keasey, R Watson and P Wynarczyk, *The Performance of Small Firms,* Routledge, (London, 1987).

14. D J Storey, R Watson and P Wynarczyk, 'Fast Growth Small Businesses', Department of Employment Research Report No.67, (London, 1987).

15. I Turok and P Richardson, 'Supporting the Start up and Growth of Small Firms: A Study in West Lothian', University of Strathclyde Papers on Planning, No.14, 1989.

Part 2
Local Studies

6
Parisian industries and national capitalism in the first half of the nineteenth century (1830–1850)

André Straus and Patrick Verley

Confirmation of the political, administrative and financial role of capital cities, such as Paris, preceded the process of industrialization of countries. More often than not such cities enjoyed a privileged position as regional centres by virtue of a tradition of proto-industrialization, of an abundance of manpower, good markets and easy access to raw materials. Even when their location was not favourable for the development of modern industry, these cities nevertheless became involved in the overall process of industrialization at two levels, which can be illustrated in the case of Paris. On the one side the industrialization proper of the city was encouraged by the importance of its market, building on the existence of a highly qualified artisan workforce.

On the other side, Paris played an unquestionable role in the gradual formation of national markets for merchandise and for capital. Apart from their intrinsic interest in the study of the demography of enterprises *les actes de création de sociétés*[1] shed light on the growth of this twin function of the Parisian region in the first half of the nineteenth century, as an industrialised zone and in the structuring of the national economy. Reflection on the motives for adopting shareholder status for enterprises and on the choice between the different forms provided under the Code, can also help in understanding the evolution of the financial structure of French capitalism. It has only been practical to take three sample years from the whole corpus of *actes de fondation,* in 1830, in 1840, and in 1850, the latter a year of economic crisis and the other two of less difficult economic circumstances.

In 1830, 103 *sociétés* principally engaged in industry were created: in 1850 there were 335. These enterprises, which were either established as *sociétés* or adopted shareholder status during the course of their existence and which have deposited their articles of association in the office of the *Tribunal de Commerce de la Seine* provide evidence about the greater part of the industrial activity in the city of Paris and its suburbs. The Articles of association provide details of the location in the conurbation of registered offices, of places of activity, of warehouses, and of commercial offices.

Table 6.1

Parisian sociétés: percentage of the number of foundations by sector.

Industries	1830	1840	1850
– des sciences, lettres et arts	19·3	13·6	13·5
– des objets en métal	14·8	15·1	15·5
– alimentaires	13·6	11·4	7·2
– textiles	13·6	9·8	12·4
– des produits chimiques	10·2	13·6	12·4
– de l'habillement	8·0	6·8	10·3
– du luxe et du plaisir	5·7	9·8	10·3
Total for 7 leading sectors	85·2	80·1	81·6

In 1830, 88 firms, or 85 per cent, of the *actes de fondation* belonged to the seven principal sectors of the economy, in 1840, 132, or 85 per cent of the *actes*, and in 1851 251, or 75 per cent. In the three years, from an analyses of the objects of all the *sociétés* established, the seven principal sectors remained the same. These are the sectors *Sciences-Lettres et Arts* (represented here principally by printers, watchmakers and booksellers/stationers): the sector *Fabrication d'objets en métal* (most frequently manufacturers of machines or implements), the sector *Industries alimentaires* (brewers, pasta makers, industrial bakers, carbonated water manufacturers): the sector *Textile* (like printers of materials, makers of shawls and trimmings): the sector of *Produits Chimiques* (the term covering in the period principally light manufacturers of finished or semi-finished products such as varnish, inks, matches, or animal fertilisers): the sector *Habillement* (hatters, glove makers, shoemakers – on the whole a ready-to-wear industry in its infancy) and finally the sector *Luxe et plaisir* (chiefly jewellers and workers in precious metal, and artificial flower makers).[2] Two types of development can be observed. To begin with the phenomena of shareholding seems to spread throughout all the sectors between the two dates (the formation of *sociétés* in the two leading sectors, represents 34 per cent of the *actes de fondation* in 1830, falling to 29 per cent 30 years later). Next, the hierarchy of sectors adopting *société* status changes. Between 1830 and 1840 the *Fabrication d'objets en métal* replaced the more traditional *Sciences – Lettres et Arts*, the manufacture of *Produits Chimiques* affirms its importance, and the relative weight of *sociétés* associated with the food industry declines. This evolution is confirmed between 1840 and 1850. The seeming depression of the *ancien* sectors in favour of more 'modern' industries is not general; because contrary to the trend the textile sector adopted shareholder status after 1840 along with the sector involved in the making of *articles de Paris* (fancy goods) which were orientated towards external markets.

Besides these *sociétés*, whose place of work was the department of the Seine, there were also registered in Paris *sociétés* whose productive capacity was situated in the provinces or abroad. In 1830 these numbered 15 or 15 per cent of foundations, in 1840 24 or 15 per cent, and 1850 84 or 25 per cent. The concentration in Paris of registered offices of *sociétés*, apparently non-Parisian in their focus, during the 1840s does not prove a growth in the industrial influence of the capital. In 1850 a very specific event caused the number of these sociétés to increase: the discovery of gold mines in California led to the creation of 36 *sociétés* whose stated objects were prospecting for and exploiting mineral deposits, in reality the colonization of American territory. If these very special categories are subtracted from the total number of *sociétés* registered in 1850, the proportion of *sociétés* whose place of work is non-Parisian returns to the same level (15 per cent) as in 1830. A sectoral approach shows a clear difference with Parisian industry, however. The two sectors most represented in 1830 are textiles and chemicals, but by 1840 and more strikingly by 1850, it is extractive industries (coal mines, quarries) and textiles. The legal forms chosen also differ according to location:

Table 6.2

	1830		1840		1850	
	Seine	Others	Seine	Others	Seine *(sauf sociétés 'Californiennes')*	Others
SNC	78%	36%	55%	43%	70%	27%
SCS	7%	36%	30%	19%	18%	18%
SCA	15%	28%	15%	38%	12%	55%
	100%	100%	100%	100%	100%	100%

(SNC = *sociétés en nom collectif*. SCS = *sociétés en commandite simple*. SCA = *sociétés en commandite par actions*).

These percentages are calculated by removing from the sample *sociétés anonymes* of which there are so few as to make little difference. The *sociétés en nom collectif* (SNC) seems to be the form most favoured in Paris, when the partnership was always in the majority for *sociétés* whose activities went beyond the Seine. As the SNC regularly brought together more limited capital than partnerships, the same division is apparent in the level of average registered and subscribed capital of Parisian and extra-Parisian *sociétés* – Table 6.3. These calculations exclude *société anonymes* as well as the SCA 'californiennes' and one SCA of 1840 of which the very significant capital and investments greatly increased the average.

It may not be necessary to infer a total division between, on the one hand, little manufacturing *sociétés* in Paris selling exclusively on the Parisian market, and on the other, the *grandes sociétés* of national, if not international, importance. Numerous Parisian enterprises had markets which extended beyond the conurbation. This is undoubtedly true of jewellers, and artistic craftsmen, like the *commandite simple* founded in 1850 with a capital of 165,000

Table 6.3

	Seine	*Others*
1830		
Average Capital	202·641 F	347·778 F
Average Investment in Cash	33·707 F	187·250 F
1840		
Average Capital	153·051 F	482·763 F
Average Investment in Cash	22·678 F	142·409 F
1850		
Average Capital	328·138 F	649·944 F
Average Investment in Cash	30·874 F	168·583 F

francs – associating Barbédienne with a merchant of wallpaper for the purpose of manufacturing and trading bronze works of art. Exports of the produce of Paris represented from 11 to 12 per cent of the whole export trade of France under the July Monarchy.[3] According to the industrial inquiry of 1847-48 Paris exported more than a ratio of 1:10 of its produce, for example, 169 on 1,464 million or 14 per cent of fashion goods.[4] But this vital contribution to export markets was not a consequence of any specific phenomena of concentration, increasing size in order to improve the capacity for penetrating markets in characteristic manner. If nominal capital, which in Paris is essentially equivalent to contributed assets in kind, grew between 1840 and 1850, this was not the case for subscriptions in cash, which declined from 1830. A great part of the export effort is in effect borne by the large numbers of enterprises which were not *sociétés:* the craftsmen and the little manufacturers of the capital who played a vigorous part in the export trade during the whole of the Second Empire.[5] Undoubtedly this great decentralization in Parisian manufacture and its seeming great paucity of capital (the enterprises with shareholders certainly are more flush with cash than those without shareholders) as late as 1850, despite its integration with the commercial world, can be explained by the structure of trade, such as the practice of 'returns' by buyers, particularly Americans, who came soliciting Parisian commission agents and wholesalers who, in turn, passed on orders to the manufacturers.[6] Provincial manufacturers evidently did not readily enjoy the same advantage of being on the spot and had, therefore, themselves to accept some of the cost of the trade.

For different reasons, the *sociétés*, which manufactured and sold in the provinces or abroad, or who manufactured in the province but had a sales office in Paris, declared their registered address in the départment of the Seine. An investigation of the typologies of these *sociétés* allows some hypothesis to be formulated on the role of the capital in the French economy. In 1830 the *sociétés,* having a place of work different from Paris, can be classified in the following fashion:

a) A third among them had a manufacturing activity near to Paris (Seine-et-Marne and Seine-et-Oise). They can be considered simply as an extension of Parisian manufacturing. Activities which require considerable equipment and large premises abandoned the central *quartiers* in favour of peripheral *quartiers* which were still in the suburbs, such as a paper-works at Grande Villette, a manufacturer of floor tiles and bricks at Vaugirard, or a maker of animal blacking at Grenelle. This extension of Parisian activity marginally spilled over into the two neighbouring departments. The constraints of location encouraged this process. Thus, in the case of the *société* Menier & Cie, whose trade was essentially in Paris, the construction of the factory at Noisiel was the outcome of a search for a site suitable for a water-powered mill. In the same way the urban development of Paris led to the exploitation of quarries and lime kilns for plaster at steadily increasing distances from the capital. This first category which in 1830 accounts for the majority of non-Parisian enterprises, merits, therefore, this final qualification that it only shows that Parisian industry must not be studied exclusively within the confines of the city walls, but in its real spatial geography which is very wide:

b) In the second category, there is an association between industrialists who manufactured directly or indirectly in the provinces and wholesalers who either traded in Paris or through intermediaries in Paris on the international market. Such an association allowed the industrialist, often engaged in textiles, to gain access to trading networks, testimony to the weaknesses in the provinces of specialised trading combines. Thus a manufacturer of printed cotton goods in Rouen linked himself to a Parisian merchant, or a shawl maker in Aisne with a Parisian business house. The sample examined is too small to be able to draw from the relative contributions of capital at the outset from the commercial and industrial concerns any conclusion about the strength of the dependence in the relationship between the commercial and industrial functions. Were these firms simply survivals of the old structures of the merchant/manufacturer type or examples of commercial firms which integrated backwards to assure privileged supplies or industrialists who were subordinated to a sales counter? The provincial location of production, which remained in the interior of the Parisian basin (Eure, Seine-Maritime, and Marne), can be attributed to two inter-related causes, wages were much lower than in the capital and the area had a tradition of craftsmanship, as is the case for those places where the proto-industrial textile industry was located.

c) Some *sociétés*, on the other hand, exhibited a very different characteristic: production and trading activity are outside Paris and sometimes in a distant province or overseas, but the registered office is declared in Paris. This is evidence of capitalism on a national scale, typified by a high degree of capital mobility. The partners, important and wealthy people, live in Paris and the capital raised by the *société* is drawn from the bourgeoisie resident in the capital city even if they often have strong provincial ties. Statistically, the *sociétés* in this category, which adopted the form *société anonyme*, accounted for a quarter of the sample by number; on the other hand the total of their registered capital made up the lion's share of that for all types of société: the Société de Saint-Gobain had a capital of 12 million francs, that of the Fonderies et forges d'Alais 6 million francs.

From 1840 and to 1850 this corporate typology was enriched. The three preceding categories were still evident, but their relative importance had changed:

a) The role of the category *extension of Parisian industries* diminished. Parisian activity still contributed but only marginally to the industrialization of the Seine-et-Oise, which a decade later were described in the industrial enquiry of 1861-1865 as giving the impression of having relatively little industry.

b) The category which linked *provincial industry with Parisian trade* was on the rise. This included more than a third of *sociétés* founded in 1840. In 1850 its relative position had retreated due to the development of the following categories. A trend, already noticeable in 1840, was confirmed in 1850: the place of manufacture, instead of being concentrated in the Paris basin, is located from now on sometimes in far distant provinces and covering a great part of the national territory. In 1840, for example, a paper manufacturer of *Angoulême* combined with one in Paris, in 1850 a firm producing orange-flower water in Grasse sold the bulk of its production in Paris, or rather through the intermediary of Paris. For if the factors of the provincial location of production remain the same, the trend indicates the growing turning of the tables on the commercial concerns in the capital, occasionally at the expense of the metropolitan region.

Certainly the increased importance of exporting for the greater part of French industry contributes to this trend. In 1850 six glovemakers – of whom two lived in Lunéville, Abraham Nathan and Charles Beer, one in Chaumont(Haute-Marne), Jules Trefousse, and three in Paris, Mayer Trefousse Pére, and his two sons having the same address – formed themselves into a société for three reasons: to augment their trading power, to find outlets for gloves made in the provinces, and to raise the elasticity of the productive potential for the Parisians. This *société* hung fire and a new foundation took its place some months after, which with seven partners, no longer included one of the manufacturers in Lunéville, but from now on incorporated three partners in New York – Charles Beer many years before from Lunéville, Cerf Beer and Antoine May. This new *société*, which relied on a familial network, no longer aimed at the national market alone but evidently at the American market, thanks to the putting out of commercial antenna across the Atlantic.

c) the *sociétés* appearing in the category 'capitalism on a national scale', which had their registered offices in Paris for other reasons than those of trade, experience a growth in number. The mining sector achieves a majority position: mines and hot blast furnaces in Terrenoire in 1840, the coal mines of Epinac and of Alès in 1850. Paris confirmed its place at the financial and decision making heart of the country because the capital needs of this sector outstripped the resources of the regions in which the activities were located. This is why amongst the seven directors of Epinac three were Parisian bankers (Mallet, Marcuard, Mathieu).

d) a category of *société* linked to landed property has not been referred to for 1830 because it only accounted then for one single case, a *société en nom collectif* which brought together five members of the nobility of whom three from the Ségur family had the intention of operating a sawmill in Aisne. This category, whose antiquity is otherwise established, comprised landed proprietors who lived in Paris and owned estates which had on them mines, hot-blast furnaces, or beet sugar refineries. In this way a *société en nom collectif* of 1850 to work a bitumen well in the Landes, comprised twelve partners, of whom eight came from the same family, a business whose foundation is directly linked to the management of a families' patrimony. There are three reasons explaining the development of this category:

    1) associated with the economic growth in the years between 1830 and 1840, demand increased for certain raw materials encouraging the owners of mines or forges to invest. In order to find the finance necessary for improving the yield from their patrimony they looked to

PARISIAN INDUSTRIES AND NATIONAL CAPITALISM

the partners with whom they were already connected.
2) associated with the urbanisation of the capital, many of the members of the provincial nobility – or their heirs – lived from now on in Paris while preserving their interests in their region of origin.
3) finally, the retreat from the regions provided opportunities to certain proprietors for the development of their land, as in the example of two *sociétés* occupying metal works in Corse, one in 1840 and the other in 1850.

e) Finally, a second new category appeared which in 1830 was only represented by one *société:* that of enterprises whose productive activities were located abroad. Until around 1840, this category scarcely existed because the sphere of action of French technicians and financiers in industrial matters remained national. In reverse Britons are to be found in the *actes de fondation* coming to France to found or participate in the establishment of *sociétés,* because they possessed technical know-how still scarce on the Continent. They had not disappeared by 1850 as three *sociétés* were established at the same time by the same partners, most of whom were English. The first with a capital of 1.5 million francs and the objective of providing gas lighting for the town of Sevilla, had two partners, R Hume and J Grafton of London, and four sleeping partners from London and one from Paris, Goldsmid. The latter, whose contribution was a works, financed a second *société* with a capital of 375,000 francs with the object of manufacturing gas meters and regulators and comprised a factory in Parish, a branch in Lyon and another in Milan: the sleeping partner was no other than J Grafton who contributed his commercial and managerial skills. Finally, the third *société* which made iron tubing at Tours, with two British partners who invested patents, machines and raw materials, and four sleeping partners, of whom one was Goldsmid again. There was a certain integrated logic to these enterprises, defined by the manufacture of materials for gas lighting, with some overlapping of partners and common sleeping partners. These *commandites par actions* are in other respects the only direct manifestation in the sample of 1850 of the contribution of British machine makers to the industrialization of the Continent.[7] Has that phase by then already passed for France?

On the contrary; at that date, the French technique had already got underway of bringing about a transfer of new technology to other countries on the Continent and French capital began to be exported in the form of direct investment in equipment infra-structure of neighbouring countries. As examples of technological transfer one finds *sociétés* whose objectives were the construction of gas works at Karlsruhe in Germany or at Sevilla in Spain. Others had need of raising significant capital which was not available in their place of business and therefore declared their *société* in Paris. Examples of this process are a Portuguese mining *société* which already had a registered office in Lisbon and whose Portuguese partners searched for sleeping partners; the *société* for gas lighting Pest, of which one of the two partners, Auguste Devin, was French; and the sleeping partners in the *Compagnie* for the gas lighting of the town of Breslau.

More generally these financial constraints are one of the means which encouraged the adoption of shareholders' status.

The corpus of *actes de sociétés* do not constitute a sample in any sense from which it is possible to infer the whole vast population of enterprises, but it does provide in itself vital information about the nature of the 'firm'. The question is to determine the motives of the merchants, and of the industrialists who created enterprises directly under shareholders' form, transforming family enterprises already in existence into *sociétés*. An analysis shows different responses according to the legal type of *société* adopted. The relative position of different forms of *sociétés* changes between 1830 and 1850.

Table 6.4

Percentage of foundations according to their legal form.

	1830	1840	1850
S.N.C.	67 %	53 %	56 %
Commandites	31 %	45 %	44 %
dont:			
S.C.S.	12 %	27 %	17 %
S.C.A.	19 %	18 %	27 %
S.A.	2 %	2 %	0 % *

(* There was only one société anonyme in 1850 out of 339 foundations).

In the 1830s the relative role of *sociétés en nom collectif* diminishes to the benefit of the *commandites,* then remains stable for the remainder of the period. The *sociétés anonymes* are so few in number that variations in the percentages have no significance. In the 1840s it is in the heart of the *commandites* that changes take place: *commandites simples* grow feverishly in popularity, while *commandites par actions,* without losing their appeal entirely were less fashionable. This evolution corresponds to the needs of enterprises between 1830 and 1850 and illustrates the differential aptitude of the *société en nom collectif* or of the *commandite* to respond (the *société anonyme* is still so untypical a form in our sample, for it to be much envisaged as an alternative form):

a) The *société en nom collectif* represents much less an association of capital as an association of identical or complementary skills. This is the reason why the registered capital is only given in 42 per cent of the *actes* in 1830, in 57 per cent in 1840, and in 38 per cent in 1850 and of capital subscribed in cash is only in 36 per cent of *actes* in 1830 and 1850 and 35 per cent in 1840. The classical family firm (two brothers, mother and sons, husband and wife, father and sons, stepsons and stepfather) is less important in Paris than in Nord, when compared with the study made by P Deyon and J P Hirsch.[8] It is rather the association of two or three professional people in the same trade which is very frequent in Paris. The complementarity between trade and manufacture is particularly evident in *sociétés* operating in Paris and in the provinces and has thus already been studied. In all these cases the capital subscribed in cash is low because the partners share in common existing establishments or equipment. One assumes that it is a question of providing legal recognition for an association already in operation (often the partners have the same address which is that of the registered office and of the workplace).

b) In 1850 the setting up of a *société* corresponds sometimes to the hopes of craftsmen to go into business on their own account, brought to attention by J Gaillard for the beginning of the 1850s.[9] In reality 'co-operatives' of craftsmen building themselves up until they adopted the form *commandite simple*. The shareholders' clauses show that these *sociétés* are, leaving aside those that are not clearly stated, of a type with variable capital, making it possible to take in new *sociétaires* - *commanditaires* (sleeping partners/ shareholders). They also show that cash is uncommon: the partners often did not have cash to invest but undertook to supply it from their subsequent salary. Two examples illustrate this type of association: a *commandite* whose object is a turner's shop for making chairs comprising three craftsmen partners: its capital was fixed at 1,800 francs which had to be increased by 30 francs with the admission of each new sleeping partner. In this case the *acte* distinguished between three founding partners who had either invested some savings or more probably plant and equipment with a combined value of 1,800 francs, and further partners whose investment would always remain modest. More egalitarian was a printing works set up by five partners – print compositors – where all the newcomers would be sleeping partners investing one to two francs a month. The clauses of these different co-operatives often provided for an obligatory incorporation of part of the profits and even salaries in the registered capital.

c) the existence of numerous small *sociétés en nom collectif* can be explained by the difficulty that small *sociétés* had in finding cash in 1850. They conform to the analysis of J Gaillard who defined a double financial circuit; finance from the banks uniquely accessible to important enterprises and an inter-professional circuit including sometimes even members of the workforce and customers.[10] The tiny size of certain investments in cash is astonishing. Association between the manufacturer who invested his business and his workers who invested a little cash is not unusual. For example, a *société en nom collectif* with a capital of 22,400 francs brought together a manufacturer who subscribed in kind one half of the capital and three workers who subscribed the other half. This shortage of cash which was solved by adopting shareholder status was still a problem for certain *sociétés* who had not made legal provision for some forms of loans, guaranteed by mortgage. This was the case in a *société en nom collectif* of harness-making and coach building which had previously existed for only five months and which brought together a saddler and a carrier who invested the cash. Sometimes the appearance of simple loans is even more explicit. For example, a couple of brocaders and satiners investing their industry linked up with a proprietor who advanced 6,000 francs to buy machinery, but a clause in the *acte* specified that the 6,000 francs would be reimbursed by the original partners and the workshops would not be part of the *société*.

The search for fresh capital for the inception or development of an enterprise, by means of forming a *société*, is a motive that is still more evident in the case of partners when they do not correspond with the configurations which have already been examined, as in the association between a provincial industrial producer and a commercial middleman based in Paris. Sleeping partners in this first case are not often found when the *acte de société* was registered. The formation of a *société* was preliminary to their search which was a condition of an increase in the firm's financial capacity.[11] An analysis of the *corpus* confirms that in the sub-totals of cases (with the exception of workers co-operatives) the number of partners are few (an average in 1830 for the *commandites simples* 1.5, for the *commandites par actions* 2.2, and respectively 2.1 and 1.9 in 1850) and that they are technicians or experts (industrialists, wholesalers, or artisans) whereas the sleeping partners (wholesalers and proprietors) are only providers of passive funds. Furthermore, from this evidence confirmed by the statistics, the partners can be split up into three groups:

a) The group with the greatest number had a need for investment which exceeded the normal capacity of an enterprise already in existence to finance itself. This is characteristic of a *commandite par actions* formed in 1850 in which the partners, a former prefect, invested mining concessions in Aveyron, valued at 1.5 million francs. He wished to construct a metal works for which he had to secure another 1.5 million francs or more. Despite this very pressing situation, the foundation of the *commandite* corresponds to a project for the creation of a new enterprise.

b) In this group two situations are possible. The first is the development of activities in a new industrial sector: in this way four sociétés registered in 1850, having for their objective the construction of gasworks or three *sociétés* wishing to undertake industrial baking. The second situation is that of holders of patents for inventions who are looking for cash to move to industrial application. In 28 per cent of *commandites* in 1830, 39 per cent in 1840, 25 per cent in 1850 (excluding 'Californian' *sociétés*) one or more partners invested patent rights. This situation is more common in the *commandites* than in *sociétés en nom collectif* where the corresponding percentages are respectively 19 per cent, 21 per cent, and 12 per cent. Most of those *sociétés* affirm clearly that their objective is the exploitation of a patent. This importance of the role of patents in the constitution of *sociétés* testifies to the creativity in the area of technical and labour-saving devices. But often successive deposits by the same *commandité* of slightly modified *actes* illustrates how difficult it had been to convince sleeping partners of the relevance of its invention. Such a *commandite par actions* was established in 1850 with a capital of 6 million francs to exploit a patent for an 'atmospheric locomotive'. It was the object of three successive *actes,* with changes in partners, undoubtedly the 6 million francs had proved difficult to raise. Stillborn sociétés are numerous in this category; one can only assume that the *commandite* which had the aim of exploiting the patent for a machine called '*pneumat-sphéroidal*' (realising perpetual motion) would have a long life!

c) Finally, as the legislation exercised no control over *commandites par actions,* it allowed swindlers to obtain money under false pretences on a grand scale. This is without any doubt the case for the great part of the 36 *sociétés,* established in 1850, which gave as their objects the transport of emigrants to California, the discovery or working of mines, and even the pursuit of agriculture and the construction of towns – one of them actually extended its projects to Africa.[12] Not frightened by great totals, these *commandites*, which had evidently no personal investments, fixed their registered capital at between 1 and 10 million francs, one of them going as far as 91 million francs. These *sociétés* only deserve a passing reference. To begin with, their existence shows that the fraudulent '*société*' is not just an exaggeration of Jerôme Pâturot, but a statistical reality (36 out of 92 *commandites par actions* in 1850). The victims targeted were little people. The 'serious' *commandites par actions* divided their capital into *actions* (shares) of 500 or 1,000 francs, but the 'Californian' *sociétés* proposed fractional shares of 100, 50, 20, even 10 or 5 francs. As the form *commandite par actions* seemed to facilitate this kind of abuse, the law of 1856 met a call for a halt in the proliferation of firms with shareholders status. In other respects the size of the capital requested did not seem unusual to the public. To have a chance of attracting subscribers, these *sociétés* had to keep pace with market possibilities in the issue of their capital and their operations. Proposal to raise several millions of francs can give the appearance of guaranteeing the seriousness of purpose. Additional comfort was derived from the fact that Paris (in itself and in so far as its market was concerned) constituted by 1850 the most important reservoir of capital on the Continent, witness the preference of registered offices of foreign sociétés to be represented directly in Paris.

If the limited sample on which this study rests does not contribute to the central task of those investigating the industrialization of France in the first half of the nineteenth century – the demography of industrial *sociétés*, its analysis nevertheless seems to illuminate several aspects – initially problematic. This is particularly true in the case of the spatial dimension. The location of very important firms in the capital is shown to be more influenced by its position as a financial centre than for the structural role of its emerging market. The form of shareholding chosen by industrial enterprises registered as *sociétés* in Seine, which accounts for nearly half of the national total, seems to have been designed to achieve two objectives: on the one hand access to savings that the system of bank credit did not provide for all enterprises and on the other side the perceived necessity of securing complementarity between manufacturing and trade.

Footnotes

1. Kept in full or in the form of excerpts in the records of the Tribunal de commerce de la Seine (*Archives de la Seine* D31 U3).

2. We use the nomenclature of the *Enquête industrielle, 1861-1865*.
3. A Daumard, *La bourgeoisie parisienne de 1815 à 1848* Paris, SEVPEN, 1963.
4. Chambre de commerce de Paris. *Enquête industrielle, 1861-1865*.
5. J Gaillard, *Paris, La Ville, 1852-1870*, Edition Champion, Paris, 1977, p.380 *et seq*, p.340 *et seq*.
6. J Gaillard, op. cit., p.391 *et seq*.
7. See the *problématique* given by K Bruland, *British Technology & European Industrialization. The Norwegian textile industry in the mid-nineteenth century*, Cambridge University Press, Cambridge, 1989.
8. P Deyon et J P Hirsch, 'Entreprise et association dans l'arrondissement de Lille', in *Entreprises et entrepreneurs XIX-XXe siècles*, Congrès de l'Association Française des Historiens Economistes, mai 1980, Paris, Presses de l'Université de Paris-Sorbonne, 1983.
9. J Gaillard, op. cit., p.389.
10. J Gaillard, op. cit., p.388 *et seq*.
11. If, in the SCSs (*Sociétés en commandite simple*), the sleeping partner(s) are generally found before the *acte de société* is declared to the court, in the case of SCAs (*Sociétés en cammandite par actions*), the *acte* makes provision for the issue of a volume of shares corresponding to the capital, and the subscribers will be found afterwards. The corporation does really exist only from the time these subscribers are found. Except in a few cases of SCAs, one can never be certain that the *acte de fondation* corresponds to a true creation. The sum of SCAs' capital (216 million francs in 1850) is a sum of 'demanded' but not yet collected capital. It would be absurd to compare it to the macro-economic aggregates of gross fixed capital formation. The real volume of collected capital was doubtless very much less; many of these corporations were stillborn; some of them fanciful or created by swindlers.
12. This *commandite par actions* is a good example of these 'Californian' corporations. It was registered on 30 September 1850. It's corporate name was 'Christophe Colomb et Cie'. The active partner was Christophe Colomb, 22 rue Duphot, naturalist-engineer, ex-envoy of the French government to the Dahomey kingdom. The corporation had seven objectives: 1) the exploitation of gold mines and other metals, resources, and products of African and Californian coasts; 2) the alliance of human races, the abolition of the negro slave trade, of human sacrifices and their consequences; 3) the civilization of Africa; 4) trade, manufacturing, colonization; 5) a general pension fund; 6) a mutual benefit society; 7) consignment, banking, and commission activities. The capital, for which provision was made, was 66 million francs for the activities in Africa and 25 million for the activities in America.

7
Companies and manufacturers of the first period of industrialisation in Marseilles: 1810–1860

Michel Lescure

Confirming contemporary accounts, several recent works devoted to industrialisation in Marseilles have emphasized the important changes that occurred in this phocean city in the second half of the nineteenth century.[1] Augustin Féraud, president of the Chamber of Commerce, explained in 1895: 'The port of Marseilles, which was only commercial in character until about 1885, has been able, since that date, to create a very important industrial base that is now the main and the overwhelming factor in its business life'.[2]

Such a chronology seems to be well-founded. As it has often been asserted, the development of the industrial function of the port was, indirectly, the consequences of the changes that occurred in international transport and trade in the second half of the nineteenth century, notably the opening of the Suez Canal and the development of steam navigation. As a result of the fall in freight rates from the 1860s, Marseilles faced serious competition from the western and northern ports of Europe that benefited from their proximity to large consumer markets. Another disadvantage for Marseilles related to the traffic which continued to go through the port itself. This traffic was under the control of the *Compagnie des Docks*, which was responsible for the combined ship-to-rail transport and was managed from Paris. But this traffic did not provide any activity for local trade.[3] These conditions, which were detrimental to the prosperity of the city as a whole, were to be overcome by industrialisation. Raw materials would be landed at Marseilles for use by local industry, manufactured goods would then be shipped abroad or sold on the French regional and national markets.

It has been argued that in the shift towards industrialisation the merchants, a group particularly concerned with the commercial future of the city, played a most important role. By supplying new industrial firms with managing partners and capital, merchants are presumed to have helped promote the industrialisation of Marseilles. Recent researches have confirmed that this is indeed the case in the so-called traditional industries, such as food processing and soap and oil manufacture. Although such a view seems convincing, it under-estimates previous achievements. As M. Roncayolo has shown, the industrialisation of the city, and more especially the development of the industrial functions of the port, had their origins in the early nineteenth century.[4] The demographic study of companies in the city (that is to say the analysis of the peaks and troughs in the creation and dissolution of companies):

1) allows for confirmation of the timing of the beginnings of industrialisation and consequently the establishment of the correct chronology for economic growth,
2) draws attention to the specific nature of the financial and social processes of this early take off,
3) helps towards understanding why these beginnings of industrialisation made so little impact on the collective memory of the city.

COMPANIES AND MANUFACTURERS IN MARSEILLES

Figure 7.1
Creations and dissolutions of industrial companies in Marseilles 1809-1859.

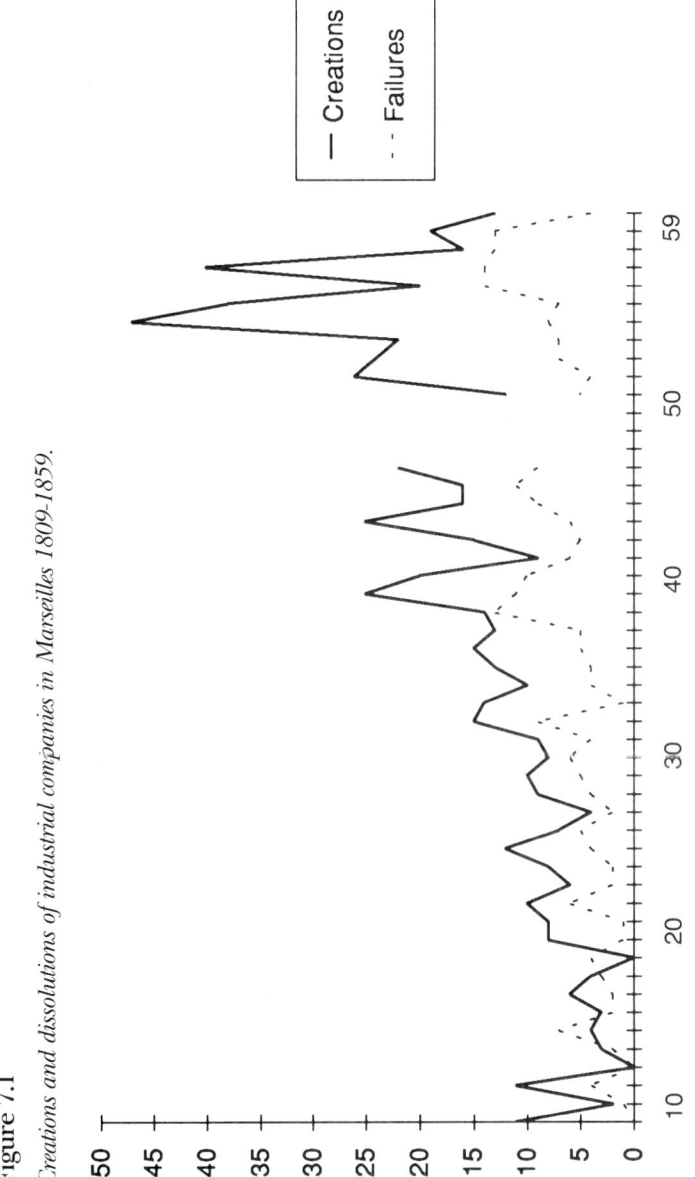

I The first successful industrialisation of Marseilles

The advantages of the historical sources used in this study will not be recited.[5] However, attention should be drawn to the close and positive correlation at the national level between the statistical data relating to the creation of the *companies* as a whole and the data concerned with industrial growth such as output and investment. For the period 1842 to 1909 the correlation with the series for industrial output (M.Levy-Leboyer, 1968) shows a coefficient of +0.957.

Table 7.1

The coefficient of correlation between national industrial product and creation of industrial and commercial companies in certain departments (1842-1860).

France	Bouches du Rhône	Gironde	Loire Inférieure	Nord	Rhône	Seine	Seine
+ 0·922	+ 0·698	+ 0·956	+ 0·626	+ 0·747	+ 0·922	+ 0·928	+ 0·737

The fact that such a positive correlation cannot be clearly found for the Bouches-du-Rhône (Table 7.1) does not mean that Marseilles and its region missed out on the first period of industrialisation. It suggests rather the overwhelming importance of trade (80 per cent of the companies founded in Marseilles in the early 1840s were non-industrial) and the relative absence of this activity in the national statistics.

Between 1809/1819 and 1850/1858 the number of industrial companies created in Marseilles grew at a rate of 4.4 per cent per annum (with a coefficient correlation with the national industrial statistics of + 0.746). The period 1818 to 1826 was characterised by a recovery in the older sectors of the economy that had run into serious difficulties during the Revolutionary and Napoleonic periods from 1789 to 1815 (Figure 7.1 and Table 7.2). Soapworks and sugar refineries provided 35.3 per cent of the new companies, so that by 1830 these two industries represented 40 per cent of local manufacturing output.[6] Industry, nonetheless, remained reasonably diversified; the revival of harbour traffic brought an increasing demand for textile and wood products. The demands created by the upturn in the staple industries had, however, more important consequences for the further development of the city. Throughout the period the expansion of soap making led to the establishment of many soda and sulphuric acid plants, as well as sulphur refineries (15.7 per cent of all new companies established were in these trades).[7] With easy access to supplies of salt, limestone and sulphur, 83 per cent of the French Leblanc soda factories were situated in the neighbourhood of Marseilles by 1847/48.[8]

Table 7.2

Manufacturing companies at the time of the first industrialization in Marseilles.

Industry	1 Number of sociétés established (% of total)			2 Legal statuts (% of total)			3 Average stock (in thousands of francs)	4 Forecasted duration (number of months)
	1820 1825	1839 1842	1851 1852	(1)	(2)	(3)		
Soap, candle, tallow	27·5	22·2	10·9	54·8	35·5	9·7	186·1	63·0
Oil	0·0	11·1	0·0	71·4	14·3	14·3	140·0	109·6
Chemicals	15·7	11·1	8·7	50·0	31·2	18·8	225·9	177·9
Sugar	7·8	4·8	6·5	70·0	20·0	10·0	361·2	70·5
Other food	2·0	4·8	4·3	83·3	16·7	0·0	208·0	100·8
Metals and machinery	2·0	6·3	39·1	26·1	17·4	56·5	839·0*	150·0
Mining	0·0	9·5	2 2	14·3	28·6	57·1	700·0	374·4
Textiles	19·5	11·1	8·7	76·2	14·3	9·5	78·1	82·6
Various	25·5	19·0	19·6	82·3	11·8	5·9	73·8	111·0
TOTAL	100	100	100	60·0	21·3	18·7	254·0	117·2
(Nb of acts)	(51)	(63)	(46)					

Source: Acts of creation of sociétés.
(1) Sociétés en nom collectif (2) Sociétés en commandite simple
(3) Société en commandite par actions.
Calculations of the columns 2, 3, 4 are based on the three sample years as a whole.
* The stock of one company totalled 5 millions of francs; the average stock of the others is only 244 571 F.

At the same time old established industries, such as candle making, sought to exploit new technologies and new industries developed. Following a decade of uncertain growth when soapworks moved away from using olive oil to seed oil, the oil industry took off in the early 1840s. Paralleling the development of mining companies, oil-mills quickly widened their share of the total number of company formations. By 1860 the value of the production of oil-mills (some 13 per cent of the total industrial output of the area) was almost equal to that of soap plants and still surpassed that of flour mills – the most important industry in Marseilles at the end of the nineteenth century. It is therefore evident that the pace of diversification and integration accelerated, even though this did not happen to any extent within the firms. During the following decade – the 1850s – the market share of most of the old established industries and even those of more recent origin (except sugar) was reduced by the rise of metalworking and machinery manufacturing companies (accounting for 39 per cent of new companies established in 1851/52). These firms were established to meet demand from local industry and harbour utilities, particularly for special items of equipment, such as elevating machinery for flour and oil mills. Although the statistical data is too unreliable even to provide a broad indication of the improvements that had taken place during this period, the facts tend to confirm that the economic growth that took place in Marseilles after 1860 marked a second phase in the process of industrialisation rather than the point of take off.

This approach which favours an early buoyancy in the regional economy is confirmed by the study of the judicial and financial structures that were established in the city during the first half of the nineteenth century. Contrary to the traditional view that characterised Marseilles' capitalism as being very shallow-rooted, these structures, from an historical perspective, appear to be the most advanced and sophisticated in the whole country. In 1853, a record year for the creation of companies in Marseilles, general partnerships (the most traditional and restrictive kind of partnership) represented only 52.6 per cent of the new (industrial and commercial) companies, whereas in France as a whole, they represented 73.6 per cent (66.6 per cent in Seine, 70-71 per cent in North and Seine-Inférieure, 82.2 per cent in Rhône). For manufacturing companies established in Marseilles, such a legal status was adopted by less than 30 per cent of the new firms. Consequently 70 per cent of manufacturing companies established in Marseilles in 1853 had *commanditaires* (sleeping partners) or shareholders. *Sociétés anonymes* (limited companies) were very unusual (just 2 per cent) but *sociétés en commandite par actions* (joint stock limited partnerships) accounted for 59.6 per cent. Admittedly the peak for 1853 was exceptional but the proportion of *sociétés en commandite par actions* had been growing steadily

Table 7.3
Distribution of the new industrial companies according to their legal statute.

		(as %)		
	Sociétés en nom collectif	Sociétés en commandite simple	Sociétés en commandite par actions	Société anonymes
1820-1825	72·9	22·9	4·2	0·0
1839-1842	61·9	22·2	15·9	0·0
1851-1852	41·3	17·4	41·3	0·0

throughout the previous half century (Table 7.3).

In addition to speculative factors, this advance in the number of firms with limited status, especially *sociétés en commandite par actions* (where sleeping partners were in fact shareholders who could buy and sell their shares without restriction) can be explained by the growing capital needs for industry and commerce. The extension of markets and important technological changes in the first half of the nineteenth century brought with them an increasing demand both for capital and credit facilities. The average capital of industrial companies rose from 73,900 francs for those created between 1820 and 1825 to 254,700 francs for those founded between 1839 and 1842 and 518,200 francs for those formed between 1851 and 1852. Promoters of firms chose the legal status which made it easiest for them to raise the capital that they required. For example, as early as the 1820s *sociétés en commandite* were not uncommon for soapworks; they accounted for 58 per cent of the companies founded between 1820 and 1825 in this industry where average capital reached 109,000 francs. During the 1830s and 1840s *sociétés en commandite* spread to the mining and chemical industries – 83 and 71 per cent respectively of the companies formed in these sectors between 1839 and 1842. In these instances, joint stock limited partnerships were preferred to simple limited partnerships because of the relative size of the fixed capital requirements. The average capital size of mining companies was 900,000 francs. In these two industries joint stock limited partnerships accounted for 50 and 43 per cent respectively of new companies formed. The new opportunities provided by issuing unregistered shares (*actions nominatives*) provided further encouragement for the adoption of this status.

At this time medium-sized enterprises engaged in metal processing, and machinery and textile manufacturer, started to switch to limited status. It was only in the late 1840s and early 1850s that some firms engaged in less-intensive industries made such a move. Although average capital size did not exceed 200,000 francs, 66.6 per cent of metalworking and machinery manufacturing companies founded between 1851 and 1852 were *sociétés en commandite par actions*. This type of organisation allowed inventive practical men to venture into manufacturing activities using speculative funds supplied by *commanditaires* (sleeping partners).

All sectors did not follow strictly this general trend. In textiles and some other industries, principally timber merchanting, paper-making, and the supply of building materials – where average capital size did not exceed 100,000 francs – *sociétés en nom collectif* and *sociétés en commandite simple* (simple limited partnerships) remained the most popular in the mid-century. These kinds of companies were only to be found in less capital saving activities. For instance, in the oil industry, the number of plants grew between 1840 and 1842 from eighteen to thirty-six; but only eight new companies were established and of these six were general partnerships.

This example should not lead to a mistaken impression of the achievements of the period. Compared with the national picture, the legal structures adopted in Marseilles were, on the whole, much more advanced than could be expected from the nature of the region's industries. Indeed, Marseilles was poorly provided with capital-intensive industries. In most sectors fixed capital was of little importance and working capital was turned over regularly. Consequently, there were no economic imperatives to adopting limited status and other factors came into play. Sugar refining provides a good illustration. This was a relatively capital-intensive industry with fixed capital representing nearly one-third of total assets by the 1860s. Most of the companies in Marseilles were converted into *sociétés en commandite par actions* between 1848 and 1864, while elsewhere in other ports (with the exception of Le Havre) they remained family concerns. Thanks to the capital that had been raised as a result of using this legal form of organization, the sugar industry in Marseilles had become the most capital intensive and the most concentrated of the sugar industry in any French port; no plant employed less than one hundred workers in 1864 while 69.2 per cent of refineries in other ports did.[9]

II   The unexpected actors

Such a comparison between the experience of Marseilles and other French harbour towns requires some explanation by a close examination of various factors such as the size and proximity of consumer markets, capital available and managerial attitudes. Some of these factors are related to the question of which individuals were involved in the process of industrialisation. As has already been mentioned, it has been frequently argued that merchants played a more prominent role in the industrial development of Marseilles than they did in other cities. For the period under review this suggestion seems to require some modification.

The sources show that, in fact, merchants were not the most important group among the founders of industrial companies. For the three sample periods they represented only 26.4 per cent of founders whose profession is known, while manufacturers represented 34.1 per cent. Only in the most capital-intensive industries (chemicals, mining, sugar) did participation by merchants exceed 40 per cent of partners. Undoubtedly, in order to avoid arbitrary bias resulting from the source itself, this conclusion should be verified by adopting other historical approaches. *Actes de société* (acts of creations of companies), although they provide information about *commandités* (active partners, managers), rarely, if ever, give any details about the *commanditaires* (sleeping partners). As a result the role of merchants and of other professions, notably bankers, as simple suppliers of capital is not reflected in the source. Moreover, merchants could engage in manufacturing activity as a purely private business; but this does not seem to have happened on any scale in Marseilles and therefore does not bias the results. During the *Restauration* period only 10 per cent of the great merchants of the city left industrial assets, totalling 13 per cent of their freehold property.[10]

Except in mining and machinery manufacture most companies were formed by industrialists. In the textile and sugar refining trades they supplied 50 per cent of the *commandités* – active partners (whose profession is known) and 41 per cent in various other industries. To a slight extent the significance of the role of the industrialists can be explained by the transfer of capital and managers from one sector to another. For instance, in 1842 A Framond set up his oil mill company with capital supplied by Roux & Bernabo, along with Tiers & Gallamand – as a result four large sugar refiners became partners in the enterprise. In most cases these transfers were organised within the family group. Indeed, in Marseilles the family rather than the enterprise continued throughout the period to support both diversification and integration of activities. The main reason for the dominance of manufacturers/industrialists was simply the long tradition of manufacturing activity in the city. Most of the founders of businesses followed a profession in the same sector as the one in which they established their company.

The other social groups involved in the formation of companies, were far behind manufacturers and merchants. The proprietors/fundholders (12.6 per cent) and employees (11.4 per cent) were of some importance only in the soap and oil industries. Although workers and craftsmen accounted for 37.5

Table 7.4

Distribution of the active partners of the industrial companies at Marseilles according to their original profession.

	Soap	Oil	Chemicals	Sugar	Other Food	Metals machinery	Mining	Textiles	Various	Tot
Unknown										
1820-25	61.5	0.0	60.0	37.5	100.0	100.0	0.0	45.8	43.3	53.1
1839-42	15.4	10.5	0.0	50.0	50.0	33.3	21.4	15.4	13.3	16.8
1851-52	0.0	0.0	0.0	25.0	0.0	25.9	0.0	42.9	6.9	14.1
Manufacturers										
1820-25	23.1	0.0	25.0	37.5	0.0	0.0	0.0	33.3	36.7	29.2
1839-42	23.1	26.3	17.6	25.0	12.5	0.0	7.1	30.8	53.3	27.0
1851-52	20.0	0.0	25.0	25.0	50.0	11.1	0.0	28.6	6.9	15.2
Merchants										
1820-25	0.0	0.0	5.0	25.0	0.0	0.0	0.0	4.2	3.3	4.5
1839-42	26.9	26.3	47.1	0.0	0.0	16.7	42.8	30.8	6.7	24.1
1851-52	40.0	0.0	75.0	50.0	50.0	7.4	66.7	0.0	31.0	29.9
Proprietors and fundholders										
1820-25	11.5	0.0	5.0	0.0	0.0	0.0	0.0	4.2	6.7	6.2
1839-42	7.7	10.6	17.6	0.0	12.5	16.7	7.1	7.7	10.0	10.2
1851-52	30.0	0.0	0.0	0.0	0.0	11.1	0.0	14.3	10.3	10.9
Employees										
1820-25	3.8	0.0	5.0	0.0	0.0	0.0	0.0	12.5	6.7	6.2
1839-42	23.1	10.6	0.0	25.0	25.0	0.0	7.1	7.7	3.3	10.2
1851-52	10.0	0.0	0.0	0.0	0.0	11.1	33.3	0.0	6.9	7.6
Workers and craftsmen										
1820-25	0.0	0.0	0.0	0.0	0.0	0.0	0.0	0.0	3.3	0.9
1839-42	3.8	0.0	0.0	0.0	0.0	33.3	0.0	7.7	13.3	5.8
1851-52	0.0	0.0	0.0	0.0	0.0	25.9	0.0	14.3	37.9	20.7
Various										
1820-25	0.0	0.0	0.0	0.0	0.0	0.0	0.0	0.0	0.0	0.0
1839-42	0.0	15.8	17.6	0.0	0.0	0.0	14.3	0.0	0.0	5.8
1851-52	0.0	0.0	0.0	0.0	0.0	7.4	0.0	0.0	0.0	2.2

Source: Acts of creation of sociétés.

The number of active partners is 113 for 1820-1825, 137 for 1839-1842 and 92 for 1851-1852.

per cent of the founders of metal processing and machinery manufacturing companies, they did not supply more than 11.4 per cent of all those involved in contracting. Together the professionals (manufacturers, craftsmen and workers) represented nearly half of the *commandités*, while tradesmen and merchants only accounted for a quarter.

Although such a distribution characterised the first phase of industrialisation in Marseilles, the pattern changed during the first half of the nineteenth century (Table 7.4). The proportion of manufacturers involved in the establishment of new firms fell quickly; they only accounted for 17.8 per cent of founders (whose profession is known) in 1851/1852 compared with 62.3 per cent at the beginning of the century. Their influence had been steadily waning throughout that time. As for merchants, who only accounted for 9.4 per cent in the 1820s, their share increased to 29 per cent in 1839 to 1842 and finally to 34 per cent in 1851 to 1852.[11] Their growing importance was particularly obvious in the so-called traditional industries of Marseilles: chemicals, soapworks and sugar refineries. Sugar refining provides a good illustration of this trend. After the Revolution the men who were the prime movers in the revival of the industry were recruited principally from a large circle of professional managers. The most important refiner in Marseilles (and for that matter in Europe as a whole) in the early 1860s was J Grandval, who had begun his career as an industrialist in the 1810s with the establishment of a distillery and then a flour mill. His main competitors were F T Roux and F Bernabo who had started out as shipowner and shipmaster respectively. However, few of the firms managed by this first generation of entrepreneurs reached a position of financial autonomy and achieved a secure basis. Consequently, by the mid century only three companies survived. As a result of economic expansion and the new tariff policy, a number of new enterprises were launched between 1857 and 1864 which made Marseilles the principal market in France for sugar refining. To a far greater extent than in the past, the promoters of these new companies came from trade. Some of them, it is true, like F. Emsens, were Belgian (or Dutch) but the majority were merchants from Marseilles itself. The sole refinery constructed in 1863, built by C. Rostand (a son and grandson of merchants and himself a merchant until 1862), raised the production capacity of the Marseilles' sugar refining industry from 60,000 to 120,000 tonnes. Moreover, at the same time, merchants seemed to have greatly strengthened their participation as *commanditaires*. For instance, at Massot Brothers, a company that was organised as a joint stock limited partnership in 1858 (with a stock of 2.2 million francs), the principal merchant subscribers held at least as many shares as M. & L. Massot themselves (20.5 per cent of the capital) and twice as much as that of the company's bankers.[11]

III The instability of the structure

This noticeable shift at about the middle of century in the social groups engaged in the process of industrialisation is probably one of the first keys to understanding why contemporaries, inspired as they were by the virtues of trade, laid such emphasis on the achievements of the second half of the nineteenth century. However, their appraisal finds some credence in the extreme instability of the structures set up during the first phase of industrialisation. As has just been explained for sugar refinery, few firms established in the first part of the nineteenth century were successful in continuing in operation until the second. Even those firms engaged in sugar refining that had been established between 1857 and 1864 were reconstructed when depression hit the industry in the late 1860s. In oil milling the origins of the largest companies of the early 1900s (Verminck, Rocca-Tassy-de Roux, Huilerie Nouvelle) dated back only to the last third of the previous century. In fact, most of the companies of the first phase of industrialisation were very short-lived. Stable companies such as Rigaud & Cremieux in chemicals, Grandval & Girard in sugar refining, or Magnam in soapworks were exceptional. While the average forecasted life of an enterprise was nearly ten years for all companies created between 1820 and 1825, 1839 and 1842, and 1841 and 1852, many companies (those dissolved during these periods themselves) disappeared after only two years and four months of existence. In the period 1820 to 1825 17.6 per cent of the companies that were established were dissolved during the first year of their life.

On a preliminary analysis such a break in continuity underlies the great risks in operating outside the local economy. Only a study of bankruptcies would provide more detailed knowledge. As everywhere else, the constraints imposed by the market made competition a driving force in the economy and no firm was spared from its pressures. Moreover, both for its supplies of raw materials and also its sales of finished products, Marseilles was dependent on fluctuating markets, most of which experienced the same low standard of life expectancy. Cycles of over-supply and shortages of raw materials threw market forecasts badly out. These factors help to explain some local managerial attitudes. To avoid bankruptcy, manufacturers tended to be cautious in making investments (many plants were leased rather than being purchased). Integration was abandoned and every effort was made to ensure rapid turnover in working capital. F. de Muizon has claimed 'fluctuations in the current prices of raw materials were so important that all manufacturers tried to sell their production even before the raw materials had been landed'.[12] As a general rule profits were expected from commercial transactions rather than from improvements in industrial productivity. Such behaviour was typical of merchant manufacturers during the second half of the nineteenth century and it seems likely that this was the case long before.

The second reason for the instability of companies was the mobility of partners. In a significant proportion of cases, dissolutions were in fact followed by new creations with the addition of some new partners. In 1870, for example, only 15 per cent of the oil mills had company names that dated back to 1855. Some degree of stability existed but rather at the level of the plant than at those of the partners and the company. Sometimes these changes were the consequence of a bankruptcy or a misunderstanding. Although most of the mobility took place inside the same sector, it is also possible that mobility was a means of preventing capital being locked up for a long time in the same business, providing an opportunity to re-assess the economic risk as either a long-term investment or merely a speculation.

Nevertheless, throughout the first half of the nineteenth century, economic structures tended to be more stable. The forecasted life expectancy of new companies rose from six years in 1820 to 1825, to ten years and six months in 1839 to 1842 and twelve years and eleven months in 1851 to 1852. The reality was almost certainly different. Those companies that dissolved did so on average when they were one year and nine months old in the first period, two years and seven months in the second and two years and eleven months in the third. Increased capital requirements led to improved life expectancies but disruption and turbulence in the markets prevented a marked advance.

Conclusion

So, with an unstable population of businesses, and without any significant participation by the merchant community, Marseilles had embarked on a journey to becoming a manufacturing city. This facilitated further development in the future and economic growth. The increasing role of the merchants brought its own benefits. While trade strengthened its grip on manufacturing industry, a major shift occurred in the scope of business operations. But was the new phase of industrialisation which began in the middle of the century so economically well-founded? Behind the buoyant performance of the local economy lay some alarming economic indicators. The share of the Bouches-du-Rhône in the creation of commercial and industrial companies in the whole of France dropped regularly from 4 per cent or more in the 1840s and 1850s to 3 per cent by the end of the century. At the same time the share of the bankruptcies of all enterprises (personal firms and companies) increased from 2 per cent to 8.3 per cent. Among all industrial départements, the Bouches-du-Rhône was the only one to show such a deficit[13] in the demography of its enterprises (Figure 7.2). This deficit had started to accumulate in the late 1860s, but the rate of bankruptcies advanced quickly between 1885 and 1902, while the peak in bankruptcies in

Figure 7.2
Creations of companies and failures of enterprises in Bouches-Du-Rhone, 1842-1909.

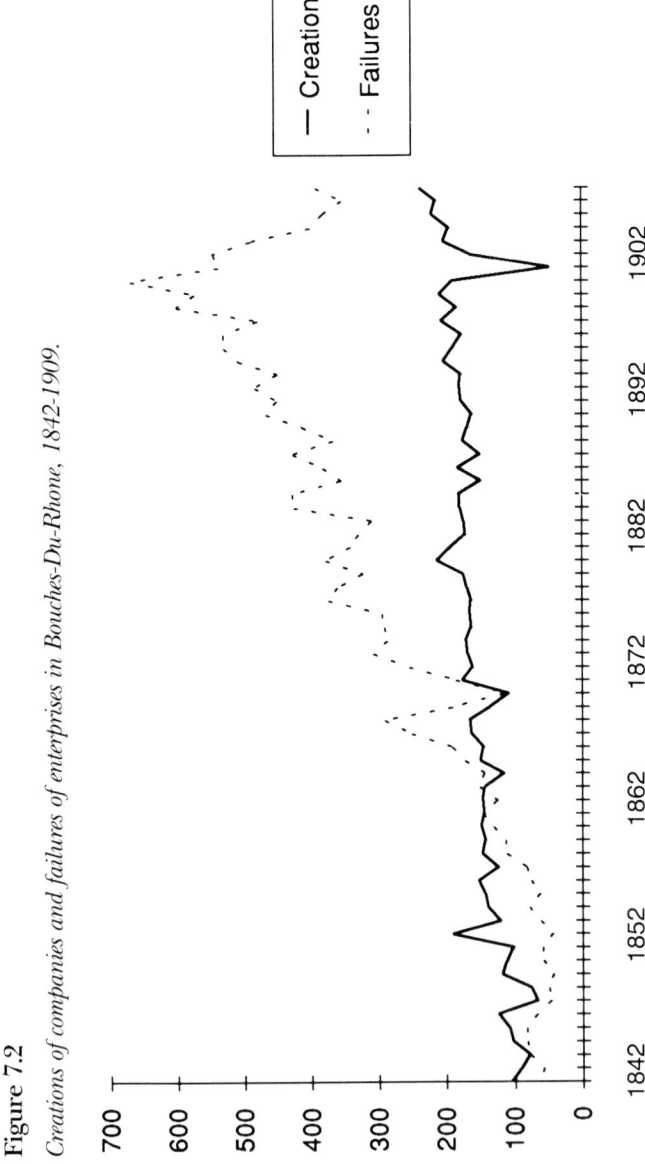

the whole of France was reached in 1886. The slowness of growth in new company formations (while creations of companies climbed rapidly in France in the early 1890s) brought the deficit to 5 per centage points. The very nature of the new companies that were founded tended to be weaker. After 1854/1856 the proportion of personal partnership (*sociétés en nom collectif* and *sociétés en commandite simple*) increased sharply at the expense of *sociétés par actions*. Although, admittedly, this was a national trend reflecting economic crises and changes in commercial law (the law of July 1856 made it more difficult to create a *société en commandite par actions*); in Marseilles the formation of *sociétés par actions* declined far more rapidly than elsewhere and the upward movement that followed in other parts of the country was delayed. As a result, by 1909, joint stock companies *sociétés en commandite par actions* and *SARL* accounted for only 13.5 per cent of new companies formed in Marseilles as against 22 per cent in the whole of France. The underlying reasons for such a decline requires new research. However, it does cast some doubt on the continuity of the achievements of the first phase of industrialisation that has been described here.

Footnotes

1. For instance, L. Piérrein, *Industries traditionnelles du port de Marseille, Le cycle des sucres et des oléagineux 1870-1958*, Marseille, 1975.
2. Quoted in L. Piérrein, *op.cit.*
3. This argument has been developed for instance by C. Fabre, Président of the Chamber of Commerce from 1881 to 1891.
4. M. Roncayolo, 'Les grandes phases de l'économie marseillaise depuis le XIXe siècle', *Revue Marseille* N°55.
5. See, for instance, P. Jobert and J.C. Chevailler, 'La démographie des entreprises en France au XIXe siècle. Quelques pistes', *Histoire Economie Société*, 1986.

6. According to the statistical data published by the Chamber of Commerce, the output of the main industries in the Bouches-du-Rhône was (in 000 F):

Table 7.5

	1830	1860	1880	1910
Oil-mill		42 120	95 000	180 000
Soap and candlemakers	30 500	46 676	62 583	97 000
Chemicals	8 101	13 316	13 000	57 700
Floormills	1 000	33 630	170 000	210 000
Sugar	16 010	36 766	82 080	87 000
Total industrial output in the B.du R.	117 359	326 213	578 481	1 308 681

7. In 1830, there were 14 sulphuric acid plants and about 20 Leblanc soda factories in Bouches du Rhône, cf. P. Baud, *L'industrie chimique en France, Etude historique et géographique,* Paris, 1932, and R. Richeux, *L'industrie chimique en France. Structure et production (1850-1957),* Paris, 1958.

8. R. Richeux, *op.cit.*

9. R. Caty and E. Richard, 'Contribution à l'étude du monde du négoce marseillais de 1815 à 1870: l'apport des successions', *Revue Historique* N° 536.

10. In text percentages are calculated with the only associates whose profession is known.

11. J. Fiérain, *Les raffineries de sucre des ports en France (XIXe-début du XXe siècles),* Lille, 1976.

12. F. de Muizon, *L'industries huilière marseillaise, 1825-1971. Le pouvoir des huiliers,* Marseilles, 1981.

13. For the interpretation of this indicator see P. Jobert and J.C. Chevailler, *op.cit.*

8
A demography of firms in Toulouse – a case study in delayed industrialisation – 1868–1940

Jean-Pierre Allinne

Why Toulouse? Because it is an example that is unique in France. This town is still today the capital of the most agricultural region in the whole of Europe. Geographically enclosed by two mountainous areas, it was not affected by the first wave of industrialisation at the beginning of the nineteenth century. On the other hand the town experienced large-scale immigration from the countryside, with a threefold increase in its population between 1850 and 1940. By then it was the fourth largest town in the whole of France with 300,000 inhabitants. An analysis of the creation of companies in the town is particularly interesting because their character is untypical. Who were the promoters of these enterprises in a town that historians have

Figure 8.1
Formation of industrial companies and average capital, Toulouse 1868-1940.
Constant francs 1914

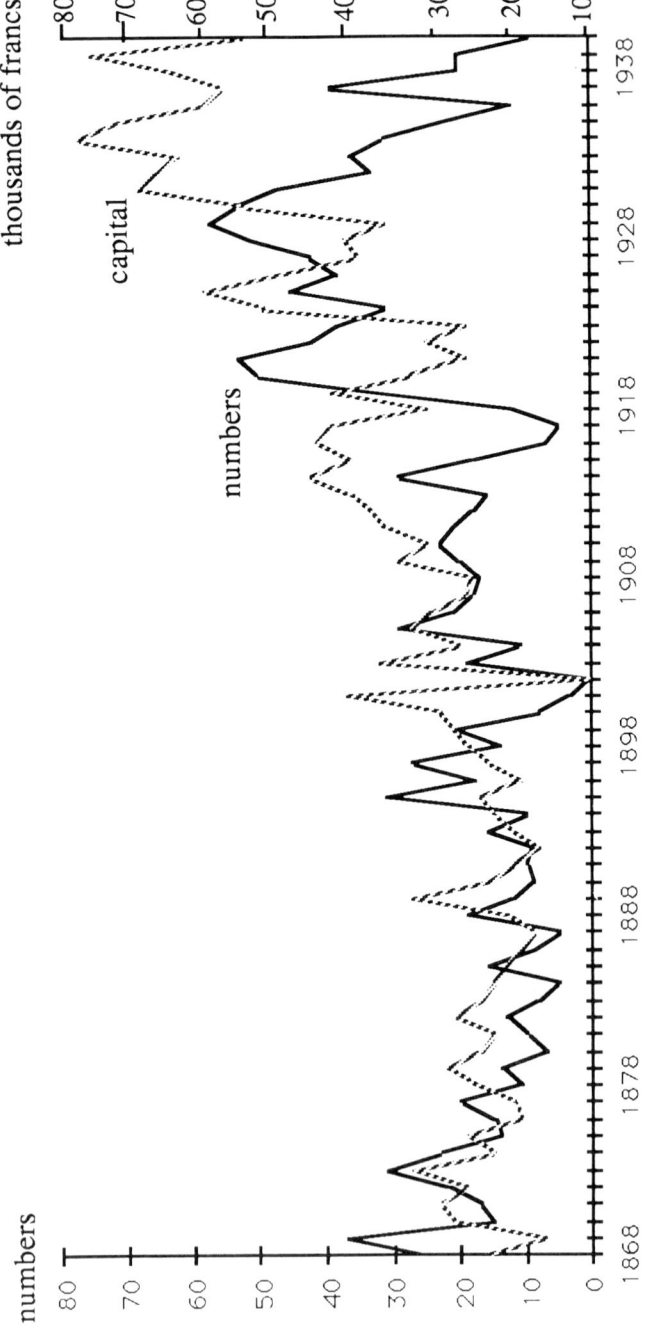

DEMOGRAPHY OF FIRMS IN TOULOUSE

termed a big village until the outbreak of the First World War?

The Toulousian series is based on 3,000 Acts registering *sociétés*, 1,600 of which related to industrial concerns either in terms of their initial production or later transformation. The series is homogeneous from 1868, the year after the *sociétés anonymes* were liberated, until the end of the Second World War. It allows for three complementary methods of approach:

1) A quantitative approach:
   To measure the movements in the Toulousian cycles:
   Teams led by Philippe Jobert and François Caron have made a start by drawing attention to the importance of comparing births and deaths of firms locally with national indicators

2) A sectoral approach:
   The Acts often show the type of activity planned by the promoters, the process to be employed and the buildings, equipment and possibly patents to be used. It will be possible in this second section to trace the long-term evolution of the most important industrial sectors in Toulouse

3) A capitalist approach:
   Investigation of partners, their professions and addresses adds a new dimension to the determinants of financial fluctuations. The type of legal status adopted and the mode of distribution of profits allows a distinction to be made between trading partnerships and investment companies. The amount and nature of capital, coupled with the origins of shareholders, allows us to evaluate better investment in Toulouse.

1. Birth cycle rhythms

1.1 Contrasted cycles

The number of creations can be broken down into four unequal parts; they decline from 1869 to 1884, then gradual recovery from 1885 to 1915, achieve very strong growth from 1919 to 1929, and experience a crisis from then until 1939, with the annual rate returning to the level of 1915. Within these general trends 8 to 12 intermediate cycles of growth can be observed in the years: 1885 to 1898, 1904 to 1915, 1919 to 1929 – all associated with very strong down swings – and 1884, 1902 to 1903, and 1923 to 1924. The wide amplitudes of the cycle in Toulouse contrasts with Philippe Jobert's findings for the departments of the Nord and the Rhône where demographic fluctuations were very small by the end of the period – 1900 to 1911. Toulouse's pulse of economic activity continued to be registered on the national scale, even if the slowing down in creations during 1860 to 1884 was less important than in Marseille (see Chapter 7). Marseille experienced its largest number of bankruptcies in 1886,

Figure 8.2
Surplus stock of industrial companies in Toulouse, 1870-1939.

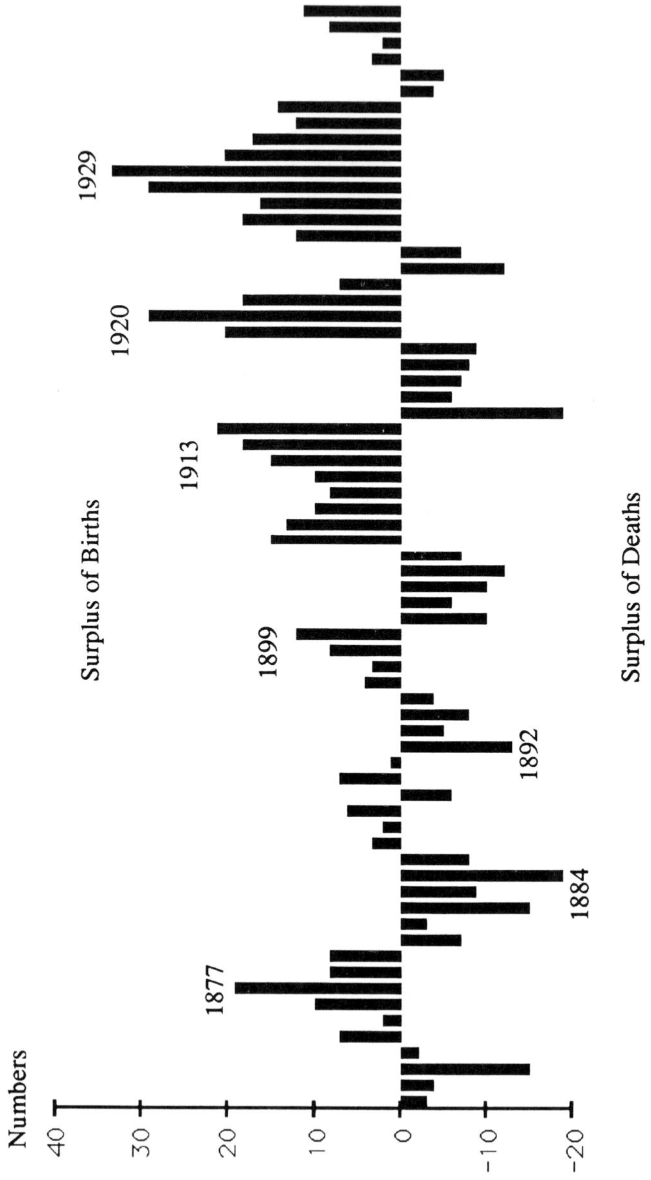

suggesting that managers had little alternative but to respond to local conditions that ran counter to national trends.

1.2 A demography determined by a combination of events.

Toulouse is very different from the industrial departments of Nord and Rhône where creations always exceeded failures. To measure the difference we have established a simple indicator by adding local bankruptcies and premature dissolutions or significant changes in articles of association. This series is imperfect: for example, bankruptcy processes do not distinguish trading from industrial firms, and craftsmen from companies. However, the series gives a truer picture of mortality. Two general observations emerge from the analysis. The first is the striking long-term decline in failures which is explained, certainly after 1820, by the development of more lenient attitudes in commercial jurisprudence. Judges preferred to authorise plans to safeguard the assets of private enterprise rather than to impose punishments on the partners. Equally important was a change after the First World War in the size and capital of individual *sociétés:* small artisan enterprises are supplemented by more important units with well organised capital divided into *actions* (shares).

Not surprisingly, mortality was greater in periods of general economic crisis, but Toulouse did not always follow the national trend – behaving idiosyncratically. In 1880, two years before the general economic crisis, the volume of bankruptcies began to increase in Toulouse and the number of creations to fall away. During this period the funds of small firms were not supplemented by over-generous bank credit in a town that was dominated by service activities. The setting up of the Société Générale in 1867 followed by the Crédit Lyonnais to improve the finance of small firms was not accompanied by a huge increase in credit as in both cases the banks prudently sought to collect deposits from savers over the counter before advancing money. The Bank of France's statistics for rediscounting bills of exchange confirms this aspect of the birth and mortality cycles. There was in Toulouse only one important local bank, the protestant Courtois Banque, which had a long tradition of discounting bills for the big food companies, the improvement and construction of houses, and towards the end of the century the provision of electricity and railway services in the Pyrénées. Only ten or twelve small banks were created in Toulouse during this period, but their objects were often too general to be taken seriously and in most cases lack of capital led to failure.

There is a global correlation between the figures for births and deaths, which is proportional to the total population of *sociétés*. Cases of dissolutions remain relatively stable at 45 per cent of the annual average for creations. Consequently there was an uncertain but definite gain in the population of enterprises in Toulouse during this period, in a country where rural departments only secured one-third of all new creations but two-thirds of bankruptcies.

1.3 Is Toulouse's behaviour anti-cyclical?

At the outset, it should be noted that it is impossible to compare the industrial creations in Toulouse with the national figures presented by Philippe Jobert and Jean-Claude Chevailler. Productive firms based in Toulouse only account for half of all acts of creation. The capital of these enterprises was smaller than firms in other trades. Toulouse certainly shows a more regular pattern of creations than other non-industrial departments. In France as a whole there were more bankruptcies than creations after 1880 until 1910 when they became less numerous except in the case of Toulouse due to a combination of circumstances. The secular fall of industrial prices does not seem to have had the same effect in inhibiting the formation of new sociétés in Toulouse as elsewhere in France. For example, in Languedoc the market for consumer goods flattened out and as a result fewer speculative *sociétés* were formed. It is with agricultural output and agricultural prices that we must look for a significant correlation in Toulouse. From this investigation two observations emerge:

a) the tendency of agricultural prices to fall after 1875 is not as pronounced in Toulouse as in Languedoc, a region composed of many small market towns. Demand from the rest of the country for goods and services from Toulouse grew steadily throughout the period. The phylloxera, which destroyed the vineyards in Bordeaux during the 1880s and led to wine being imported from other areas, brought about a revival in the old-established wine trade in Toulouse. Until the outbreak of the First World War wine, vinegar and other alcoholic liquors accounted for about 40 per cent of the food and drink produced in the area. This growth in sales of agricultural produce was only possible because the railways had opened up the largest rural market in France.

b) The hazards resulting from the instability of agricultural prices, however, encouraged merchants and landowners to look for other types of investment. This contention is borne out up until 1913 by the fact that there is no correlation between short-term upward movements in prices and the growth in the number of creations. The two years that recorded the greatest fall in prices – 1885 and 1895 –

also achieved the largest number of new creations, particularly in the food and agricultural industries which took advantage of the fall in prices to exploit new markets. In contrast the number of creations actually fell when agricultural prices rose as in 1900 to 1903 and 1910 to 1913.

Apart from these specific instances, Toulouse follows the national trend. In France as elsewhere agricultural prices are themselves related to industrial prices. There is a steady decline from 1860 to about 1890, followed by a period of stability which parallels the industrial price indices. The investment cycle, described by Maurice Lévy-Leboyer, entered a new phase in 1886 in France as a whole as well as in Toulouse[2]. The correlation between local and national growth is even more obvious during the so-called golden age of the 1920s, which came to an abrupt end in 1930 when the pace of creations fell sharply. This chronology agrees with that proposed by Jacques Marseille who located in 1929 the beginning of the crisis which at first was 'Franco-French' in character. The monetary and political events began to be felt immediately in Toulouse. As Philippe Jobert and Jean-Claude Chevailler have shown little can prevent national shifts in production from having an effect on every region in France, with, of course, local variations. In these long swings in the economy, the demography of enterprise is a vital engine for and a consequence of growth. There is a kind of 'feed-back' effect. This is particularly true in Toulouse after 1920 with the establishment of sub-contractors to larger industrial concerns.

2. The creative industrial sectors

2.1 The long predominance of the semi-craftsmen, 1870-1914

Three traditional activities related to the rural world produced a majority of firms until the outbreak of the First World War (Figure 8.3). The first of these was the food and agriculture industry. There were in Toulouse about 1,000 very small flour mills employing roughly 3,000 workers. Two hundred of these mills were controlled by private companies, often twinned with the grain trade. Much the same was true for the clothes, shoe and textile trades. There were, for example, some 500 shoe making businesses. Customers for all these concerns came mainly from the countryside. Factories making clothes, worn by agricultural workers, were numerous. Clothing was the driving force behind the development of this local market. The only big clothes firms were either controlled by Basques (Etchepare) or Catalans (Soler-Puig). The First World War encouraged the concentration of clothing companies. One-quarter of French production of military overcoats and shoes was turned out in Toulouse by a smaller number of firms with more capitally intensive workshops. The importance of the housing industry is not surprising in a town whose population was growing quickly as people left the countryside. The town's population grew rapidly during the First World War to meet the needs of the munitions' industry and afterwards as a result of political exodus from Poland, Italy and Spain. The statistics of imports of bricks and cement from Spain drawn from records of tolls charged correlate very well with the data for the population and creation of building *sociétés*. Woodworking is a complementary activity to house building. This sector is interesting because of its co-operative tradition in the furniture trade. Another complementary activity was the manufacture of flat glass. In 1894 two big building employers established a glass-making *SARL* in Carmaux alongside coalmines.

The artisanal companies which were established after 1890 had a strong added value component in their trade. The number of patents registered in France grew at the end of the century. In Toulouse they were used first to improve services to the town's country hinterland. For example, a chemist in partnership with a dealer began manufacturing tartar from deposits found in wine barrels, and also producing ammoniac from public sewerage for use as a fertilizer. The development in Toulouse of a fertilizer industry led many craftsmen to acquire real chemical 'know-how'. When the Nitrogen National Office was established in 1924, 2,500 workers in Toulouse were enrolled.

Another service provided by the town to the local countryside was specialised metal-work, particularly brass-working, cartwrighting, and the production of farm equipment. In the cartwright trade the first artisanal cycle developed after 1890. The first motor-car companies were established in the town from 1910, for example the production to order of the light car 'Micron' and the 'Bébéli' car. It should be remembered that in France as in Great Britain by 1914 there were over ninety different makes of car on the market. During the same period the growth in the readership for newspapers and the use of schoolbooks resulted as in Paris in the rapid development of lithographic and printing works, with machinery driven by electric power. The use of electricity led directly to the establishment in Toulouse of new industry assisted by the coming of Pyrénées hydro-electricity.

DEMOGRAPHY OF FIRMS IN TOULOUSE

Figure 8.3

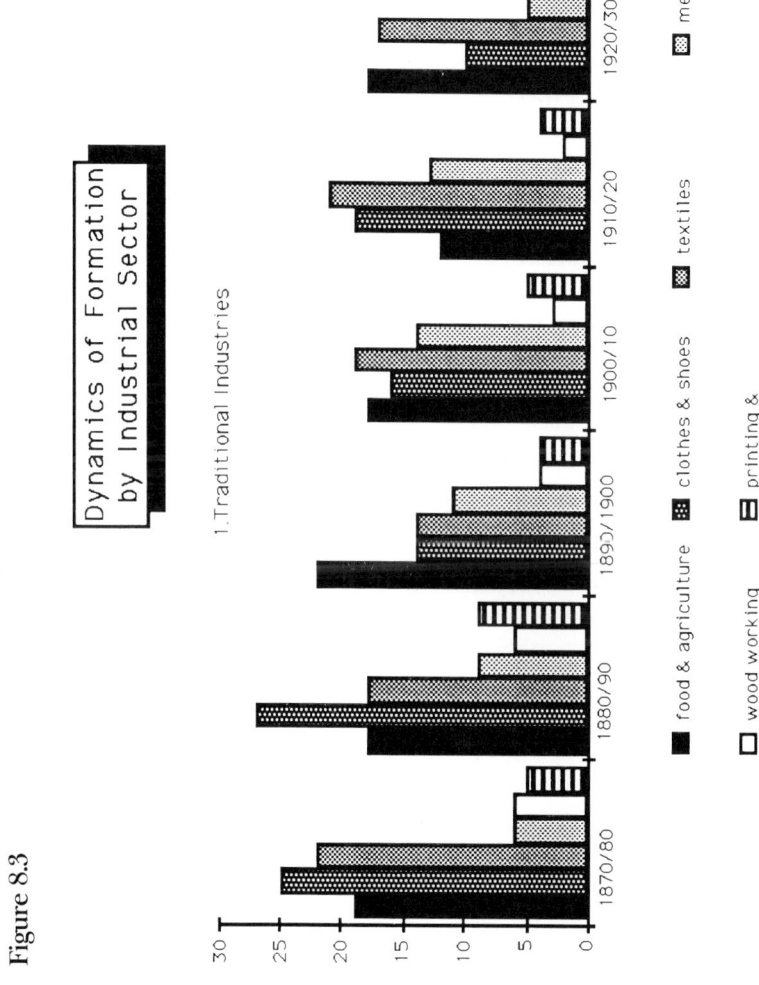

Figure 8.4

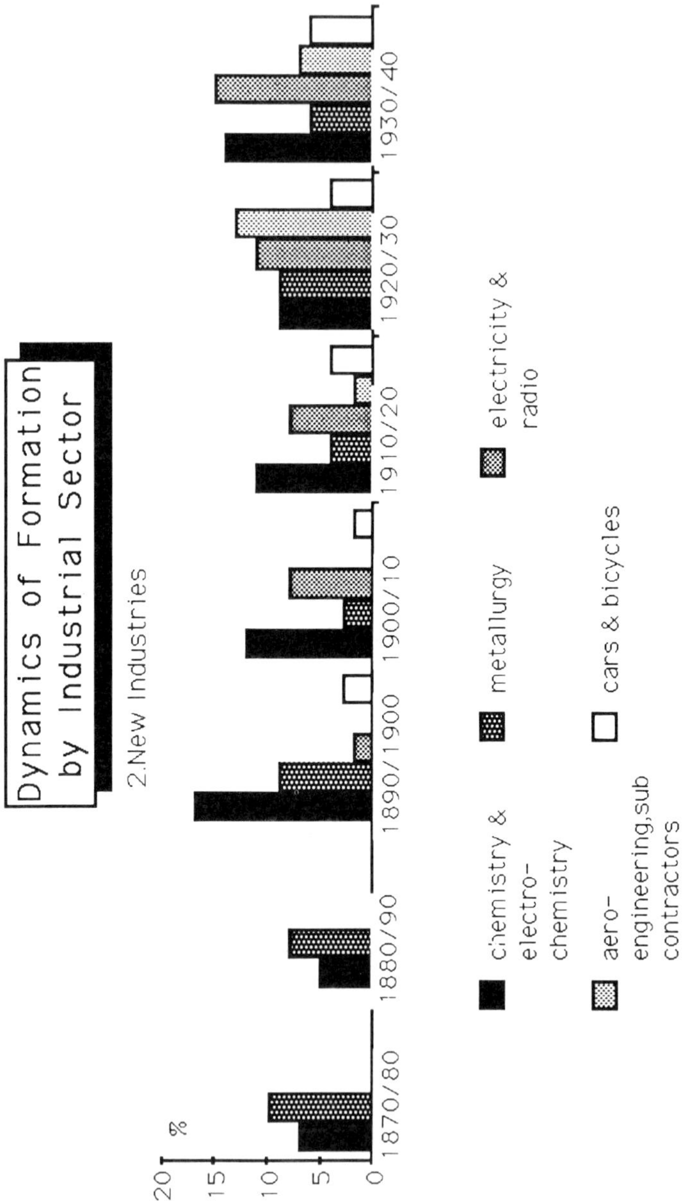

Dynamics of Formation by Industrial Sector

2. New Industries

■ chemistry & electro-chemistry
▨ metallurgy
▦ electricity & radio
■ aero-engineering, sub contractors
□ cars & bicycles

2.2 Power industries and sub-contractors: 1919-1939

After 1924 public utilities became the principal employers in the region. They provided the impetus for the establishment of many small innovative industries. The paper industry can be considered to fall into this category as it had either to adopt mechanized production techniques or disappear. After the First World War the 'Job' cigarette paper firm became the principal sub-contractor of the public tobacco industry in Toulouse. The outstanding feature of the twentieth century is undoubtedly the rise and application of electricity. The promoter of hydro electricity in the region, the engineer Paul, wanted Toulouse to become the 'Pyrénées' Grenoble'. His ambition was only partly realised. The production of electricity and the construction of a network of lines provided the catalyst for changes in the demography of enterprise which passed Toulouse by. However, electricity supply did have a beneficial effect on the industry of Toulouse, with the establishment of innovative firms supplying the electrical industry itself, especially the manufacture of engines, ceramic insulators, and radios (Figure 8.3). As a result after 1920 a second high-technology industrial sector began to develop in the town, with rich promise for the future – opening the way for expansion after 1950.

Before the Second World War employment in Toulouse remained roughly in equilibrium. Jobs created in the new know-how industries more or less balanced those lost in traditional activities. The 1906 and 1931 industrial censuses show that the working population had remained almost constant at 100,000. Traditional activities were still predominant in both years. Rapid urbanisation supported the building trades and also the food and agricultural industries. The function of Toulouse as a regional capital with locally owned businesses and an active business community allowed the town to survive the inter-war depression without serious loss of jobs.

3. The profile of creators of sociétés

3.1 The predominance of trades- and craftsmen

In about 1850 the difference between trade, craft and small industries is difficult to determine. This remains so in Toulouse until 1940. The professions of those involved in the establishment of firms remains somewhat antiquated (see Figure 8.5 *over*). The number of craftsmen and tradesmen, who set up businesses, remains almost constant until 1930, a feature reminiscent of proto-industrialisation. Much the same is true for farmers, who were often involved in the formation of businesses to

Figure 8.5

The occupations of founders of companies in Toulouse in the years at the beginning of the cycles.

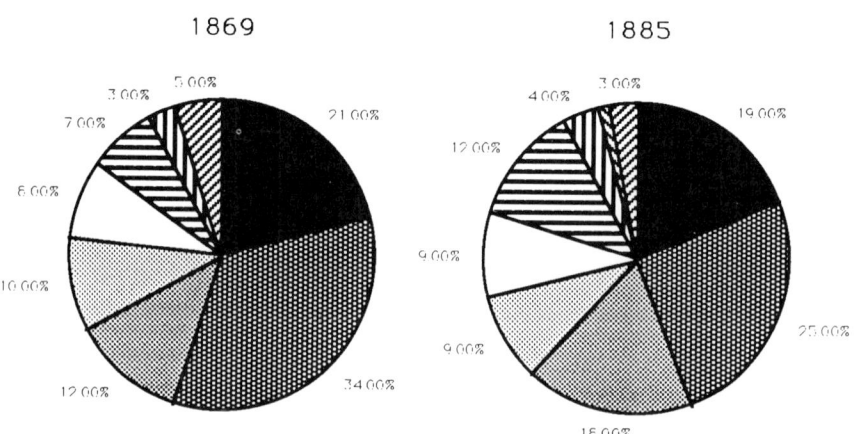

DEMOGRAPHY OF FIRMS IN TOULOUSE

133

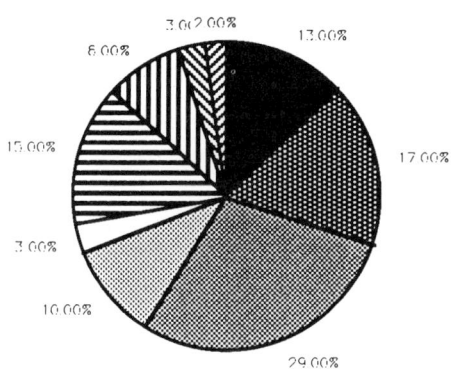

1920

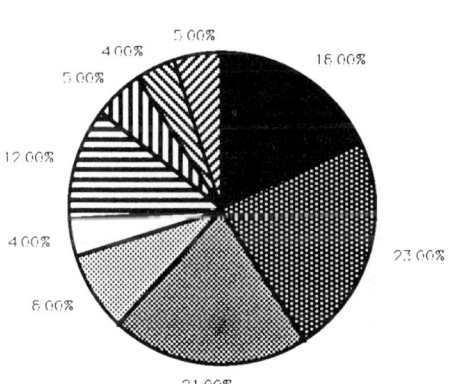

1929

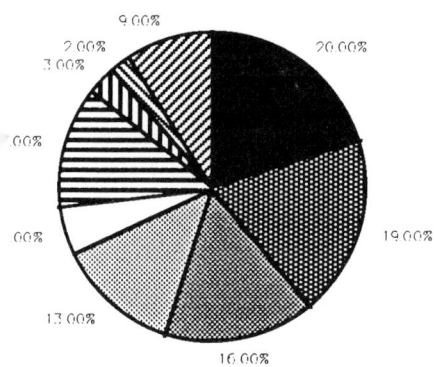

1937

operate flour mills and preserved food factories. Throughout the period it was common for merchants to go into partnership with their sons to form small *sociétés* to manufacture goods. Some widows also went into partnership with the clerks of the firms operated by their deceased husbands to carry on the business. In general the creation of small firms looks far more like family agreements rather than any determined search for new capital.

The rise of engineering in the town after 1920 (Figure 8.4) set a new trend, a patent-holder going into partnership with a trader or a property owner in order to raise capital. This is a very late variant of the old *commandite*. There are few workers co-operatives as compared with the example of Marseille (see page 114). Workers' co-operatives in Toulouse usually had a very short life. The only significant example of this type of *société* were partnerships between the owner and his clerk, sometimes a covert way for the employer to ensure the succession of his trusted employee to the ownership of the enterprise.

Notaries (lawyers) often appear as partners. The drafting of the acts of formation led them to invest in the *société* on behalf of their clients or of themselves in what they considered to be safe businesses. They also acted as corporate consultants to banks and financial houses. The legal status chosen by partners for their *société* reveal that the *sociétés en nom collectif* – the personal partnership between two individuals was the rule until 1920. Few *sociétés en commandite par actions* (limited partnerships) were formed, but several of the small *sociétés* set up in 1925 adopted the status of *SARL*, private limited companies. This gives rise to the question of where their capital came from.

3.2 The origins of outside capital

The whole population of Toulousian enterprises experienced an increase in capital after 1920. However, this increase must be set in the context of the origin and control of the capital raised. Throughout the period large limited companies represent half of the capital registered in Toulouse. For example, a wire-drawing firm established in an old mill in 1877 was, in fact, simply a branch of the Martin Steel business formed to manage the invention of the open-hearth furnace. Martin imported steel to Toulouse, despite the proximity of the Carmaux coalmines. These mines themselves were managed, not by local people, but by two Parisian aristocrats and two Parisian bankers.

Where did the capital for smaller *sociétés* come from? More often than not it was provided by the promoter himself, and very rarely raised from outside partners. The totals for registered capital are over-estimates but nevertheless, in the long term the average capital of all enterprises increased from 10,000 constant francs in the 1890s to 40,000 by 1930. So why was it that *sociétés* were formed rather than businesses being conducted simply by sole traders? The primary motive was almost certainly judicial and financial, to limit the liability in the case of bankruptcy. On the other hand there is evidence of a desire to extend, albeit modestly, productive capacity: for example, in the case of functionally-linked businesses – printer/typographer, cartwright/coachbuilder, and mason/carpenter. In these cases the capital is only a legal formality.

The example of aircraft manufacture, which remained in the hands of private companies, does not impress. In 1921, 650 jobs were created by Pierre Latécoère, 130 in the firm of his rival, the engineer Dewoitine. Latécoère's example illustrates the lack of capital and the process of financial colonisation in Toulouse. Coming from Lille in the north, Pierre Latécoère tried to convert his business to civil production after the First World War, manufacturing aeroplanes and wagons, and setting up air mail services. As early as 1924 he was forced to look for *commanditaires* (sleeping partners) in Paris and Madrid and the Franco-Spanish Company with a capital of 20 million francs. Only two of the seven directors of this company were from Toulouse. In 1927 he was obliged to give the air mail company its autonomy and accept the appointment of a Parisian banking group to administer his main business before it was sold in 1939 to France's biggest aircraft builder, Bréguet. On the other hand, Dewoitine had his principal factory in the Parisian suburbs and only two of the thirty shareholders were from Toulouse, holding sixty shares out of 20,000. Dewoitine himself held 12,400 preference shares.

For many firms Toulouse, with its strong immigration, was simply a source of cheap labour. Industrial investment only found 'polite acceptance' in local high society. The Toulousians only invested 44 per cent of their fortunes in stocks and shares, and even out of this total only 7 per cent was invested locally in the town's industries. The preference was first and foremost for safe investments, like foreign government securities and stocks in railway and electricity utilities. Toulouse bears little resemblance to individual centres like Lille or Marseille, while shortage of capital coupled with its geographical location had a negative effect on Languedoc.

Conclusion

Finally, was Toulouse simply a big village? This was probably so until 1920:

however, things began to change during the inter-war years. Despite its isolation from the industrial north, Toulouse did not escape from the effects of industrial cycles. Throughout this period the French economy was becoming more national. As in the Alpes, the coming of hydro-electric power was a powerful influence for national integration. Foreign models suggest that the Toulousian case is not completely unique. Rural Japan has changed without a transition from textile labour to electronic technopoles. Its example suggests an interesting parallel. Is Toulouse our French Japan?

Footnotes

1. Philippe Jobert et Jean-Claude Chevailler, 'La démographie des entreprises en France, quelques pistes', *Histoire, économie, société,* Paris, 1986 et François Caron, 'Commerçants et industriels de la Côte d'Or vus à travers les actes de sociétés', *Annales de Bourgogne,* 1983, pp.90-121.
2. *The Cambridge Economic History,* tome VII, I, 1978, p.292.

9

Industrialisation and financial networks: regional disparities in nineteenth century France

Jean-Luc Mayaud

The present article is based on a systematic analysis of the deeds constituting, modifying and dissolving companies declared to two *tribunaux de commerce* in the Franche-Comté. The results presented – if incomplete – nevertheless reveal the need for qualitative accuracy in serial analysis, and also, using the example of the Franche-Comté, the wide disparities to be found within a single region. Thus, the notion of a business should doubtless be replaced with that of a financial network.[1]

I. Quantitative and qualitative methods

This article analyses the company deeds declared to the *tribunaux de commerce* of Besançon[2] and Belfort[3] between 1880 and 1914. For each deed, all the information needed to use them for serial analysis has been collected, permitting relatively easy consultation: the nature of the company, the date of its constitution, modification or dissolution, its object and its registered capital, are immediately to hand; along with either the full name, occupation, place of residence and respective investment of every active or sleeping partner, or each shareholder. For *sociétés en commandite par actions* and *sociétés anonymes*, the list of shareholders is copied verbatim, specifying the number of shares held by each. Using these deeds creating or modifying or dissolving a firm where they were declared, it is now possible to reconstitute each company's career, and analyse lists of business promoters. Before such investigations can be undertaken, some methodological decisions have to be taken.

The initial *corpus* of 1,282 deeds was reduced by eliminating companies which did not enter the criteria of commercial and industrial activity as defined by the Franche-Comté: for example, buyers' co-operatives for industrial or agricultural workers, and workers' housing syndicates with very little registered capital, generally less than 5,000 francs. The examination of deeds of these enterprises shed more light on the organisation of labour and of employer paternalism rather than on the region's economic activity. Also eliminated are large industrial and commercial companies which registered with the local tribunals when opening a branch office – the registered capital declared is that of the head office, and the deed of constitution declared in the Franche-Comté records neither any increase in capital nor the presence of local investors. Their registered capital, generally very large – several hundred thousand or several million francs – if included would gravely distort the shape of the graph of capital raised in the region.

A name index of company promoters has also been created without the use of a computer since one promoter investing in several companies would receive several identification numbers, making him difficult to trace. Consequently, 7,884 files have been manually reconstituted, noting at a minimum the full name, profession, and domicile of every shareholder and of every active (*commandité*) or sleeping partner (*commanditaire*); also the character of each company concerned and the amount of each investment. After producing a simple list of promoters' names, two distinct indices were constituted for the two *tribunaux de commerce*, one listing investors in *sociétés en nom collectif* and *sociétés en commandite simple*, the other listing investors in *sociétés en commandite par actions* and *sociétés anonymes*. The alphabetical list provides details of promoters investing in more than one company: as a result the total number of files, 7,884, was reduced to 6,648 individuals, 801 of whom had multiple investments. Individual promoters of *sociétés en commandite par actions* or *sociétés anonymes* numbered 5,697 out of 6,808 files or investments[4] out of a total of 116,014,020 francs invested in the companies scrutinized, 29,561,427 francs – or 25.5 per cent was invested by the 801 multiple investors.[5] Finally, these investors have also been disaggregated

Table 9.1

Investors and their Investments in Commercial and Industrial Companies.

Company's legal status		Commandite simple and Nom collectif			Commandite par actions and société anonyme		
Commercial court		Besançon	Belfort	Total	Besançon	Belfort	Total
Number of Investments		615	461	1076	5,275	1,533	6,808
Number of investors with n investments	1	484	364	848	3,685	1,314	6,499
	2	52	32	84	441	69	510
	3	6	11	17	78	16	94
	4	1		1	51		51
	5	1		1	13	1	14
	6				13	1	14
	7				4		4
	8				2		2
	9				2	1	3
	10				1		1
	11				2		2
	12				1		1
	13					1	1
	21				1		1
Total Investors		544	407	951	4,294	1,403	5,697

according to their place of residence at the time of a company's formation. From these data a twofold map, showing the distribution of the number of promoters and the capital invested, has been generated.[6]

Table 9.2

Capital contributed by Investors to Commercial and Industrial Companies.

Company's legal status		Commandite simple and Nom collectif			Commandite par actions and Société anonyme		
Commercial court		Besançon	Belfort	Total	Besançon	Belfort	Total
Investors with 1 Investment	Amount	15·916·014	19·954·909	371·870·923	21·501·070	29·080·600	50·581·670
	%	67·4	78·7	74·3	69·3	80·6	75·5
Investors with 2 investments	Amount	6·526·039	2·867·350	9·393·389	3·278·125	3·707·400	6·985·525
	%	27·6	11·3	18·4	10·6	10·3	10·4
Investors with more than 2 investments	Amount	1·164·833	2·532·000	3·696·833	6·230·180	3·255·500	9·485·680
	%	5	10	7·3	20·1	9·1	14·1
Total investors	Amount	23·606·886	25·354·260	50·961·145	31·009·375	36·066·900	67·076·275
	%	100	100	100	100	100	100

All in all, the choice of this approach demanded much laborious counting and classification. If the intrinsic interest of these deeds as a result is no longer in doubt, it nevertheless becomes clear that they do not cover the total number of companies in existence, largely because proto-industrial establishments, though extremely common, rarely constituted themselves as a registered company. As they do not appear in the *corpus*, their absence led to a reconsideration of the objectives of this analysis. This is why it was decided to devote attention to the identification of the individuals who played a part in the Franche-Comté's economy. In addition to the present study of companies involved in the region's development, a parallel study provides a prosopography of industrialists and merchants in the region, using the indices assembled and the deeds.[7] Despite these limitations, the source allows different patterns of industrialisation to be distinguished. While the district of Belfort is marked by a dramatic growth in industry, that of Besançon – given

Table 9.3
Finances and Investors in Companies in the Besançon district (1883–1914).

Company Status — Shareholders Active partners Sleeping partners — Domicile	Commandite simple Nom collectif			Commandite par actions sociétés anonymes			Total Companies		
	Number	Amount/ francs	%	Number	Amount/ francs	%	Number	Amount/ francs	%
Besançon	414	18,857,510	76·1 / 79·9	1,636	13,292,100	38·1 / 42·9	2,050	32,149,610	42·4 / 58·9
Doubs (1)	33	593,120	6·1 / 2·5	547	1,708,125	12·7 / 5·5	580	2,301,245	12 / 4·2
Haute-Saône	6	282,450	1·1 / 1·2	73	1,136,200	1·7 / 3·7	79	1,418,650	1·6 / 2·6
Jura	7	165,000	1·3 / 0·7	142	174,300	3·3 / 0·6	149	339,300	3·1 / 0·6
T. de Belfort	3	82,110	0·6 / 0·3	10	62,200	0·2 / 0·2	13	144,310	0·3 / 0·3
Total Franche-Comte	463	19,980,190	85·2 / 84·6	2,408	16,372,925	56 / 52·8	2,871	36,353,115	60·2 / 66·6
Paris	14	1,821,0000	2·6 / 7·7	190	3,725,475	4·4 / 12	204	5,546,475	4·2 / 10·2
Lyon	1	5,000	0·2 / –	883	3,607,000	20·6 / 11·6	884	3,612,000	18·3 / 6·6
France (2)	18	467,830	3·3 / 2	579	3,803,875	13·5 / 12·3	597	4,271,705	12·3 / 7·8
Total France (3)	33	2,923,830	6·1 / 9·7	1,652	11,136,350	38·5 / 35·9	1,685	13,430,180	34·8 / 24·6
Abroad	11	735,550	2 / 3·1	79	1,482,100	1·8 / 4·8	90	2,217,650	1·9 / 4·1
Unknown	37	603,470	6·8 / 2·6	155	2,018,000	3·6 / 6·5	192	2,621,470	4 / 4·8
TOTAL	544	23,613,040	100 / 100	4,294	31,009,375	100 / 100	4,838	54,622,415	100 / 100

(1) Excluding Besançon   (2) Excluding Paris, Lyon and Franche-Comté   (3) Excluding Franche-Comté

Table 9.4
Finances and Investors in the "Territoire de Belfort" (1883-1914).

Company Status Shareholders Active partners Sleeping partners --- Domicile	Commandite simple Nom collectif			Commandite par actions Société anonymes			Total Companies		
	Number	Amount/francs	%	Number	Amount/francs	%	Number	Amount/francs	%
T. de Belfort	277	14,586,160	57.5	737	11,756,200	32.6	1,014	26,342,360	42.9
Doubs	18	360,000	1.4	66	2,361,750	6.5	84	2,721,750	4.4
Haute-Saône	6	211,100	0.8	15	148,600	0.4	21	359,700	0.6
Jura	0	0	0	2	6,000	—	2	6,000	—
Total Franche-Comté	301	15,157,260	59.8	820	14,272,550	39.6	1,121	29,429,810	47.9
Paris	18	3,405,500	13.4	101	4,878,700	13.5	119	8,284,200	13.5
Lyon	1	50,000	0.2	4	20,000	0.1	5	70,000	0.1
France (1)	39	2,098,250	8.3	354	12,265,900	34	393	14,364,150	23.4
Total France (2)	58	5,553,750	21.9	459	17,164,600	47.6	517	22,718,350	37
Abroad	17	3,290,750	13	60	3,107,900	8.6	77	6,398,650	10.4
Unknown	31	1,343,500	5.3	64	1,521,850	4.2	95	2,865,350	4.7
TOTAL	407	25,345,260	100	1,403	36,066,900	100	1,810	61,412,160	100

(1) Excluding Paris, Lyon and Franche-Comté   *(2) Excluding Franche-Comté*

its relative lack of capital concentration – seems to have missed out, surviving thanks mainly to small trade.

II. The comparative industrial failure of Besançon

With a dozen or so *sociétés* created each year between 1883 and 1914, the profile of economic life in the Besançon region seems to continue in the same pattern, evident between 1827 and 1857.[8] However, when looked at from year to year, the rhythm seems less even, and a cyclic evolution is discernible: periods of multiple creations between 1893 and 1898, and 1906 and 1911 – follow periods of stagnation – 1884-1892, 1899-1905, and 1911-1914. The analysis of creations of *sociétés en nom collectif* confirms a similar rhythm, apart from the years 1902-1904 which saw the formation of a large number of new *sociétés*.

The predominance of trade

Nevertheless it appears that the rhythm of creations of *sociétés* does not follow the same cycle as that for industrial companies alone. On the whole, the phases of this advance may be explained by the growth in the number of non-industrial companies – among which, business houses have a clear majority. This reinforces Besançon's commercial position. A similar impression is gained with equal clarity by examining the total capital raised: variations in investment are a function in large part of the creation of business houses. With the exception of the peaks of 1890 and 1896, due to the setting up of the Chardonnet artificial silk-works in Besançon (6 million francs in 1890, 2 million in 1914 and to the opening of a soda-works and distillery at Roche-les-Beaupré 2.3 and 2 million francs) advances come from trade capital: 2.3 million for two banks in 1884, 1.2 million francs for another in 1893. This should not disguise the expansion in the number of small commercial enterprises.

The predominance of commercial activity in Besançon is not a matter of massive establishments. Most of the businesses (118 out of 138) had a capital of less than 200,000 francs, and 74 percent had a capital of less than 100,000 francs. The bias toward non-industrial activities tended to increase during the first years of the twentieth century: from 1905 to 1913, capital invested in Besançon industry dwindled steadily (100 to 300 francs a year), while that invested in commerce expanded (to more than a million francs a year). Overall, the Besançon district exhibits a pre-disposition towards medium-scale commercial ventures.

An industrialisation influenced by clockmakers

Apart from the large sums of money invested in setting up the Chardonnet artificial silk works, Besançon industry appears to stagnate. The number of industrial companies created remained relatively stable from 1883 to 1914, while the capital invested declined. Clockmaking alone remained buoyant. Out of 179 industrial companies created between 1883 and 1914, 87, or 49 per cent, were involved in clockmaking. This expansion of Besançon's industrial specialisation in clockmaking continued a trend which had its origins in the early nineteenth century. Clockmaking was introduced by Swiss refugees – and its development after the French Revolution helped strengthen the economic axis between Besançon and the border region of the *Haut-Doubs*, a strengthening made all the more necessary by the departmentalisation of France in 1790. Still dependent on up-country handicraft production methods, Besançon clockmaking remained closer to the workshop than the factory: 77 per cent of clockmaking companies had capital investment of less than 100,000 francs; none of them had capital of more than 700,000 francs. Metalworking activity, extant in the first half of the nineteenth century, had completely disappeared by the end. The boom in artificial textiles seems an anomaly. The only industrial sector to have anything like a continuous history was clockmaking. Still medium-scale, Besançon's clockmaking industry was distinct from the *domestic system* and from proto-industrialisation throughout the nineteenth century: even at the beginning of the twentieth century, it remained entirely separate from true industrialisation. It thus seems a useful index of Besançon's comparative industrial failure.

The diversification of methods of capitalisation

The legal status of the *sociétés* in the Besançon district was clearly dominated by *sociétés en nom collectif*, increasingly challenged at the end of the century by the emergence of *sociétés anonymes*. Thus, from 1827 to 1887, 75 per cent of the companies were *en nom collectif*, as against 65 per cent for 1883-1914; in the same periods, the fraction of *sociétés en commandite simple* declines from 16 per cent to 8 per cent, and that of *sociétés en commandite par actions* from 8 per cent to 2 per cent, that of *sociétés anonymes* climbs from 1 per cent to 24 per cent. In fact, the great reduction in the number of *sociétés en commandite simple* and the near-extinction of *sociétés en commandite par actions* illustrates the competition between *sociétés en nom collectif* and *sociétés anonymes*. However, the relationship between these two legal forms is precisely inverted when the capital invested is examined: 24 per cent of the total was invested in *sociétés en nom collectif*, 67 per cent in *sociétés anonymes*, and just 2 per cent for *sociétés en commandite simple* and 5 per cent for *sociétés en commandite par actions*.

This justified the procedure adopted in assembling the indices of investors, separating *sociétés en commandite simple* and *sociétés en nom collectif* from *sociétés en commandite par actions* and *sociétés anonymes*. The former index contains 72 per cent of the companies and 26 per cent of the capital, the latter contains 26 per cent of the companies and 72 per cent of the total sum invested in *sociétés* of the Besançon district.

Here, the dominant model was that of a small company, with relatively little capital: average capital for *sociétés en nom collectif* as for *sociétés en commandite simple* lies between 85,000 and 90,000 francs. Even at the start of the twentieth century, the majority of clockmaking and trading *sociétés* remained within these legal forms and were distinguished by the middling sums invested. By contrast, *sociétés anonymes* and the few *sociétés en commandite par actions* controlled a registered capital of at least seven times this amount: their average is 665,000 francs, raised for the most part by a few banking houses and the new industries set up in Besançon. Here again we can discern the constants of a model of economic development which explains all too clearly Besançon's comparative industrial failure.

Equally revealing is the division of capitals between the various investors. Active and sleeping partners, in *sociétés en commandite simple* and *sociétés en nom collectif*, made 615 investments. Although the 52 backers with two investments and the eight with three, four or five, represent just 11 per cent of the total of 544 investors,[9] the proportion of their capital investment is more significant. From a total capital of over 23.5 million francs, 27.6 per cent came from double investors and 5 per cent from those with more than two investments.[10] In general, capital was distributed almost exclusively amongst different investors, and only a small group were prepared to diversify and add – however modestly – to their investments. The capitalism of the *sociétés en commandite simple* and *sociétés en nom collectif* of the Besançon district remained very concentrated and individualist. By contrast, that of the *sociétés en commandite par actions* and *sociétés anonymes* was more fragmented. Active and sleeping partners were distinctly more common: 4,294 out of the 5,275 investments; 441 – or 10.3 per cent – held two investments and 168 – or 3.9 per cent – more than two. The sums involved were larger: over 31 million francs, spread between single investors (69.3 per cent), double investors (10.6 per cent), and those with 3 or more investments (20.1 per cent). This second group of companies hints at the beginnings of capitalist concentration in the region.

With an average of 43,395 francs for investors in *sociétés en nom collectif* and *sociétés en commandite simple,* and an average of 7,222 francs for those in the second group of companies, the distribution of capital seems equally differentiated. Choosing the status of a *société anonyme* or a *société en commandite par actions* allowed smaller investors to share in a company's capital. The geography of their recruitment is equally significant.

The strictly local financing of traditional activities

The traditional activities of the Besançon district – small trade and clockmaking – were mainly organised into *sociétés en nom collectif* and *sociétés en commandite simple*. The geographical spread of investors and of the capital they provided can therefore be linked with that of these traditional activities. Out of 544 active and sleeping partners, 414 – 76.1 per cent – lived in Besançon and 33 – 6.1 per cent – were domiciled in the department of Doubs. Among the latter, 25 lived in communes in the Besançon district. This massively local membership barely extended beyond the Franche-Comté, with 33 investors from other French departements and eleven from abroad – of whom ten were Swiss.

A similar concentration is revealed in the geographical distribution of capital held by investors: 79.9 per cent of the total registered capital of 23,613,040 francs was subscribed from the town of Besançon itself. The contributions from the département of Doubs was proportionally less significant than the number of investors resident there; Montbéliard, though, is distinguished by the contribution of 160,000 francs from three sleeping partners. Apart from Paris with subscriptions of 1.8 million francs – the few investments from outside the Besançon district came from neighbouring regions: Haute-Saône 282,000 francs, Jura 165,000 francs, Côte-d'Or 175,000 francs, and Switzerland 735,000 francs.[11]

Besançon's traditional industrial and commercial activity therefore remained predominantly locally financed. The lack of interest on the part of investors outside the Franche-Comté bears further testimony to the comparative failure of Besançon's early industrialisation.

A regional and inter-regional opening for new activities

More diverse is the geography of investors in *sociétés anonymes* and *sociétés en commandite par actions*. Out of 4,294 shareholders, only 38.1 per cent were resident in Besançon, bringing in 42.9 per cent of the 31 million francs collected by these types of companies between 1883 and 1914. Those resident in the departement of Doubs represented 12.7 per cent of the shareholdings. Although the cantons of the Besançon district stand out, the interest of investors from Haut-Doubs was not negligible: 24 shareholders and 76,000 francs from the canton of Pontarlier; 30 and 69,000 francs from that of

INDUSTRIALISATION AND FINANCIAL NETWORKS IN FRANCE   147

Figure 9.1

French and Foreign Investors in **"Societes Anonymes"** *and* **"Societes en Commandite par Actions"** *in the Besançon District (1883-1914).*

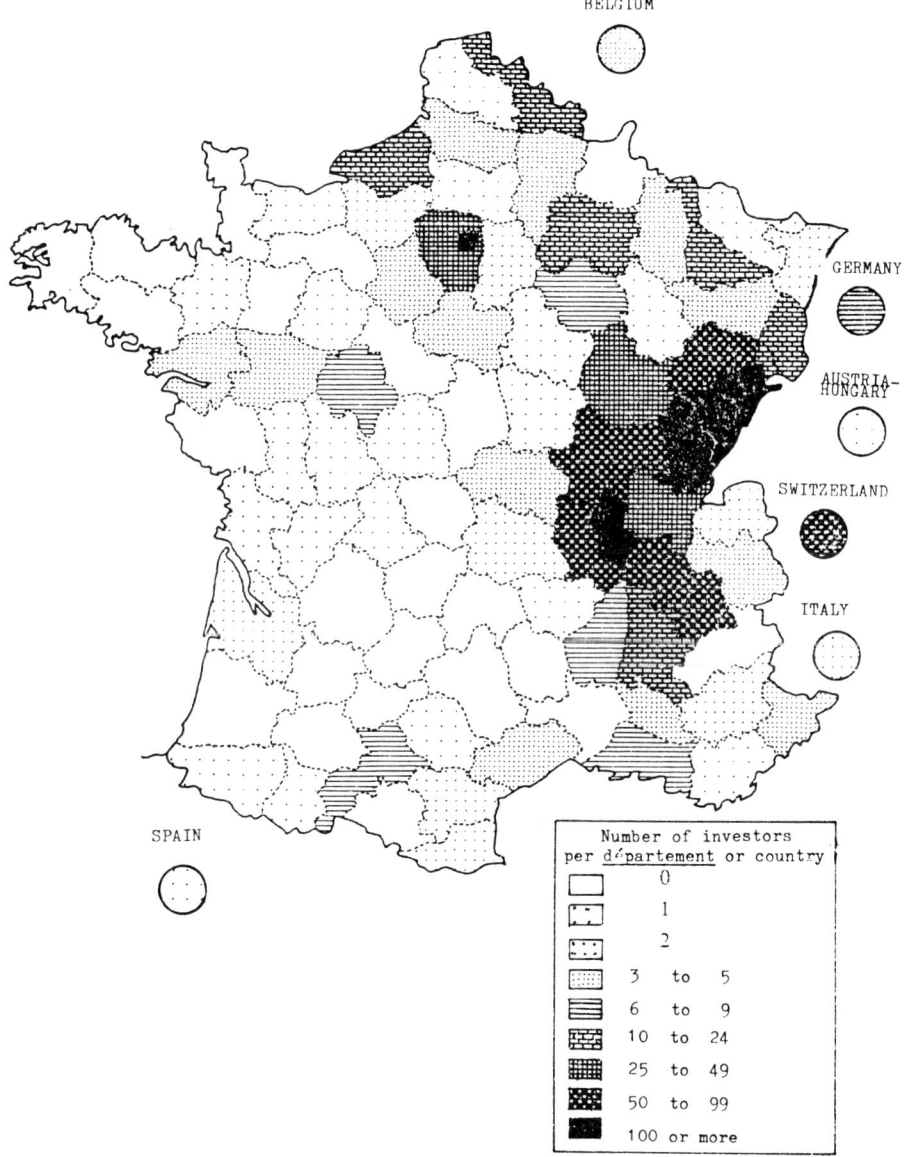

Figure 9.2

French and Foreign Investors in ***"Societes Anonymes"*** *and* ***"Societes en Commandite par Actions"*** *in the Besançon District (1883-1914): Capitals Contributed.*

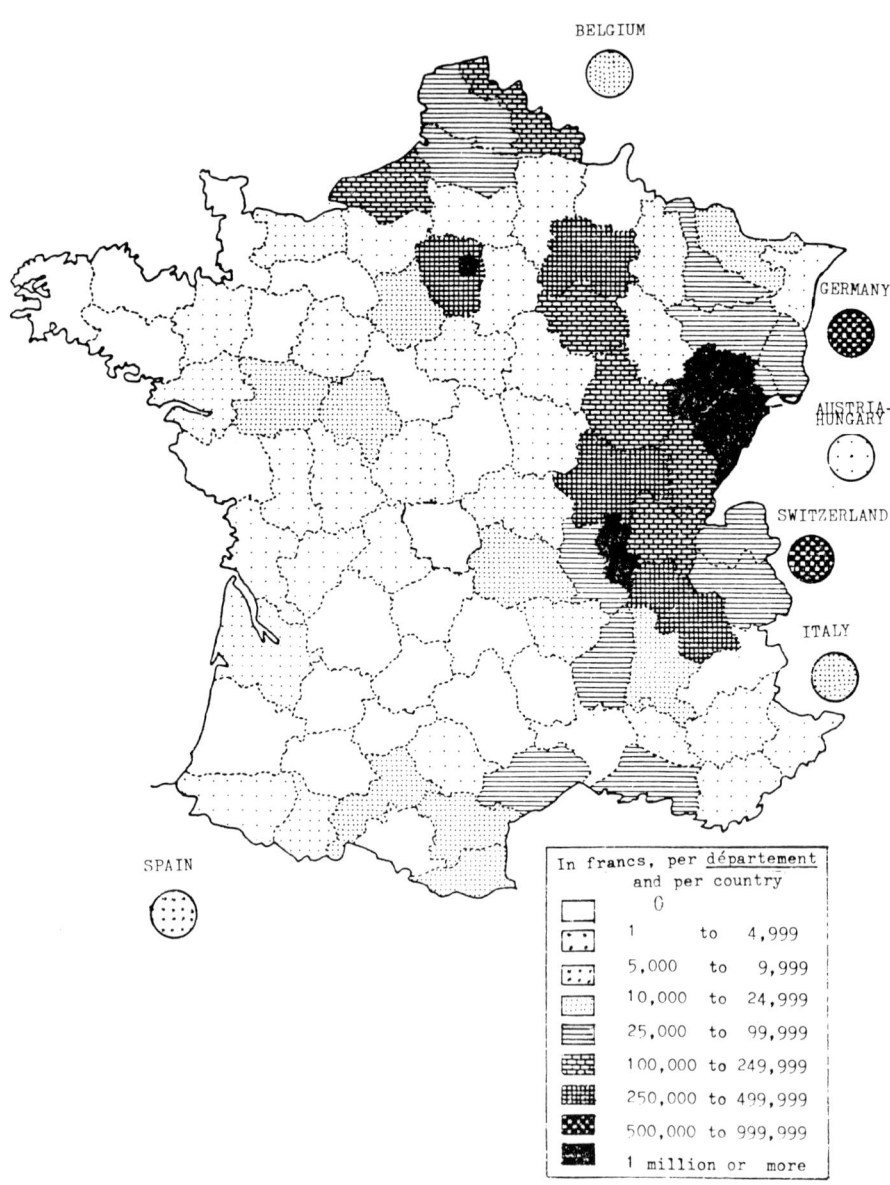

Maîche; and 35 and 30,000 francs from that of Morteau. Similarly, some shareholders from the Pays de Montbéliard, from Vesoul, Dole and Lons-le-Saunier, participated in Besançon's development. Nevertheless, Besançon did not resume its role as a regional capital.

Besançon's financial outlook was also inter-regional. The proportion of shareholders and capital coming from outside the Franche-Comté – 44 per cent and 47 per cent respectively – suggests a wider interest in Besançon's new economic activities. The establishment of the silk-works and the distilleries, the creation of companies to manage hot springs and for electrification, particularly attracted investors from neighbouring regions. The majority of shareholders came from neighbouring departements: excluding contributions from Paris and the Paris region which accounted for 5 per cent of the shareholders and 13 per cent of the capital, the North of France with 16 shareholders and 194,000 francs and the departement of Seine-Maritime – 11 shareholders and 127,000 francs.[12] The orientation of Besançon's financial geography followed the Rhône-Rhine economic axis, Besançon's companies looked to Lyon rather than to Paris. With 883 shareholders – 20 per cent – the town of Lyon ranked second after Besançon for the number of its investors; when the contributions of the departement of Rhône's 81 shareholders were added, the assembled capital totalled 4 million francs. The Besançon-Lyon axis was reinforced by the weight of investment from neighbouring departements: Saône-et-Loire with 39 shareholders and 327,000 francs; Ain with 47 shareholders and 171,000 francs; Côte-d'Or with 38 investors and 244,000 francs; and even Isère with 74 shareholders and 423,000 francs in total. Lastly, the involvement of Swiss investors was not insignificant, with 66 individuals subscribing 928,000 francs.[13]

The new industrial activities in the Besançon district allowed financial links to be forged with neighbouring departements orientated toward the Lyon region. This geography of shareholding should be set in the context of the markets created by the Franche-Comté's proto-industrial enterprises.[14] The commercial dynamism and product quality of businesses like those engaged in the edge-tool industry of Nans-sous-Sainte-Anne certainly caught the attention of investors ready to speculate in true industrialisation. In short, Besançon's financial extension allowed at least a partial integration into national, indeed international, money systems. True enough, at the end of the nineteenth century and the beginning of the twentieth centuries this extension remained primarily extra-regional. The pursuit of this analysis after the First World War might show whether this expansion stretched to the traditional activities which lost out later in the century.

III. The territory of Belfort: an example of successful industrialisation

Compared with that of the Besançon district, the industrialisation of the Territoire of Belfort appears to be clearly successful. Nevertheless, Besançon might seem more dynamic if dynamism were gauged solely on the gross number of companies created. Before drawing any conclusion from this fact, it is worth pointing out that of the two towns in question: Besançon was more populous than Belfort, and the latter's new departement was much smaller than that of the Besançon district. The 331 company creations registered at the *tribunal de commerce* describe a slow progression tempered by moments of sudden acceleration: 1873-1875, 1890-1893, 1898-1907 and 1910-1913. The comparison of the cycles of rapid growth at the very end of the nineteenth and the start of the twentieth centuries reveals an economic gap.

An industrial stronghold

A simple analysis of the company creations retained in our corpus reveals a similar progression, which clearly accelerated after 1898. Industrial companies follow the same pattern, though in less marked fashion: uncommon before 1898 – 1 to 3, or, rarely, 4 to 5 creations a year – they underwent a sharp and lasting expansion up to 1913. However, during this period, other companies also developed at least as much: the simple examination of the number of companies created suggests an equivalent expansion in commercial and industrial companies. In contrast, the graphs showing registered capital subscribed to all the companies and that assembled by industrial companies are parallel. Excepting the peak of the years 1912-1913 caused by the creation of two large shops (with a capital of 1 million and 1.5 million francs respectively), every peak is explained by industrial capital: 1873 by the 6,948,000 francs for the Japy de Beaucourt clockmaking factory; 1877 by the 2 million francs for two spinning-mills; 1880 by a gas factory (2 million francs) and another spinning-mill (800,000 francs); 1890 by the Giromagny mines (1.5 million francs); 1902 by a wire-drawing mill (1,120,000 francs); 1907 by the forge and foundry of Châtenois (45 million francs); and finally 1917 by the Danjoutin cloth mill (3.4 million francs). Overall, the shape of the graph for capital assembled by all companies is governed by that for industrial companies. Without being negligible, commercial activity was not the dynamic sector of Belfort's economy.

Companies with significant registered capital

With an average registered capital of 207,000 francs, companies in the

Territory of Belfort were better financed than those in Besançon, whose average registered capital is 161,000 francs. This difference is clearer still in industrial companies alone: 353,000 francs for Belfort establishments, only 169,000 francs for those of Besançon. Although for the decade 1883-1892, Besançon's industrial companies had more than average registered capital than those of Belfort – 288,000 francs against 258,000 francs – opposite tendencies emerged in the following two decades. In Besançon, the average fell to 156,000, then 83,000 francs, while in Belfort it rose from 200,000 to 315,000 francs. The industrialisation of the Territoire of Belfort is triumphant, with companies becoming even better financed. The great rarity of industrial companies with registered capital under 10,000 francs stands in marked contrast to the situation in Besançon. Industrial companies take first place in the scale of finance. The five companies with capital over 2 million francs were all industrial companies; 12 out of 14 companies with capital between 1-2 million francs, 11 out of 16 with 500,000-1 million francs were also industrial. Across the whole scale, the Territoire of Belfort's industrial enterprises are shown to be better financed: 50.8 per cent of its companies controlled over 100,000 francs, against 30.7 per cent in Besançon. The success of industrialisation is also the triumph of financing.

The legal status of companies was adapted to their financial needs. Out of 277 companies whose status is known, 71 per cent were *en nom collectif* and 6 per cent were *en commandite simple*. They controlled in total over 25 million francs, an average of 118,000 francs per company. In contrast, *sociétés en commandite par actions* (2 per cent of the total number) and *sociétés anonymes* (20 per cent), which only really emerged after 1889, controlled 36 million francs, an average of 600,000 francs per company. Some were formed for the opening of new economic sectors in Belfort, like the tramway and electrical companies, but the majority of them were set up to pursue traditional activities whose scale increased with the growth in available finance: mines, metal-works and engineering; and also textiles – with the expansion in spinning-mills – and dye-works. The shift from people companies to capital companies allowed full-scale industrialisation. It also attracted new investors.

From local to international financing . . .

Sociétés en commandite simple and *sociétés en nom collectif* remained the most popular corporate form in nineteenth century Belfort, reflecting the old model of financial concentration for groups of people engaged in commerce and in the first stages of industrialisation. In Belfort, the average capital invested by each active or sleeping partner was over half again as much as in Besançon: 62,295 against 43,395 francs. Out of 407 investors, 10 per cent held

Figure 9.3

French and Foreign Investors in **"Societes Anonymes"** *and* **"Societes en Commandite par Actions"** *in the* **Territoire de Belfort** *(1880-1914).*

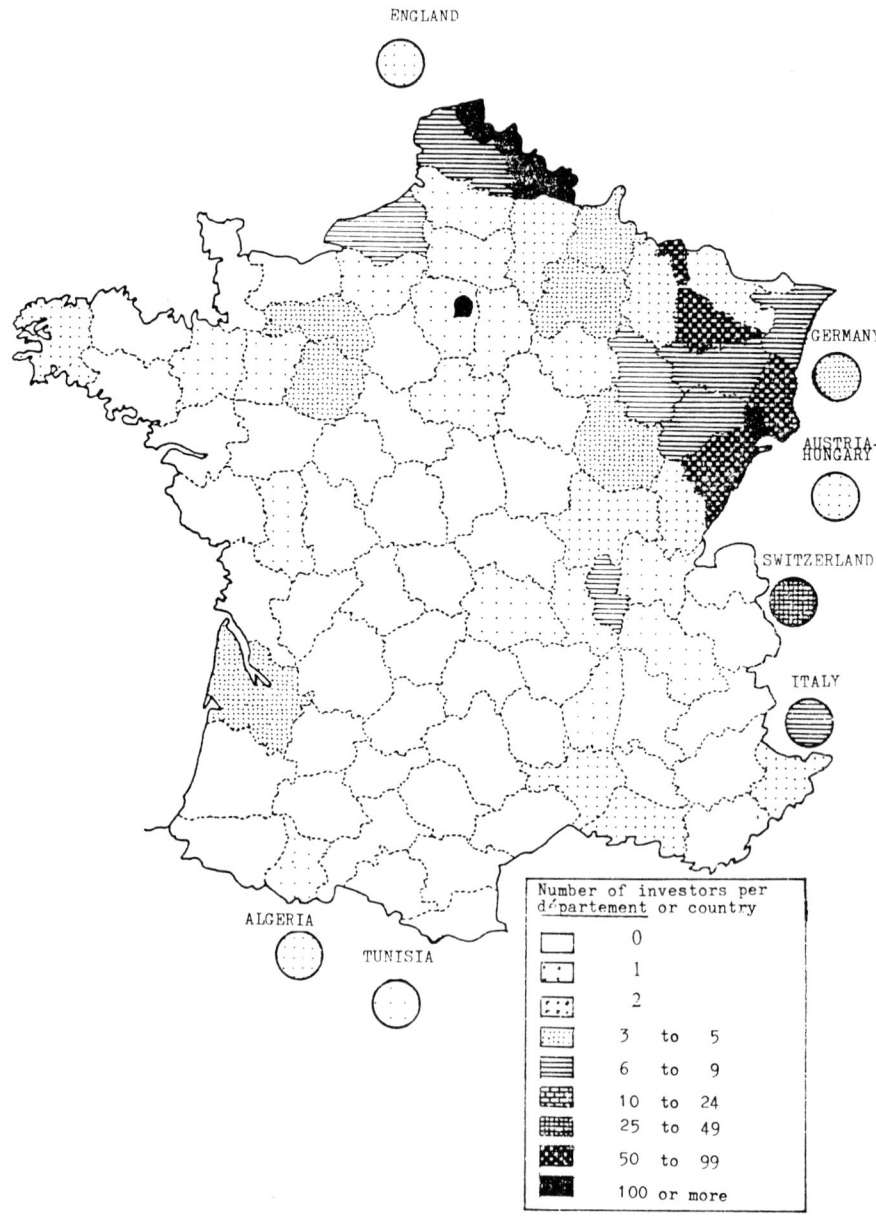

two or three investments, representing 21.3 per cent of the total registered capital.[15] The low number of investors – less than two per company – suggests an early financial concentration. These essentially family businesses, nevertheless, succeeded in drawing capital from distant investors into Belfort.

Although 68 per cent of investors resided in the Territoire of Belfort, and of those 67 per cent lived in the Belfort canton itself, contributions respectively 14,586,000 and 9,548,000 francs – that is 58 per cent and 38 per cent of the total figure respectively, a significant fraction of investors and capital came from outside the Franche-Comté. There were 39 investors from other provincial areas, 18 Parisians and 17 foreigners. In total, this amounted to 40 per cent of total capital: 3.4 million francs from Paris, 1,187,000 francs from Haut-Rhin, 2 million francs from the Netherlands and 1 million francs from Belgium. This geography indicates that the early industrialisation of the Territoire of Belfort was not exclusively local. Moreover, it was oriented toward Paris – a sign of national integration – as well as towards Alsace and northern Europe. Following the Rhine axis, it seems to have been more tied to the Rhine orbit than to that of the Franche-Comté, from which it was totally independent, doubtless because it was added to it so late.

. . . to national integration

The development of *sociétés anonymes* and *sociétés en commandite par actions* at the end of the nineteenth and the start of the twentieth centuries was accompanied by a second industrialisation which contributed to placing the Territoire of Belfort among France's main industrial centres. During this phase, 36 million francs was subscribed by 1,403 individual shareholders. The average capital invested – 25,707 francs – is 3.5 times greater than that subscribed by shareholders in Besançon – a difference in scale, but also a difference in geographical origin of investments. The 52.5 per cent local investors only contributed 32.6 per cent of the total capital. This second industrialisation, therefore, depended on outside finance. But just like the *sociétés en commandite simple* and the *sociétés en nom collectif*, investors in the *sociétés anonymes* and *sociétés en commandite par actions* were not drawn from the Franche-Comté: out of the departement of Doubs' 66 shareholders, 59 resided in the Pays de Montbéliard, contributing 2,264,000 francs, or 6.3 per cent of Belfort's total capital investments.

In fact, the core financing of the *sociétés* came from shareholders outside the Franche-Comté. Their geographical origin was very diverse:[16] if the Alsace and Vosges represented a bastion, the financial network extended to the North and West of France: Ardennes and Meuse, but also Nord-Pas-de-Calais, Seine-Maritime, Orne and Sarthe. In all, the French departements

Figure 9.4

French and Foreign Investors in **"Societes Anonymes"** *and* **"Societes en Commandite par Actions"** *in the* **Territoire de Belfort** *(1880-1914): Capitals Contributed.*

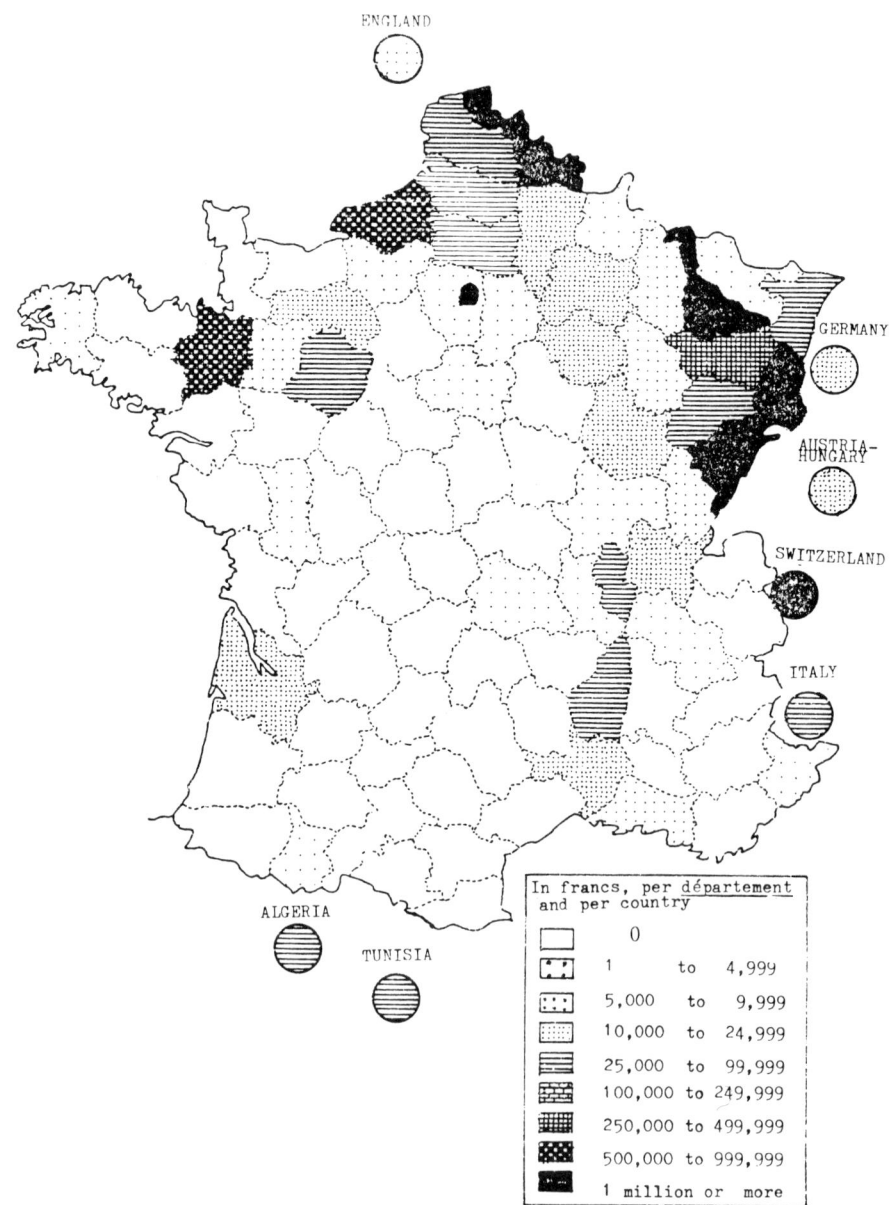

subscribed 48 per cent of the total capital: 4,993,000 francs from Paris and its environs; 7 million francs from Haut-Rhin; 205,000 francs from Bas-Rhin; 251,000 francs from Vosges; 1.5 million francs from Meuse; 1.5 million francs from Nord; 537,000 francs from Ile-et-Vilaine; and 636,000 francs from Seine-Maritime. The geography had become truly national; the *sociétés anonymes* were no longer looking for investors only in the Rhine area. Before the First World War, the Territoire of Belfort had already been relentlessly integrated within a national network. The 43 Swiss shareholders and the 2.3 million francs they contributed were the sole exception to the Belfort economy's national position. But as in the case of Besançon, this weak Swiss participation should be considered from the perspective of frontier economic relations.

A study of company deeds thus confirms the absence of true regional networks in the financing of industry. Despite the existence of small local networks – interacting weakly with each other – the Franche-Comté could not itself generate the financial resources required for full industrialisation. The solution was by recourse to the facilities of neighbouring or distant regions, following the logic of centuries-old trading traditions. Integration within a national economic unit developed out of inter-regional financial circuits. Thus, the Franche-Comté offers no more unity in the financing of its industrialisation than it presents in its agriculture and in its political, religious and cultural behaviour.[17] Even at the start of the twentieth century, it is a mere aggregate of divergent industrial centres. Above all, this study pleads for the value of a delicate analysis of small- and medium-scale financial networks, since they too are agents of industrialisation.

Footnotes

1. On this subject, see Louis Bergeron, 'Les espaces du capital', in Jacques Revel (dir.), *Histoire de la France*, vol. I, *L'espace* (Paris, 1989), pp.288-371.
2. These deeds are in the archives of the Besançon *tribunal de commerce* for the period after 1883.
3. Deeds presented by the Belfort *tribunal de commerce* to the Territoire of Belfort's departmental archives.
4. Table 9.1: Investors and their investments in commercial and industrial companies.
5. Table 9.2: Capital contributed by investors to commercial and industrial companies.
6. Tables 9.3 and 9.4: The number of maps presented here has been reduced for reasons of space. Maps concerning Franche-Comté investors, those from

Franche-Comté or elsewhere engaged in *sociétés en nom collectif* or *sociétés en commandite simple* have thus been removed.

7. Jean-Luc Mayaud, *Les Patrons du Second Empire en Franche-Comté*, Paris – Le Mans, to appear in 1990.
8. Jean-Marc Olivier, *Les Sociétés commerciales dans l'arrondissement de Besançon (1827-1857)* (Université de Besançon 1985), p.276™.
9. Table 9.1.
10. Table 9.2.
11. Table 9.3.
12. Figure 9.2.
13. Figure 9.1.
14. Claude-Isabelle Brelot, Jean-Luc Mayaud, *L'Industrie en sabots. Les conquêtes d'une ferme-atelier aux XIXe et XXe siècles: la taillanderie de Nans-sous-Sainte-Anne* (Paris 1982), 278 pp.
15. Table 9.4.
16. Figure 9.3 and 9.4.
17. Clause-Isabelle Brelot, Roland Fietier (dir.), *Histoire de la Franche-Comté* (Toulouse, 1977).

10

Birth, growth and death of firms in a proto-industrial economy – the experience of the Ahmedabad textile industry, 1858–1929

Dwijendra Tripathi

An active search for a general theory of the growth of firms is of a recent origin. Since the publication of Edith Penrose's[1] seminal work on the subject about thirty years ago, some competent studies have appeared.[2] Most of these, however, are based on generalized understanding of the authors. The few empirical studies that exist deal with western economies;[3] late industrializers have received little attention, if any at all.

It is necessary to review the experience of the countries in the latter category to assess the general applicability of the existing formulations. This paper is a step in this direction. It seeks to examine the growth process of firms in India which took the first halting steps towards industrilization around the middle of the 19th century. Our focus is on cotton textiles and that too in one solitary location. While the reasons for choosing the cotton industry are obvious – as in most other countries, it is this industry that heralded the industrial age in India – our choice of Ahmedabad needs some explanation. The city was among the first, preceded only by Bombay by a few years, to start cotton manufacturing in India. The size of its cotton industry has been second only to that of Bombay which has a population several times larger. More importantly, while Bombay and other smaller centres of cotton production developed a variety of industries, textiles has remained the backbone of the industrial economy of Ahmedabad as a result of which the city is called the Manchester of India.[4] And lastly, the development of the industry was the handiwork of local entrepreneurs. No major industry anywhere in India had such a cohesive social base. Our focus on the period between 1858 and 1929 is justified by the fact that the first cotton mill in Ahmemdabad was registered in 1858 and by 1929 the industry had reached a saturation point.

For the purpose of our analysis, we have divided this long span into three time-blocks: (i) from 1858 to 1898, (ii) from 1898 to 1916, and (iii) from 1916 to 1929. During the first period, the industry attained, slowly but steadily, a measure of maturity and faced no major crisis. The beginning of our second time-block was marked by the rise of a variety of adverse factors – growing competition, imposition of excise duties on the domestic production of cotton goods, currency difficulties causing grave uncertainties in international trade, and mounting attack on company managements in the press – followed by a decade of very favourable conditions generated by the onset of the swadeshi movement in 1905 and later the First World War. The boom was beginning to recede by the end of 1916 – the beginning of the third time-block, paving the ground for the emergence of a more competitive environment.

Our concern in this paper is essentially with growth and relative changes in the size of firms. There are various ways to determine the size. Capital employed may not be a good indicator for Ahmedabad mills which raised their working capital through public deposits, keeping their paid-up capital rather low. Time series data for net fixed assets and volume of workforce in case of all companies are not available. We have, therefore, used the number of spindles as a criterion. Though this choice is forced on us because of the nature of data available, we are not the worse for it. For, few mills in Ahmedabad had added processing facilities during our period and in the case of composite mills we have adjusted the spindle figures to incorporate the looms, using commonly accepted principles of equivalence.[5]

We are also concerned with the decline and death of firms. While the meaning of 'decline' is obvious and needs no elaboration, 'death' in our analysis does not mean simply physical extinction or the stoppage of production; it also means the change in control of a unit following its liquidation or take-over. The extended connotation of the term is justified by the fact that the managing agency system – the dominant form of corporate management prevailing in India then and until very recently – enabled a family to control and manage a number of public limited companies as if they were proprietary concerns or different divisions of a single unit. Thus, the loss of control over a unit by a family was tantamount to the 'death' of that unit for the family concerned though its acquisition, even under a new name which was sometimes the case, by a new owner did not mean the birth of a new unit. The challenge and risk in reorganizing an existing mill cannot be of the same magnitude as in setting up a brand new unit.

All these concerns for growth, size, decline, and death revolve around one basic question: whether age, size, growth, decline and death were in any way inter-related. This requires us to determine the criteria for size, age, growth and decline. For the formative phases of an industry, particularly an industry heralding industrial change, we cannot go by fixed notions in these respects – notions that may inform a study relating to a more mature economy or more developed state of an industry. We have, therefore, evolved our own criteria. We have taken the median or average figures of spindlage, whichever is lower, to distinguish between large and small units and between the fast-growing and slow-growing companies in each of our reference time-blocks. As for the age criterion we have assigned a period of two to three years to the childhood phase of company. This is because of the fact that most early mills in Ahmedabad started declaring dividend at the end of the first year of production and there was a time-lag of two to three years between registration and production.

With these preliminaries out of our way, let us see what our data tell us about the first time-block? During this period Ahmedabad witnessed the registration of twenty-seven textile firms in different years. Out of these, we know very little about the size of sixteen companies and have only the figures of spindles for the remaining eleven. In view of the fact that most mills had only spinning operations in the beginning or very few looms, we are justified in depending on the spindle figures alone for our analysis of this block. The eleven companies in our sample (appendix 10.III on page 177) at the time of their birth had altogether 98,095 spindles (median 9120: average 8,918) and added another 177,801 spindles (median 16,612; average 16,164) by 1898. To determine the size as well as growth we have taken the lower of the two figures for reasons explained earlier. In other words, a mill with less than 8,918 spindles at the start of its career has been treated as a small firm and if the increase in its number of spindles by 1898 was less than 16,164, it has been regarded as less than average growth. Table 10.1 presents the picture that emerges from applying these criteria to our sample.

It is clear from the above that in the first time-block, neither size nor age provided any significant advantage or disadvantage to a firm. Young, old, large and small all were equally susceptible to liquidation or take-over and no company of whatever size or age became defunct in this period. While the solitary young and large firm in the sample showed no sign of growth, the pattern in case of old and large units was by no means consistent. Old and small firms were the only ones in our sample which maintained more than normal upward trend.

These results, however, are open to question. For, the exclusion of as many as sixteen firms from our sample, for want of complete data, might have distored our analysis. Our data for the next time-block (ie 1898-1916) fortunately are more complete. None of the twenty-seven companies that existed in 1898 became defunct, though as many as thirteen changed hands. These units together had a total of 665,148 spindles (average 24,635; median 22,068) in 1898. The twenty-six new units (excluding a knitting company which does not concern us) set up between 1898 and 1916 cannot be included in our sample for this block since none of the new firms existed in the base year, i.e. 1898. This means that we will have to fix the normal size of a firm at 22,068 spindles at the base year. The twenty-seven firms in our sample registered an increase of 672,063 spindles between 1898 and 1916, giving us a median figure of 21,048 spindles (in preference to average figure of 24,891 which is higher) to measure the growth in size between the base year and the end of the time-block. The results of applying these criteria are given in Table 10.2 (*over*).

The table seems to indicate that (i) small firms were more vulnerable to liquidation or take-over than the larger units, particularly those which continued to be small even beyond the childhood stage, and (ii) age or size at the base year did not provide a substantial advantage to a firm in relation to growth although the young and small firms had a slight edge in this respect. These results are somewhat, though not substantially, different from those relating to our first block of time where old and small firms fared better than the rest.

Comparison between the first block and second block, however, may not be valid because of the unsatisfactory data base for the former. But

Table 10.1
Growth Pattern of Firms, 1858-1898.

	Category	No.	Defunct	Surviving: Change Control	Static	Mobile Upward Less than normal	Mobile Upward More than normal	Downward	Total
According to Size	Small	5	0	1	0	1	4	0	5
	Large	6	0	1	1	2	2	1	6
	Total	11	0	2*	1	3	6	1	11
According to Age	Young	1	0	1	1	0	0	0	1
	Old	10	0	1	0	3	6	1	10
	Total	11	0	2*	1	3	6	1	11
According to Age & Size	Young & Small	0	0	0	0	0	0	0	0
	Young & Large	1	0	1	1	0	0	0	1
	Old & Small	5	0	1	0	1	4	0	5
	Old & Large	5	0	0	0	2	2	1	5
	Total	11	0	2*	1	3	6	1	11

* Not included in the total as these firms reappear in the static or mobile columns.

Table 10.2
Growth Pattern of Firms, 1898-1916.

	Category	No.	Defunct	Surviving				Total
				Change Control	Static	Mobile		
						Upward	Downward	
						Less than normal	More than normal	
According to Size	Small	14	0	12	0	6	8	0	14
	Large	13	0	1	0	6	5	2	13
	Total	27	0	13*	0	12	13	2	27
According to Age	Young	8	0	6	0	2	6	0	8
	Old	19	0	7	0	10	7	2	19
	Total	27	0	13*	0	12	13	2	27
According to Age & Size	Young & Small	7	0	5	0	1	6	0	7
	Young & Large	1	0	1	0	1	0	0	1
	Old & Small	7	0	7	0	5	2	0	7
	Old & Large	12	0	0	0	5	5	2	12
	Total	27	0	13*	0	12	13	2	27

*Note: totals do not add to the total as these workbear in static or mobile columns.

comparison between the second and third blocks would not suffer from this disability as our data for the third block are as complete as for the second. At the beginning of the third block (1916-1929), Ahmedabad had a total of fifty-three mills but the number was reduced to thirty-nine by 1929 because eleven units had become defunct and five companies (nos.9,26 and 50 and nos.18 and 32, see appendix 10.I on page 171) had merged into two. Consistent with the logic applied to the second block, this would form our sample for the third block. For the same reasons as before, eighteen companies added between 1916 and 1929 have been excluded from this analysis.

The median figure for spindles operated by the mills existing in 1916 is 34,048 (as against an average of 36,934 which is higher) and the surviving mills cumulatively added a total of 1,570,013 new spindles (median 38,248 against average 40,359) by 1929. This means that our yardstick to measure the size at the base year and growth at the end of this block of time would be 34,048 and 38,248 respectively. Looking at the entire sample with reference to size, age and growth, we get the results shown in Table 10.3 (*over*).

This analysis seems to confirm our finding deduced from the data of the first and second time-blocks that small firms, particularly those which refused to outgrow their 'smallness' even during their adulthood, encountered greater risk of extinction, liquidation, or take-over. But contrary to our earlier finding, it was the old and large firms – and not the old and small as in case of the first time block or the young and small as the second – which had an edge over others in the matter of growth. Even if we ignore our analysis of the first time-block, we still do not find a clear pattern of relationship between size and growth on one hand or age and growth on the other.

Before coming to any definite conclusion, however, we must re-examine the performance of these companies with reference to the various managing agency houses which controlled them. For, it is possible that the growth pattern of companies in our sample in different time-blocks had something to do with the strength or the weakness of the respective clusters they belonged to, as there was no restriction on inter-company transfer of resources within a house. We have, therefore, grouped the companies according to the families controlling them from time to time, determined the sizes and ages of these families – large or small and old or young – in the same manner as in the case of individual companies, and then attempted to establish the relationship, if any, between the growth pattern of the managing agency houses and the companies under their control. This exercise has been done only in relation to the last two time-blocks as the complete data for the first block are not available and the process of the formation of clusters in a meaningful sense began only a few years before 1898.

Table 10.3
Growth Pattern of Firms, 1916-1929.

	Category	No.	Defunct	Surviving					Total
				Change Control	Static	Mobile			
						Upward		Downward	
						Less than normal	More than normal		
According to Size	Small	17	7	7	2	7	7	1	17
	Large	22	4	3	0	10	12	–	22
	Total	39	11	10*	2	17	19	1	39
According to Age	Young	1	1	1	0	0	1	0	1
	Old	38	10	9	2	17	18	1	38
	Total	39	11	10*	2	17	19	1	39
According to Age & Size	Young & Small	1	1	1	0	0	1	0	1
	Young & Large	0	0	0	0	0	0	0	0
	Old & Small	16	6	6	2	7	6	1	16
	Old & Large	22	4	3	0	10	12	0	22
	Total	39	11	10*	2	17	19	1	39

* Not included in the total as these reappear in static and mobile columns.

The twenty-seven companies that existed in Ahmedabad in 1898 were controlled by twenty-one families. One house born and defunct before this date has been excluded from our reckoning. Going by the average figure of spindles per mill to distinguish between large and small clusters and a three-year time lag from birth (the birth of a managing agency house is deemed to coincide with the birth of the first company floated or acquired by it) as the cut-off point between the young and old, we get the picture of the state of these houses by 1916 shown in Table 10.4 (*over*).

Four things become clear from these tables: (i) survival rate among the large and old houses was far better than among the small and young ones; (ii) a small house, if young, faced greater danger of extinction than an old one in this category; (iii) while the large and old houses were more aggressive towards expansion through acquisition or new floations, they were much less enthusiastic about adding new machinery to the existing units; (iv) on the other hand, the strategy adopted by small clusters was to expand the capacity of their existing companies. This seems to suggest that the larger and more experienced houses had greater capacity to bear the risk inherent in acquiring or floating new units and thus quickening the process of expansion – as compared with young and small houses.

Our second time-block coincided with the most expansionist interlude in the entire history of the Indian textile industry. The next time-block in contrast, witnessed the end of the war boom and the rise of stiff competition not only because of larger number of domestic units but also because of the consumption of imports from Manchester and the entry of Japan in Indian markets around 1920. Between 1898 and 1916 as many as thirty new houses (all were small except one by the 1916 standard) appeared on the scene in different years, but one was a knitting firm and seven perished before the beginning of this time-block. All the seven were small houses which had only one company each. Since we do not have the figures of the spindles in the companies controlled by them between their birth and extinction, we have to exclude them from our analysis. We, thus, have a sample of thirty-four houses, excluding a house which split into two a few years before 1916. Using our criteria for determining the size and age, we get the result shown in Table 10.5 (*over*).

This analysis confirms the first two conclusion we have derived from the previous block, ie (i) the large and old houses were able to avert extinction more successfully than the young and small clusters and (ii) more experienced houses, irrespective of size, had better survival rate. However, the above table seem to suggest two conclusions running counter to our last two findings relating to the previous block. We find here that the houses of all

Table 10.4
Growth Pattern of Managing Agency Houses, 1898-1916.

	Category	No. of Houses in 1898	No. of Cos. controlled	Static Cos.	Mobile Cos.			No. of Cos. lost	No. of Cos. gained	No. of houses defunct by 1916	No. of houses surviving upto 1916
					Upward		Downward				
					Less than normal	More than normal					
According to Size	Small	16	17	0	8	8	1	10	11	7	9
	Large	5	10	0	4	5	1	2	5	1	4
	Total	21	27	0	12	13	2	12	16	8	13
According to Age	Young	6	7	0	1	6	0	5	2	4	2
	Old	15	20	0	11	7	2	7	14	4	11
	Total	21	27	0	12	13	2	12	16	8	13
According to Age & Size	Young & Small	6	7	0	1	6	0	5	2	4	2
	Young & Large	0	0	0	0	0	0	0	0	0	0
	Old & Small	10	10	0	7	2	1	5	9	3	7
	Old & Large	5	10	0	4	5	1	2	5	1	4
	Total	21	27	0	12	13	2	12	16	8	13

Table 10.5
Growth Pattern of Managing Agency Houses, 1916-1929.

	Category	No of Houses in 1916	No of Cos controlled	No of Cos defunct by 1929	Surviving cos.				No of Cos lost	No of Cos gained	No of houses defunct by 1929	No of houses surviving upto 1929
					Static Cos.	Mobile Cos.						
						Upward		Downward				
						Less than normal	More than normal					
According to Size	Small	25	25	4	3	8	9	1	11	3	11	14
	Large	9	26	7	0	9	10	0	10	1	2	7
	Total	34	51	11	3	17	19	1	21	4	13	21
According to Age	Young	5	5	1	0	2	2	0	3	2	3	2
	Old	29	46	10	3	15	17	1	18	2	10	19
	Total	34	51	11	3	17	19	1	21	4	13	21
According to Age & Size	Young & Small	5	5	1	0	2	2	0	3	2	3	2
	Young & Large	0	0	0	0	0	0	0	0	0	0	0
	Old & Small	20	20	3	3	6	7	1	8	1	8	12
	Old & Large	9	26	7	0	9	10	0	10	1	2	7
	Total	34	51*	11	3	17	19	1	21	4	13	21

* The discrepancy between this and table 3 is because we have counted here company no. 32 separately which was controlled by a different house before its integration with no. 18 sometime before 1929.

types were more reluctant or less able to add new companies to their respective clusters; expansion through installing new machinery to the existing units found greater favour with all categories. Also, although the percentage of defunct houses in this block remained almost the same as in the previous one, the small houses, both old and young, could fight against the threat with greater success than the large ones. Even in the matter of net gain to the number of companies controlled by the various types of clusters, the small houses seem to have had an edge.

Taking the entire span covered by this study, it seems that during the formative period, when the industry was still developing and there was enough space for everyone, no company went out of existence and the variations in the growth pattern of large and small firms on one hand and the old and young on the other were rather marginal. The managing agency houses showed a somewhat similar pattern. Though some families, which perhaps had rushed into the scene under the impact of demonstration effect and without adequate preparation, left the textile scene during this phase, there were enough takers for the companies they had floated, making sure that no concern became defunct. During the period of competition and crisis following the First World War again, the variations in the pattern of growth of individual firms as well as the clusters represented by the managing agency houses remained marginal. Houses in all categories were cautious in acquiring or floating new companies with the result that a large number of firms were allowed to go out of existence altogether.

Our account also indicates that some small companies as well as the clusters improved their status during both phases of the industry. Out of five small companies born before 1898, as many as three became large by 1898; three out of fourteen and seven out of seventeen did likewise in the next two time-blocks. As regards the managing agency houses, out of nine in the small category surviving up to 1898 as many as five grew into large cluster by 1916. However, only three out of fifteen small survivors in 1916 entered the large category by 1926. More perhaps would have achieved this status if the conditions during this time-block were less daunting.

What about the change in the status of large units? Going by individual companies, we find that three out of six firms, though born large, were reduced to small size by 1898. Only three out of thirteen large survivors up to 1898, however, changed their status by 1916 and there was no change in the position of the large firms surviving up to 1916 in the next time-block. If we look at the houses, all large survivors retained their status during the long period from 1898 to 1929 although one prominent house was holding on to this position rather precariously. Only four large clusters (one before 1898 one between 1898 and 1916, and two between 1916 and 1929) became extinct during this period but their demise was due to some very peculiar circumstances, unrelated to size or age.[6] We may discover special difficulties causing the disappearance of several small houses as well. But there is no denying the fact that the large and old companies as well as the houses displayed greater capacity for survival and growth than their small and young counterparts. But a significant number of small and young units survived and grew into larger units in each time-block and some large and established firms had to succumb to the challenge of circumstances.

This reminds us of the dictum advanced by Alfred Marshall who linked the business firms with the trees in the forest growing according to their 'share of light and air'. Writing about hundred years ago he visualied 'a constant rise and fall of large business' with 'some firms, being in the ascending and others in the declining phase'.[7] How many in various categories would get atrophied or killed and how many would go up or down the ladder and with what pace would depend on specifics rather than any fixed pattern. Apparently deduced from the industrial scene in the late nineteenth century England when competition rather than monopoly was the order of the day, Marshall's formulation seems to apply eminently to firms in a proto-industrial economy[8] – as Ahmedabad, in fact India as a whole, was during our period of study. However, more studies relating to other industries and locations are required before we come to a definitive conclusion.

Footnotes

1. Edith T Penrose, *The Theory of the Growth of the Firm* (Oxford, 1959s).
2. Some of these are G C Archibald, *The Theory of the Firm* (Harmondsworth, 1970); C J Hawkins, *Theory of the Firm* (London, 1973); Joan Robinson, *Economic Heresies: Some Old-fashioned Questions in Economic Theory* (London, 1971). For a somewhat old survey see B Loasby, 'Hypothesis and Paradigm in the Theory of the Firm', *Economic Journal,* Vol.82 (1972).
3. See for example J Steindle, *Small and Big Business : Problems of the Size of Firms* (Oxford Institute of Statistics, Monograph No.1, 1945) which deals with American experience; and R Lloyd-Jones and A A LeRoux, 'Marshall and the Birth and Death of Firms: The Growth and the Size Distribution of Firms in the Early 19th Century Cotton Industry', *Business History,* Vol.24 (1983).
4. S D Mehta, *Cotton Mills of India, 1854-1954* (Bombay, 1954); Howard Spodem, 'The Manchesterization of Ahmedabad', *Economic Weekly,* Vol.17 (13 March 1965). For general account of the industry we have drawn on S D Mehta. Also see D Tripathi, *Business Houses in Western India: A Study in*

Entrepreneurial Response, 1858-1956 (New Delhi, 1989), 36-112.

5. All Ahmedabad mills except one produced coarse or medium quality goods during the period of our study. For the one which produced better varieties our conversion rate is 50 spindles = 1 loom. For the rest it is 40 spindles = 1 loom. These conversion rates are based on the advice of Professor Manubhai D Shah, until recently the General Manager, Arvind Mills, Ahmedabad, whose help we gratefully acknowledge.

6. These are the Houses of Motilal Ghelabhai (No.14), Ranchhodlal Mankiwala (n.7), Ranchhodlal Chhotalal (No.1) and Jagabhai Motibhai (No.41). Acute family differences killed the first two of these in their very infancy; the second met its doom because it was left with a minor child and an indulgent widow who proved unequal to the task suddenly thrust on them; and the heads of the fourth, steeped in neckdeep speculation, gambled their companies away. The House of Mansukhbhai Bhagubhai (No.3) among the largest up to 1916, was holding on to this status precariously during the 1916-1929 time-block. Its decline was due to the absence of male heir and the inability of a widow to sail through the crisis of the 1920s. See for details N N Desai, *Directory of Ahmedabad Mill Industry, 1929-1956* (Ahmedabad, 1957), 208,367, 368; D Tripathi, *Dynamics of a Tradition: Kasturbhai Lalbhai and His Entrepreneurship* (New Delhi, 1981), 64-65; idem, *Business Houses in Western India* (No.4), 49.

7. Marshall, *The Principles of Economics* (London, 1967), 263-64.

8. Our characterization of the Indian economy as proto-industrial is due to two reasons: (i) industrialization had touched only the fringe of the Indian economy during our period of study, and (ii) the industrial firms, depending entirely on imported technology, were not in a position to embark on technological innovation – a critical instrument of growth at a maturer phase of industrialization.

Appendix 10.I
Textile Mills in Ahmedabad 1858-1929.

Sr No (1)	Year of Birth (2)	Name of Mill (3)	Managing Agent (4)	Date of Change (5)	New Agent (6)	Change of name of Company (7)
1	1858	Ahmedabad Spinning & Wvg	Ranchhodlal Chhotalal (1)	–	–	
2	1864	Bechardas Spg & Wvg	Bechardas Laskari (2)	–	–	
3	1876	Ahmedabad Ginning & Mfg	Ranchhodlal Chhotalal (1)			
4	1876	Calico Printing	Bholanath Sarabhai	1880	Karamchand Prem (4)	Ahd Mfg & Calico Print
5	1877	Gujarat Spg & Wvg	Mansukhbhai Bhagubhai (3)			
6	1881	Gujarat Ginning & Mfg	Mansukhbhai Bhagubhai (3)			
7	1888	Trikamlal Harilal Spg & Mfg	Harilal Harivallabh (5)	1891	Harilal & Girdhar (5)	Maneklal Harilal Spg & Wvg
8	1889	Motilal Hirabhai Spg & Wvg	Tricumlal Jamnadas (10)	1895	Mansukh Bhagubhai (3)	
9	1890	Rajnagar Spg & Wvg	Motilal Hirabhai (6)	1902	Mangaldas Parekh (8)	Rajnagar no 1
10	1892	Aryodaya Spg & Wvg	Ranchodlal G Mankiwala (7)			
11	1892	Ahd Vepar Urtejak Spg & Wvg	Mangaldas Parekh (8)	1908	Lalsankar Umiyasan (38)	
			Lallubhai Raichand (9)	1913	Mangaldas Parekh (8)	Aryodaya Ginning Mfg
12	1893	Manekchawk Ahd Mfg	Tricumlal Jamnadas (10)			
13	1893	Hitechhu Spg & Wvg	Nagindas Lallubhai (11)	1913	Harilal Harivallabh (5)	Harivallabh Mulchand Mill
14	1893	Purshotam Spg & Wvg	Mansukhbhai Bhagubhai (3)			
15	1894	Ahd Cotton Mfg (Bagicha)	Amrutlal B Shodhan (12)			
16	1895	Gujarat Cotton Spg & Wvg	Amulkrai Mahipatrai (13)	1913	Chandulal Karsan (47)	City of Ahd Spg & Mfg
17	1895	Gujarat Cotton Mills	Motilal Ghelabhai (14)	1897	Tribhowan Motichnd (18)	New Gujarat Cotton Mills
				1901	Shantilal Bhagwan (24)	
18	1895	Ahd New Spg & Wvg	Lallubhai Rajitbhai (15)	1909	Naran J Girdhar (12)	
19	1895	Hatheesing Mfg Co	Manibhai Premabhai (16)	1903	Mansukh Bhagubhai (3)	Ahmedabad New Textile
20	1896	Ahmedabad Sarangpur (Bordi)	Motilal Haribhai (16)			
21	1896	Bharatkhand Cotton Mills	Kevaldas Tribhowandas (18)	1912	Motichand Jaikisan (43)	
22	1896	Ahd Commercial Co	Tricudas Bhogilal (17)			
23	1897	Saraspur Mfg Co	Lalbhai Dalparbhai (19)	1912	Jagabhai Motibhai (41)	
				1924	Kasturbhai Lalbhai (42)	
24	1897	Ahd Jubilee Spg & Mfg	Chunilal Jaychand (20)	1901	Chunilal Nagindas (11)	
25	1897	Ahd Advance Mills	Laxaisankar Eavshankar (21)	1903	Tata & Sons (26)	

Appendix 10.1 Continued

(1)	(2)	(3)	(4)	(5)	(6)	(7)
26	1898	Rajnagar Gin & Mfg	Ranchodlal G Mankiwala (7)	1902	Mangaldas G Parekh (8)	Rajnagar Spg, Weg & Mfg
27	1898	Ahd Fine Spg & Weg	Sorabji D Karaka (22)	1910	Hiralal I Patel (39)	
28	1900	Ahd Cotton & Wast Mfg	Rustonji & Govindlal (23)	1929	Dhirajlal Chunilal (57)	
29	1900	Hitwardhak Cotton Co	Sorabji D Karaka (22)	1914	Nagin M Jaychand (49)	Asarwa Mills
				1923	F E Dinshaw (54)	
30	1902	Ahd Merchants Spg Mill	N A	1902	Vaikunth A Desai (25)	
				1913	Raman Kanaiyalal (45)	Ahmedabad Kaisare Hind
				1914	Motilal Hirabhai (6)	
31	1904	Ahd Silk & Cotton Mfg	Ramanbhai Dahayabhai (27)	1924	Jiwanlal Girdhar (12)	New Textile Mill no 2
32	1904	Zaveri Spg & Mfg	Manibhai Premabhai (16)	1913	Kalidas Umabhai (46)	
33	1905	Himabhai Mills	Nagarseth Chimanbhai (28)	1914	Khusaldas Gokuldas (48)	
34	1905	Ahd Shorrock Spg & Weg	Mafatlal Chandulal (29)	1912	Kasturbhai Lalbhai (42)	
35	1905	Raipur Mfg	Lalbhai Dalpatbhai (19)	1915	Jagabhai Motibhai (41)	
36	1905	Ahd New Edward Mfg	Lalbhai Tricumlal (17)	1920	Jiwanlal Girdhar (12)	
37	1905	Ahd Industrial Mills	K L Mehta & Co (30)			
38	1905	National Mills Co	Chimanlal G Nagri (31)			
39	1905	Ahd New Manekchawk Spg & Weg	Lalbhai Tricumlal (17)			
40	1905	Ahd New Cotton	Girdharlal A Shodhan (12)	1915	Jagabhai Motibhai (41)	Govinddas Maneklal
41	1905	Shrinagar Weg & Mfg	Dahyabhai Kripasankar (32)	1923	Govinddas Maneklal (53)	
42	1905	Sarangpur Cotton Mfg	Balabhai D Shodhan (33)			
43	1905	Bharatkhand Tex Mfg	Jivanlal Giridharlal (12)			
44	1906	Ahd Swadeshi Spg & Mfg	Manilal Maganlal (34)	1923	Shivnara S Nemani (55)	New Swadeshi Mills of Ahd
45	1906	Ahd Jahangir Vakil Mills	Rustomji Divetia (35)	1915	Mangaldas Jaysingh (51)	
46	1907	Ahd Shri Ramkrishan Mills	Chimanlal M Munshaw (36)			
47	1908	Fine Knitting Co	Baldeodas V Parikh (37)			
48	1909	Ahd Astodia Mfg Co	Girdharlal Amratlal (12)			
49	1912	Ahd Gomitpur Spg Weg	Mohd Ali Taiyab Ali (40)	1925	Chunilal K Patel (48)	Patel Mills
50	1912	Haripur Spg & Weg	Mangaldas G Parekh (8)			
51	1913	Ahd Laxmi Cotton Mills	Jayantibhai A Shodhan (12)			
52	1913	Raipur Mills	Patel Shah & Co (44)	1928	Bhikha J Patel (56)	New Raipur
53	1914	Ahd Gordhan Spg & Mfg	Narsidas Jaikisamdas (50)			
54	1916	Ahd Vaso Mumbai Mills	Chinubhai Balabhai (52)	1923	Mangaldas Jaysing (51)	Rustom Jahangir Vakil

Appendix 10.1 Continued

(1)	(2)	(3)	(4)	(5)	(6)	(7)
55	1920	Silver Cotton Mills	Balabhai D Shodhan (33)			
56	1920	Marsden Spg & Weg	C Marsden & M Munshaw (36)			
57	1920	Sri Vivekanand Mills	Nanubhai M Munshaw (36)			
58	1920	Ahd Jupiter Spg & Weg	Fulchand Maganlal (58)			
59	1920	Bharat Laxmi Mills	N A	1927	Amrat D Shodhan (12)	Ahd Jaybharat Cotton
60	1920	India Skinning Mills	Dakwala Bros (59)	1924	Mangaldas Girdhar (8)	Bharat Suryodaya Mills
61	1920	Asoka Mills	Kasturbhai Lalbhai (42)			
62	1925	Nagri Mills	Chimanlal H Nagri (31)			
	1925	National Mills	Chimanlal H Nagri (31)			
63	1926	Oriental Mills	N A	1926	Harivallabh Kalidas (5)	Ambica Mills
64	1927	Vikram Mills	Motilal Hirabhai (6)			
65	1927	Monogram Mills	Manilal M Munshaw (36)			
66	1927	New Commercial Mills	Ratilal Nathalal (60)			
67	1928	Bhalakia Mills	Jethalal P Bhalika (61)			
68	1928	Aruna Mills	Kasturbhai Lalbhai (42)			
69	1929	Vijay Mills	Haridas Acharatlal (62)			
70	1929	Sarangpur Cotton no 2	Balabhai D Shodhan (33)			
71	1929	Lalbhai Tricumlal Mills	Chimanbhai Lalbhai (17)			
72	1929	Amruta Mills	Jayantilal A Damodar (63)			

* *Figures in ( ) indicates managing agents' serial numbers.*

Appendix 10.II
Spindle Growth in Ahmedabad Mills, 1898-1929.

Year of Birth (1)	*Mill No. (2)	Size in 1898 (3)				Size in 1916 (4)					Size in 1929 (5)				
		*Mg. Agmts (3.1)	Spindles (3.2)	Looms (3.3)	Total (3.4)	*Mg. Agents (4.1)	Spindles (4.2)	Looms (4.3)	Total (4.4)	Growth Over 1898 (4.5)	*Mg. Agents (5.1)	Spindles (5.2)	Looms (5.3)	Total (5.4)	Growth Over 1916 (5.5)
1858	1	1	33268	689	60328	1	35103	794	66868	6040	1	Defunct			
1864	2	2	16768	314	29328	2	14500	336	27940	-1388	2	18156	868	52876	24936
1876	3	1	44912	375	59912	1	65516	1608	129836	69924	1	Defunct			
1876	4	4	27000	401	47050	4	40768	1111	96318	49268	4	68412	3336	235212	138894
1877	5	3	33400	917	70080	3	26472	668	53192	-16888	3	26800	1346	80640	27448
1881	6	3	19798	482	39078	3	74504	1838	148024	108946	3	Defunct			
1888	7	5	25000	0	25000	5	23752	471	42592	17592	5	34012	1534	95372	52780
1889	8	3	32860	372	47740	3	30848	700	58848	11108	3	Defunct			
1890	9	7	11384	119	16144	8	18912	528	40032	23888	8	47936	2370	142736	102704
1892	10	8	24712	312	37192	8	38264	1250	88264	51072	8	45120	2390	140720	52456
1892	11	9	10310	0	10310	8	23856	0	23856	13546	8	36128	1654	102288	78432
1893	12	10	12992	304	25152	10	17128	438	34648	9496	10	35174	1709	103534	68886
1893	13	11	7040	0	7040	5	17040	0	17040	10000	5	17648	862	52128	35088
1893	14	3	10816	297	22696	3	13040	384	28400	5704	3	Defunct			
1894	15	12	14984	304	27144	12	25116	608	49436	22292	12	28800	1408	85120	35684
1895	16	13	15000	0	15000	-47	18572	0	18572	3572	47	24000	1006	64240	45668
1895	17	18	10000	0	10000	24	25529	392	41209	31209	24	29540	1355	83740	42531
1895	18	15	14130	0	14130	12	20288	344	34048	19918	12	35908	1826	108948	74908
1895	19	16	8848	0	8848	3	15316	0	15316	6468	3	Defunct			
1896	20	6	14000	0	14000	6	26764	384	42124	28124	6	24800	1080	68000	25876
1896	21	18	12576	0	12576	43	16344	432	33624	21048	43	Defunct			
1896	22	17	8256	0	8256	17	22984	462	41464	33208	17	28512	1280	79712	38248
1897	23	19	11516	0	11516	41	33824	630	59024	47508	42	29760	1382	85040	26016
1897	24	20	9600	0	9600	11	20812	351	34852	25252	11	36008	1746	105848	70996

THE AHMEDABAD TEXTILE INDUSTRY, 1858–1929

Appendix 10.II Continued

(1)	(2)	(3) (3.1)	(3.2)	(3.3)	(3.4)	(4) (4.1)	(4.2)	(4.3)	(4.4)	(4.5)	(5) (5.1)	(5.2)	(5.3)	(5.4)	(5.5)
1897	25	21	9460	0	9460	26	30612	600	54612	45152	26	30692	1369	85452	30840
1898	26	7	10228	296	22068	8	18912	578	42032	19964	8	Integrated			
1898	27	22	0	125	5000	39		376	15040	10040	39	Defunct			
1900	28					23	1092	0	10920		57	20296	723	49216	38296
1900	29					49	18975	400	34976		54	13048	1064	55609	20632
1902	30					6	17033	396	32873		6	23300	979	62640	29587
1904	31					27	0	198	7920		27	0	198	7920	0
1904	32					16	0	500	20000		12	Integrated			
1905	33					48	0	300	12000		48	0	378	15120	3120
1905	34					29	16816	628	41936		29	28208	1368	82928	40992
1905	35					42	26680	411	43120		42	36000	1760	106400	63280
1905	36					41	14500	250	24500		41	35000	0	35000	10500
1905	37					30	17640	330	30840		12	Defunct			
1905	38					31	15196	0	15196		31	15196	0	15196	0
1905	39					17	25380	561	47820		17	27896	1353	82016	34196
1905	40					12	28516	576	51556		12	28516	1423	85436	33880
1905	41					41	0	217	8680		53	13048	1064	55608	46928
1905	42					33	26754	334	40124		33	27080	1253	77200	37076
1905	43					12	16400	432	33680		12	34240	1734	103600	69920
1906	44					34	20985	625	45985		55	25824	1328	78944	32959
1906	45					51	17124	438	34644		51	29060	1404	84220	49576
1907	46					36	0	374	14960		36	0	408	16320	1360
1908	47					37	Knit	Knit	Knit		37	Knit			
1909	48					12	17500	0	17500		12	Defunct			
1912	49					40	7712	0	7712		48	12182	305	24382	16670
1912	50					8	10810	0	10810		8	Integrated			
1913	51					12	25346	114	29906		12	34100	853	68220	38314
1913	52					44	0	334	13360		56	0	226	9040	-4320
1914	53					50	9688	200	17688		50	Defunct			
1916	54					52	8340	0	8540		51	16444	769	47204	38664
1920	55										33	19420	992	59100	
1920	56										36	16748	893	52468	

Appendix 10.II Continued

| (1) | (2) | (3) | | | (4) | | | (5) | | |
		(3.1)	(3.2)	(3.3)	(3.4)	(4.1)	(4.2)	(4.3)	(4.4)	(4.5)	(5.1)	(5.2)	(5.3)	(5.4)	(5.5)
1920	57										36	0	304	12160	
1920	58										58	9028	614	33588	
1920	59										12	16488	412	32968	
1920	60										8	Defunct			
1920	61										42	31824	1731	101064	
1925	62										31	15808	395	31608	
1926	63										5	11360	540	32960	
1927	64										6	15276	697	43156	
1927	65										36	21000	1053	63120	
1927	66										60	14224	752	44304	
1928	67										61	13752	780	44952	
1929	68										42	0	0	0	
1929	69										62	17117	476	36157	
1928	70										33	20884	1098	64804	
1929	71										17	0	0	0	
1929	72										63	0	0	0	

Sources: Data for this as well as for Appendix I have been compiled and calculated from N N Desai, *Directory of Ahmedabad Mill Industry, 1923-1933* (Ahmedabad, 1935) and *ibid, 1929-1956* (Ahmedabad 1957); S. Playne, *The Bombay Presidency, the united provinces, The Punjab etc.* (London, 1917-20), 64-103; Thacker Spink & Co, *Thacker's Indian Directory, 1899* (Calcutta, 1900), 1374-75; *Prajabandhu* (Ahmedabad), issues for the years 1898-1900; *Indian Textile Journal*, X (September 1900); Govt of Bombay, *Provincial Reports on the Working of Indian Factories Act in Bombay Presidency* for the years 1884-1899; idem, *General Reports on the Administration of the Bombay Presidency* for 1864-65 to 1898-99; and M. Mehta, *The Ahmedabad Textile Industry Genesis and Growth* (Ahmedabad, 1982), 151-165.

Appendix 10.III

Ahmedabad Mills, 1858-1898.

Sr No	Mill No	Spindles at birth	Spindles in 1898	Growth
1	1	2500	33268	30768
2	2	10000	16768	6768
3	3	9120	44912	35792
4	4	7000	27000	20000
5	5	11561	33400	21839
6	7	9422	25000	15578
7	8	5000	32860	27860
8	10	8100	24712	16612
9	12	5100	12992	7892
10	15	20292	14984	−5308
11	17	10000	10000	0
	Total	98095	275896	177801
	Average	8918	25081	16164
	Medium	9120	25000	16612

Part 3
Sectors

11

The life-cycle of firms in late nineteenth century Britain

Stana Nenadic

Introduction

This chapter offers a brief, for the most part descriptive and in some respects speculative survey of certain life-cycle characteristics of firms and their owners in later nineteenth century Britain. It additionally considers the problems that beset attempts to understand the demography of nineteenth century firms in a period when most were small and short-lived, and when there was limited division between the ownership and control of the firm on the one hand, and the ownership and control of other personal or family assets on the other. The paper represents an initial statement drawn from work that is still in progress and is intended to formulate themes for discussion; it should not be regarded as a definitive account since the results contained here may well be modified in the light of future research.[1]

Two contrasting case studies, one urban and one rural, are employed in the paper. Inevitably these demonstrate their own unique characteristics; but the firms described here provide a useful illustration of certain basic demographic experiences that may, with further investigation, prove to be typical of British business in the later nineteenth century. The first case, and the one most amenable to statistical analysis, is derived from a sample of 285

Table 11.1

Number of firms in each area of activity, 1861 to 1819.*

	1861	1871	1881	1891
Paper makers	4	6	5	9
Ink manufacturers	1	5	3	6
Type founders	3	2	2	2
Printers	67	63	103	125
Engravers, lithographers	56	78	90	102
Paper rulers	6	5	9	13
Envelope manufacturers	0	8	7	9
Book binders	36	31	39	39
Publishers	36	42	42	60
Paper stock merchants	0	0	2	11
Stationers, wholesale	22	36	37	43
Stationers, retail	32	82	146	201
Book sellers	119	121	138	149
Circulating libraries	5	12	16	18

* *Note:* many firms engaged in more than one distinct activity and were listed accordingly.

firms that were engaged in the manufacture, wholesale and retail of books and other paper products in the city of Edinburgh between 1861 and 1891 (a 25 per cent sample). The data and illustrations are drawn from the trades lists that were published annually in the *Edinburgh Post Office Directory* and from the sequestration records of a sub-sample of fourteen firms that went bankrupt during or immediately following the period of study. Firms engaged in the book and paper trades formed a major sector in the nineteenth century Edinburgh economy. As indicated in Table 11.1 the sector manifested a complex and changing range of activities. There was a three-fold increase in the number of firms over the period, with peaks of new firm formation in

THE LIFE-CYCLE OF FIRMS IN BRITAIN

Figure 11.1

Entries and Exits 1861-91.

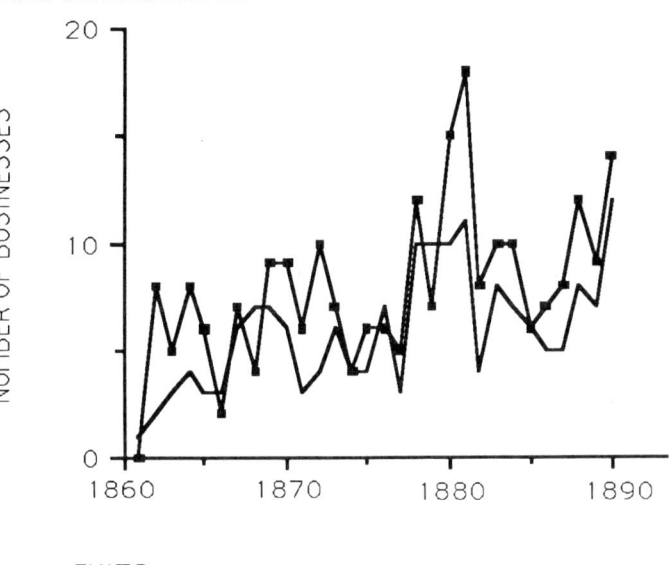

— EXITS
■— ENTRIES

the years 1862-65, 1869-72, 1878-1881 and 1888-91 (Figure 11.1).[2] The sector supported both larger and small firms, barriers to entry were fairly low (paper making excepted), but not so low as to give rise to a dominance by 'penny capitalists', and the nature of both markets and products gave scope within individual firms for growth, specialisation and diversification, particularly in response to such developments as the bureaucratisation of government and business.[3] The second case is drawn from a study of 28 small and personal or family owned businesses that existed in the predominantly rural and agricultural township of Whittington in Lancashire (five miles south of Kirby Lonsdale) between 1864 and 1914. These firms include shopkeepers, joiners, builders and carriers. Again the principal source of data is a series of trade lists, but these are supplemented by information from an extensive record of the activities of one business family.[4]

Firm types and sizes

Many historians and business analysts have identified hierarchies of firm types and sizes based on such criteria as employee numbers, the capital invested or the structure of ownership and management. Such hierarchies are designed to represent the spectrum from small to large and are to some extent life-cycle determined since younger firms will tend to be small and concentrated at a lower end of the hierarchy. The following model (Table 11.2), loosely derived from Chandler and the work of Scase and Goffee, is a fairly typical illustration.[5]

Table 11.2

Hierarchy of Firms.

1. **Owner directed firms**
    1.1 Self-employed. An individual or family worked for themselves with no outside labour but relied on the unpaid labour of women and children. Place of home and work was probably the same.
    1.2 Small employer. An individual, family or possibly a non-family partnership worked alongside their small paid labour force (probably drawing an equivalent wage) and also undertook the task of firm management. There was a reliance on unpaid family labour and place of home and work was often the same.
    1.3 Personal owned/directed and managed. An individual, family or non-family partnership owned and directed the firm, but did not work alongside the employees and were solely and singularly responsible for management. Place of home and work was probably separate.
    1.4 Personal owned/directed and managerial managed. An individual, family or non-family partnership owned all of the firm and undertook personal direction through an established hierarchy of salaried professional managers who were non-family members.

2. **Managerial directed firms**
    2.1 Personal owned and managerial directed. An individual, family or partnership owned all or a substantial part of a firm but all significant day-to-day direction was undertaken by salaried professional managers.
    2.2 Finance owned and managerial directed. Owned by many individual or corporate shareholders and directed and managed by salaried professionals.

It is well established in the history of British business development that large, multi-operational, vertically integrated managerial firm did not exist in any significant numbers prior to the First World War.[6] Though historians of nineteenth century business have frequently overlooked the fact, preferring to concentrate their energies on exceptionally large industrial enterprises, all existing evidence and most contemporary commentaries would indicate that in Britain in the nineteenth century the vast majority of firms were small and exhibited a range of characteristics that would have placed them in the lowest ranks of such a hierarchy as that described above.[7] One of the most compelling and systematic demonstrations of the small scale bias of nineteenth century business is provided in Richard Roger's study of the structure of industry in mid-Victorian urban Scotland. Drawing principally from evidence on the number of employees per firm, Rogers has shown that the median workforce size across a range of business sectors, including retail, wholesale and manufacturing enterprises, was less than four employees.[8] Though the data so far available from the Edinburgh and Whittington case studies does not provide any regular evidence on workforce size, it does furnish some limited indications that tend to reinforce the impression of a business world in which very small, owner directed firms were the norm. In rural Whittington, as one might expect, many firms were those of the self-employed and even a relatively substantial undertaking such as the long established family firm of John Hodgeson, joiner and builder, never exceeded a workforce of six.[9] In Edinburgh, of those fourteen firms from the sample of 284 that had experienced the legal process of bankruptcy sequestration, only one, the firm of Brydone and Luke (sole partner Robert Luke), a printer and publisher, sequestered in June 1893, with a weekly wages bill of 19 gives any indication of a significant workforce.[10] Another firm, that of R M Cameron, school board stationer and publisher, sequestered in March 1882, had a workforce of ten.[11] In most cases the typical pattern appears to have been that of the owner working with family members and one or two assistants, as in the firm of John Chisholm, a publisher, sequestered in May 1890, whose work force consisted of an unmarried female relative and a shop boy.[12] In addition to evidence on workforce size, in both Edinburgh and Whittington the vast majority of the sample firms had business titles that suggested they were single proprietorships.[13] Such modest and obscure undertakings were very unlike the more substantial and famous firms that tend to be associate with the book and paper trades in nineteenth century Edinburgh. The largest according to one contemporary estimate of 1869 was that of Thomas Nelson and Sons, printers, publishers, booksellers and stationers, with a workforce of over 400.[14]

Age of firms

Some nineteenth century firms had a very long lifespan. The Edinburgh sample included several, such as the firms of W & R Chambers, A & C Black or William Blackwood and Sons, that were founded in the late eighteenth or early nineteenth century and in some cases continued in existence through to recent years.[15] But though such undertakings have tended to dominate twentieth century perceptions, in the nineteenth century mature firms, as with large firms, were always a minority. Data on the lifespan of the Edinburgh sample firms that were formed between 1862 and 1890 (and not recorded in existence in 1861 or 1891) suggest a very short average life and a high annual rate of mortality among young businesses. In the book and paper trades, a third of firms were in existence for one year only, 62 per cent had died by the end of their third year and only 5 per cent survived beyond ten years (Table 11.3). It is worth remarking that from a sample of 284 cases, only

Table 11.3

Lifespan of businesses that were formed between 1862-1890 and were not in existence in 1891 (n = 152)**.

1 Year	34%	7 Years	3%
2 Years	16%	8 Years	5%
3 Years	12%	9 Years	3%
4 Years	11%	10 Years	3%
5 Years	5%	11 Years +	5%
6 Years	2%		

** *Note:* the exclusion of firms in existence in 1891 but founded during the period 1862-1890 skews the sample toward the young. These figures should be read in conjunction with the age profile data given in Table 11.3.

sixteen firms were in existence in both 1861 and 1891. In effect, this study of the age of firms would indicate that in parallel with a striking pattern of size dualism among urban businesses as described by Roger, the age of firms was widely divergent. Although annual listings were not available for the rural case study, the Whittington area suggests an equivalent structure of age distributions. Fourteen of the 28 Whittington firms were recorded only once in the series of trade directories between 1864 and 1914, six were recorded twice, and eight were recorded more than twice (three of the longest surviving firms being associated with the Hodgeson family). Overall these figures suggest a shorter lifespan than that found in other studies of late nineteenth century business, though the emphasis elsewhere has tended to be on large or corporate enterprises. Payne has demonstrated, for instance, that the mean average life of Scottish limited liability companies incorporated between 1856 and 1895, and dissolved before 1975, was 16.4 years.[16] But instructive parallels are uncovered when the Edinburgh and Whittington findings are compared with data from the well charted experience of smaller firms in the second half of the twentieth century. A recent study of manufacturing firms in the North East of England has demonstrated, for example, that nearly 40 per cent of new businesses ceased to trade within three years of being founded.[17] While an earlier study has established that of firms with an employed capital of less than 250,000 in 1960, an estimated 59 per cent would have been subject to take-over or liquidation by the end of 1969.[18]

It should be fairly clear from what has been said already that on the basis of the studies described above the majority of firms in the latter part of the nineteenth century were both small and short lived. Another perspective on the demographic experience of nineteenth-century businesses, and one that points to changes through time, can be derived from snapshot age profiles of firms at specified dates. Again drawing on the Edinburgh data, Table 11.4 reveals that for all those firms in existence in 1891, 25 per cent were aged

Table 11.4
Age profile of businesses in 1875 and 1891.

	1875 (n = 67)	1891 (n = 112)
Younges quartile	2 years	4 years
Median	5 years	10 years
Oldest quartile	15 years	20 years

Source: Trade directory as recorded in the *Edinburgh Annual Post Office Directory* (Edinburgh, 1861 to 1891).

twenty years or older, ten years was the median average age and a quarter were aged four years or younger. The age profile of firms in 1875 was significantly younger, with half of those sampled being less than five years old. Though the Edinburgh book and paper trades were probably following a pattern of chronological development that was unique to that sector (and possibly also to that city), the relative ageing of firms over the period suggests parallels with evidence from a study of businesses engaged in cotton manufacturing in the early nineteenth century.[19] The latter has indicated, and this is reinforced by certain studies of twentieth century business concentration that the relative ageing of a population of firms is associated with the tendency towards larger enterprises.[20] There is little systematic evidence from the present case study to support the contention that the ageing process was linked to significant growth in average firm size, and there are, indeed, many individual counter indications of the mature firm that remained small and unchanging over many decades.[21] Though the precise implications of the ageing process on business size and experience in this period is as yet unclear, the phenomenon is worth remarking.

In concluding this analysis of the size and age of firms, one can state (and in this there are no surprises) that in conjunction with the 'small-scale labour-intensive mode of industrial production' that was still so important in nineteenth century Britain,[22] a significant reason for the predominance of small businesses was the tendency for most firms to die in infancy and be constantly replaced by other firms with low life expectancy.[23] To plunder the terminology of demographers, with regard to the birth and death of nineteenth century firms what we observe is a 'high pressure' regime consistent with a period of rapid expansion within an existing structure of industrial and commercial activity. If the evidence suggested by the changing age profiles of the firms engaged in the Edinburgh book and paper trades can be taken as indicative of a wider experience, it may be the case that the demographic transition, that is the transition to a more stable population regime in which low rates of birth were coupled to low rates of mortality and rising life expectancy, was about to take place. But it should not be assumed that such a transition necessarily imperilled the dominance of small firms.

Life-cycle characteristics

The last part of this paper consists of a tentative account, elaborated where appropriate with speculative asides, of the life-cycle characteristics of the Edinburgh sample firms that existed in 1891 and had been in existence for more than five years (82 in all) plus those predominantly younger firms that had been born and died between 1862 and 1890 (a further 152). The paper concludes with a survey of aspects of the relationship between businesses and their nineteenth-century owners that challenge the precision of business demography and cause one to reflect on the meaning of the terms 'birth' and 'death' when applied to firms in this period. It should be stressed at the outset that an exercise that endeavours to establish some basic life-cycle characteristics for firms defined according to age criteria is inevitably attended by uncertainties and doubts; more particularly since the data is largely drawn from a single source and the cases available to illustrate the older age groups are few in number. Nevertheless, on the basis of evidence on business location, on changes in business name and on the range of activities in which firms were known to engage,[24] the following account tends to suggest that business life-cycles typically conformed to a pattern of internal stability irrespective of the age at death. When changes occurred, especially in those firms that survived to maturity, they were apparently gradual and relatively late in life.

a. Young firms, life of 1-5 years (n = 124 or 53 per cent of cases) On the data available from the Edinburgh sample the term 'life-cycle' cannot be applied to firms in this age category in any meaningful sense. In addition to their short lifespan, the majority remained in the same premises and appeared to engage in the same activities, predominantly retail and jobbing printing, from birth to death. Only sixteen of these firms moved premises during their life, mainly in the year prior to their exit. Most deaths did not represent business failures in a formal sense; bankruptcy sequestrations and the related process of *cessio bonorum* were rare in this group, being only five in number.[25] The majority of non-sequestration deaths occurred in years of high firm formation, which were also, for the most part, years that coincided with peaks in the business cycle. It seems reasonable to surmise, and this is reinforced by Payne's work on limited liability companies, that a large proportion of deaths among young firms were the result of either voluntary liquidation or a decision to sell the business as a going concern.[26] Since, according to their business titles,[27] the great majority firms in this youngest age group were personally owned, the pattern of births and deaths should be understood in the light of the changing circumstances and expectations of the kinds of individuals who formed those businesses, in conjunction with the availability to such individuals of other opportunities for securing an appropriate income. We can hypothesise that the personal life-cycle stage of the business owner may have been a greater influence on the experience of the personal firm than commercial considerations. Though this has still to be established in statistical terms, the owners of short-lived businesses in the large urban centres were probably dominated in their numbers by young men who regard business formation as one of several income generating options available to them and were able to move rapidly in and out of business concerns as opportunities presented.[28] The desire for income stability, arguably the primary aim of the family enterprise owner, was probably not their first objective.[29]

b. Medium aged firms; life of 6-15 years (n = 66, or 28 per cent of cases) Although the dominant pattern was again, apparently, one of unchanging activities and situations, firms in this age group tended to have more distinctly identifiable life-cycle patterns. Twenty-seven moved premises during their life, with almost all of the moves taking place in the first seven years of existence. Proportionately this was a greater level of movement than seen in the youngest age group. There may, in such movements, be evidence of business expansion. But conversely it may be the case that such movements are representative of business difficulties, for there are indications of a higher level of identifiable failure than seen among the younger firms. This age category contains the largest number of sequestrations, six in all, clustered on the sixth to ninth years of existence. Most firms were again personally owned, but there were a small number that on the evidence of business title had begun in life as non-family partnerships and private companies, and might, therefore, be expected to be somewhat larger than the first category of firms.

c. Mature firms: life of 16 to 30 years (n = 28 or 12 per cent of cases) Sixteen of the firms in this age group moved premises during their life with most of these movements taking place between the years of six and fifteen. This may represents a pattern of late and cautious expansion in contrast to the possible early expansion noted above. There were only three sequestrations among firms in this group. Again, it was the case that personal ownership dominated, but firms showing evidence of inter-generational succession in their changing business titles, were also present.

d. Long established firms: life of 30 years and more (n = 16 or 7 per cent of cases)

There were few firms in this category and their experience prior to 1861 was not traced in a systematic fashion. Nine were identifiable as established family businesses with evidence in their changing business titles of inter-generational succession. One of the sixteen became a public limited company in the 1880s, two appeared to be non-family partnerships and four were individually owned. The dominant feature exhibited by these firms was that of modest and gradual development. During the thirty years from 1861 to 1891 most (ten out of sixteen) retained a fairly stable profile of activities and did not move their premises.

Life-cycle complexities and the problems of measurement

The illustrations employed in this paper are taken, for the greater part, from a single type of source. Lists of trades in Post Office or commercial directories were usually annual, and since they were employed by businessmen as a form of advertising they tended to be comprehensive and therefore broadly representative of a population of local firms. In showing the dynamics of the mass of smaller nineteenth century businesses, trade lists are widely recognised as being of particular value.[30] In reflection of this fact, it has been assumed throughout the present paper that the appearance of a new name in such a list of firms is held to represent a 'birth', and a disappearance to represent a 'death'. But such assumptions, it must be admitted, are excessively sanguine. The data certainly possesses an indicative value, but the precision that trades lists appear to bestow in the generation of statistics on the demography of firms, should be recognised as being in some respects illusory. There are necessary reservations to be born in mind when dealing with this or, indeed, any other form of information that appears to represent the birth and death of populations of firms in the past. This is for reasons that are partly connected with the nature of the source – which tends, for instance, to be under-representative of ephemeral firms, notably those that were owned by women[31] – but is more directly the consequence of the particular types of relationship that sometimes existed between businesses and their owners in the nineteenth century.

It should be stressed, that when applied to firms the terms 'birth' and 'death' do not, and cannot, represent the same certainties of experience as those equivalent events among animate populations. Birth should imply the creation of a new and independent entity, while death should imply that entity's demise. Yet some firm 'births' consisted of businesses, or substantial parts of businesses, that had previously existed under earlier ownership and with different names, and been purchased by their new owners as going concerns. Were these new firms? Some recorded 'deaths' arose from the sale of viable concerns to other owners and consequent changes in the name of the firms. Had such businesses died? At the other extreme certain firms could remain in existence over several years with their names unchanged, yet have been bought, sold and even failed on several occasions. How should the life-cycle of these firms be defined? Though the fourteen sequestrated Edinburgh firms mentioned above probably represent a biased group, it is worth noting that seven of these enterprises had been partially or wholly purchased as existing concerns (in two cases by employees within the firm) and at the bankruptcy of their owners, five were sold to new owners on a similar basis. A good illustration is the firm of Boyd and Bell, booksellers in Edinburgh, whose sole proprietor at sequestration in August 1880 was David Ross. One imagines that at some stage in the past there had been both a Mr Boyd and a Mr Bell with an interest in this undertaking. Immediately prior to 1875 (when Ross, the former manager, purchased the firm) the business was in the hands of a Mr Stillie. At sequestration the firm was sold as a going concern and retained its name and pursued the same activities apparently unchanged until 1890.[32] Finally, how should one deal with those individuals (there were two in the Edinburgh sequestration sample) whose firms had encountered bankruptcy on previous occasions yet remained in business, again apparently unchanged?

Pursuing this point further, certain firm 'deaths' may not have been deaths at all if one views the business from the perspective of the owner and in the context of the owners other income generating activities. Businesses, where these were identified with a single personality, could and commonly did mutate as the owner grew older. Family life-cycle events could sometimes result in a change of business name and premises or even activities, which might have given the impression of a business 'death' when none had occurred . Family businesses sometimes merged – indeed, this may have been an important aspect of growth – but does such a merger represent a birth or a death? With births as with deaths the relationship between the family and the firm could give rise to complexity. Some new firms were created with a dependent relationship on existing family firms. They existed as part of a network of concerns and relative to the market may not have been independent. A form of business paternalism prevailed in the nineteenth century and it can be hypothesised that networks of family firms were an important mechanism for securing stable markets and for reducing the costs of transactions.[33] One of the differences between the mass of short lived firms and those that experienced a longer life-span might have been the link between firms in the latter category and networks of family enterprises. To understand such relationships is one of the objects of continuing research. Another objective is to establish a more sophisticated method for understanding the demography of nineteenth century firms.

A final illustration serves to reinforce the point that the task of defining the birth and death of firms in the past will ever be complex. This is the case of the firm of R M Cameron, school board stationer and publisher of Edinburgh and Glasgow, which was owned by a Robert Cameron, was formed in 1873 and sequestered for bankruptcy in March 1882. The firm was closely connected with an earlier enterprise, engaged in a similar line of business, named McNiven and Cameron, in which Robert Cameron and his brother Duncan were partners. The firm was saved from total failure in 1882, partly as a result of the financial interventions of Cameron's sisters, the Misses Sarah and Catherine Cameron, stationers in Melrose. After 1882 the firm remained in Robert Cameron's hands, seemingly thriving, and from 1887 to 1891, the year at which this study ends, it came to be know as R M Cameron and Son.[34]

Footnotes

1. This paper is partly derived from work associated with a current ESRC funded research project entitled 'The family and the small firm: Edinburgh 1861 to 1891'. This project is the joint undertaking of S Nenadic, R J Morris and J Smyth in the Department of Economic and Social History, University of Edinburgh, and the financial assistance of the ESRC is gratefully acknowledged.
2. The pattern of firm entries shown in Figure 11.1 broadly coincides with pattern of company formations among Scottish limited liability firms, which in turn coincide with positive stages in the Scottish business cycle. See P Payne, *The early Scottish limited companies, 1856-1895*, (Edinburgh, 1980), p.20.
3. The most comprehensive study of the evolution of the book and paper trades in this period is F Barbier, 'Livre, économie et société industrielles en Allemagne et en France au XIX siècle (1840-1914)', (These Doctorat, Universite de Paris IV, 1986). I am grateful to Emmanuel Chadeau for this reference.
4. *Post Office Directory of Lancaster and vicinity* (1864); Topography and directory of Lancaster and sixteen miles round (Preston, 1881); Topography and directory of Lancaster, Morecombe, Carnforth and Milnthorpe (Preston, 1886); Lancaster, Morecombe and district directory (Lancaster, 1896, 1899 and 1901); History, topography and directory of Lancaster and district (Preston, 1912). The records of the firm of John and Christopher Hodgeson, joiners and builders in Whittington, which consist of day-by-day account of work undertaken between 1864 and 1914 with miscellaneous papers, are in the possession of the author.
5. See A D Chandler, 'Comparative business history', in D C Coleman and P Mathias, eds., *Enterprise and history* (Cambridge, 1984), pp.3-26; R Scase and R Goffee, *The real world of the small business owner* (Beckenham, 1987), p.24-27.
6. A concise, comparative account of the relationship between small and large firms is provided by M G Blackford, *The rise of modern business in Great Britain, the United States and Japan* (1988).
7. For a contemporary view see A Marshall, *Industry and trade: a study of industrial techniques and business organization* (1919). Recent accounts, sensitive

to the role of the small firm include P Payne, 'Family business in Britain: an historical and analytical survey', in A Okochi and S Yasuoka, eds., *Family business in the era of industrial growth: its ownership and management* (Tokyo , 1984), pp.171-206; also V Gattrell, 'Labour, power and the size of firms during the second quarter of the nineteenth century', *Economic History Review*, 2nd ser. XXX (1977), pp.95-139.

8. R Roger, 'Concentration and fragmentation: capital, labour and the structure of mid-Victorian Scottish industry.' *Journal of Urban History*, 14 (1988), pp.178-213.

9. Most of the Hodgeson workforce, though identifiable by name over long periods, was employed on a casual basis to undertake specific building contracts. See note 4 for details on the source.

10. CS318/39/32: Scottish Record Office, West Register House, Edinburgh.

11. CS318/29/63 – location as above.

12. CS318/39/49 – location as above.

13. Company name is not, in all cases, an accurate indicator of the structure of ownership. This point is elaborated in the final section of the paper. But given that most companies were young and recently formed, one reasonably might expect that their names be indicative of their ownership. Among those fourteen firms that encountered sequestration all but one were single proprietorships, and this despite the fact that two of these single proprietorships had business titles that suggested they were partnerships, and one the phrase '& Co' appended to the owners name.

14. D Bremner, *The industries of Scotland: their rise, progress and present condition* (Edinburgh, 1969, facsim reproduction of 1869 edition), p.502.

15. See W Chambers, *Memoir of Robert Chambers with autobiographical reminiscences of William Chambers* (Edinburgh, 1874); *Adam and Charles Black 1807 to 1957: some chapters in the history of a publishing house* (1957); M Oliphant, *Annals of a publishing house: William Blackwood and his sons* (Edinburgh, 1897)

16. Payne, *Scottish limited companies*, pp.34-38.

17. D Storey, R Watson and P Wynarczyk, *Fast growth small businesses: case studies of 40 small firms in North East England* (Research Paper No 67, Department of Employment, c.1989). I am grateful to David Storey for pointing out this parallel.

18. J M Samuels and P A Morrish, 'An analysis of concentration', in C Levicki, ed., *Small business: theory and policy* (1984) p.26

19. R Lloyd-Jones and A A Le Roux, 'Marshall and the birth and death of firms', *Business History*, 24 (1982), pp.141-155.

20. See discussion in Payne, *Scottish limited companies*, pp.96-104.

21. Some modern firms remain small by choice, see Scase and Goffee, *Real world*, p.163.
22. Roger, 'Concentration and fragmentation', p.187.
23. This assumes, of course, that in the past as in the present, most new firms began life as small. On this see M Binks and J Coyne, *The birth of enterprise: an analytical and empirical study of the growth of small firms* (1983) pp.18-20.
24. See reference 13 above. It should be noted that because of the advertising functions of trade lists, firms that engaged in a range of connected activities were listed several times under the different trade headings. It was possible, though with reservations (see discussion in the final part of the paper), to identify when an established firm had embarked on new activities.
25. Relative to the number of firms, business bankruptcy at any age was a rare phenomenon. Though concerned with an earlier period, J Hoppit, *Risk and failure in English business: 1700-1800* (Cambridge, 1987) provides an instructive account of the bankruptcy phenomenon.
26. Payne, *Scottish limited companies,* pp.23-24.
27. See reference 13.
28. A good illustration of such behaviour is given in 'The autobiography of an unsuccessful man by George W Muir', (1865), MS SR205427075, Mitchell Library, Glasgow.
29. See J M Scheid, 'The family business: remnant or elixier of the market economy', *German Yearbook on Business History 1985* (Berlin: 1986). The role of income stability is discussed in S Nenadic, 'The family and the small firm in late nineteenth century Britain' (unpublished paper presented to the 1989 pre-congress meeting of the A4 session, 'Structure and Strategy of Small and Medium Enterprise', of the 10th International Economic History Congress).
30. It should be noted that this issue is discussed in detail in Chapter 12, page 200.
31. See, S Nenadic, 'Record linkage and the exploration of nineteenth century social groups: a methodological perspective on the Glasgow middle class in 1861', *Urban History Yearbook* (1987) p.34.
32. CS318/25/65 location as in reference 10.
33. On transactions associated with family contracts see, Y Ben-Porath, 'The F-connection: families, friends and firms and the organisation of exchange', *Population and Development Review* 6 (1980), pp.1-30.
34. CS318/29/63 location as in reference 10.

12

Building by numbers: the lifecycle of Scottish building firms, 1793-1913

James Carroll, Nicholas J Morgan, Michael S Moss

Although much contemporary economic and management literature is devoted to theories of the firm and empirical analysis of individual enterprise, the firm and the entrepreneur as concepts have until recently received little attention from historians in the United Kingdom. There have been attempts to rank and list the largest companies by a variety of criteria, and to identify and examine the most successful businessmen, but such studies, useful as they are, have contributed little to the definition of the typical firm.[1] Likewise, histories of companies and collections of business archives are equally unrepresentative since they invariably relate to enterprises that have both survived for long periods and are relatively large. Sectoral studies[2], enquiries into bankruptcy returns[3], and investigations of limited liability registrations[4], approach the firm more directly, addressing historically such questions as typical capitalisation, life expectancy, modes of entry and exit, conditions for growth and failure, and the relationship of large enterprises to tiny concerns.

Some historians have claimed that it is an impossible task even to begin to calculate historical business populations in the United Kingdom. While this may be true nationally, it is demonstrably not true for businesses that require to be registered for the conduct of their trade; for example, with the Excise.[5] In most towns and cities in the United Kingdom, it is practical, if time consuming, to calculate the number of enterprises in operation at least for individual sectors from trade and general directories which were widely published from the late eighteenth century.[6] By the 1840s the compilers of those for the largest towns and cities had established systematic methods of gathering information annually from trade and other associations. Although there are inevitable doubts about the comprehensiveness and consistency of the information, directories contain the names and activities of more businesses than can be gleaned from any other source because the vast majority were (and are for that matter) sole traders or informal or formal partnerships.[7] To evaluate the utility of this approach for the study of the life-cycle of companies a pilot study was designed to investigate the building trades in Glasgow in the 1870s, based on an analysis of companies listed in the *Glasgow Post Office Directories*.[8]

The early 1870s witnessed an unprecedented boom in Glasgow's building industry which was abruptly terminated by the depression of 1877 and the crash of the City of Glasgow Bank in 1878. Between 1872 and 1878 the City's Dean of Guild Court[9] approved plans for some 25,179 new houses (the majority contained in tenements); at the same time large areas of congested housing in the city centre were cleared by a combination of local authority initiative and private enterprise. As a result of this phrenetic activity by 1881 the city contained 19,957 residential properties and 119,166 houses, increases since 1861 of 18 per cent and 37 per cent respectively.[10] These new buildings were provided partly by a surge of new companies which were formed with rapid succession, much to the dismay of informed contemporaries: 'It must be remembered', said the prominent ex-builder and property valuator Thomas Binnie, 'that the years 1872-1875 were years of excessive speculation in the building trade. Never before nor since has speculation run so high.' 9 The easy availability of capital, particularly from building societies, was alleged to be one of the principal causes for promoting new building firms and projects: 'they began to advance the money as soon as the first joists were on, and continued to advance in proportion as the building proceeded, but that system spelled ruin in very large letters . . .' Unparalleled opportunities existed for company formation during these years: 'these building societies advanced money to an enormous extent, and on the most reckless terms, to builders who were absolutely penniless, or very nearly so. I have known a man starting a building which would cost him £5,000, and all he had in the world was £70, and yet he managed to build and finish it. At the same time these opportunities for enterprise were matched by pitfalls for the unwary or unfortunate: 'he failed of course' concluded Binnie's story, 'in the end.'[11]

As a first step in the research all the names of the firms and individuals listed under the main headings involving construction in the trades directory were entered into a simply structured dataset: these included builders, contractors, gasfitters, glaziers, masons, painters and paperhangers, plasterers, plumbers, slaters, and wrights and joiners.[12] These were cross-referenced with the personal directory, where job descriptions, business address, and home address, if different from the business address, are to be found. This information was also abstracted and entered into the dataset. Not surprisingly, there was duplication between headings, with a few firms listed four times. Altogether, however this first survey identified 1,353 firms and individuals as being engaged in these trades in 1875.

On further scrutiny, 130 of these firms were discovered to have nothing to do with the building trades. The category that contained the majority of unrelated businesses was contractors, which included such disparate activities as cartage contractors, cowfeeders and contractors, steamship brokers and contractors, coal merchants and contractors, and even J Defries & Sons, 'contractors for fêtes and rejoicings'. The intrusions into the other categories of extraneous occupations was far less pronounced and included such activities as hot house builders and unspecified engineers. All the obviously non-building enterprises were deleted from the dataset. However, where there was any doubt the entry was allowed to stand, as in the case of 'wright and vat builder', or 'shipwright and joiner', on the grounds that there is a probability from the job descriptions that they were involved in building. Similarly firms whose addresses were outside the city of Glasgow (for example in Argyllshire or Ayrshire) were also removed, as were offices for large contracting firms whose headquarters lay elsewhere (for example the London based public works contractor Thomas Brassey). The resulting population comprised 1,206 firms.

The question remains as to how representative this number of firms is of the total involved in building activity in the city at the time. The Directories themselves provide some reassurance on this point, despite the fact that the Preface to the 1872 Directory offered an apologia for the fact that it was 'neither an official nor perfectly got up work'. First published in 1828 the Glasgow Post Office Directories were compiled annually by officials at the

City Post Office. The new Post Office Directory usurped the position occupied by McFeat's Glasgow Directory (published between 1799 and 1828) which solicited entries through the local press. Fees were not charged for entries in either Directory, so barriers to inclusion were limited. Information for the new Directory was obtained through the issue by the Post Office of a preliminary circular asking the public to supply the required information, subsequently the 'upmost care and attention' was 'exerted to procure authentic information' by checking and seeking out confirmation on business from local trade organisations and societies. 'In a work so minute in detail and as a whole of such magnitude it is pleasing to reflect how few complaints of errors inadvertently committed have been bought under the notice of the publishers' wrote the editor in 1854. The Directory was demonstrably responsive to change; its expanding bulk (and the sporadic increase in cost to would be purchasers: 'the annual increasing size of the volume has been attended with great added expenditure') pays testimony to the increasing numbers of businesses and individuals listed in its pages in the nineteenth century. The editors of the volume for 1877-78 were disingenuous when they claimed 'they can with confidence recommend it as a safe and correct guide to the business places and private residences of the principal inhabitants' for there were few business of any size that were not included within its pages. Nor did the banking catastrophe that year go unnoticed by a publication whose *raison d'être* had previously lain in annually enlarging its size; the editor of the Directory for 1878-79 noted the difficulties in accurate compilation, complaining of 'the removals this year being more numerous than usual'.

Company titles are not a foolproof means of describing the nature of a particular firm. Nonetheless the names taken from the Directory tell us something about the typical unit of enterprise. Perhaps not surprisingly only two of these businesses were limited liability companies. Few firms in the sector took advantage of limited liability until the early twentieth century; as the scale of businesses grew in the inter-war years so the limited company slowly became a common form of organisation. This apparent lack of sophistication in structure should not however blind historians to the importance of the industry, which probably accounted for 'a larger share of total investment than any single industry'[15] both within Glasgow (where it stood at the fulcrum of a complex and to the historian largely impenetrable informal capital market), Scotland, and the United Kingdom as a whole.

Although another sixty-four firms of the total population added the epithet '& Co' to their names, and 209 involved a combination of either individual's surnames or forenames, indicating the possibility of some type of formal partnership, it seems likely that the overwhelming form of enterprise was the individual or family firm: 57 firms used the title '& Sons' or '& Son', four incorporated the phrase 'Brothers'. The remainder were simply named after an individual, presumably in most cases the sole owner. Nine businesses were identified as being owned by women, very probably widows. Five firms indicated in a directory entry that the business was in the hands of a manager; two of these were the limited companies already mentioned, Frederick Braby & Co Ltd,[16] the Glasgow Working Men's Investment & Building Society Ltd (which had been deliberately listed as a building firm) and a third the Associated Joiners Building Company, a syndicate managed by the successful mason and builder John Morrison, later a partner in the public works contracting firm of Morrison & Mason Ltd. Of these firms only a handful (79) listed an identical workplace and home address, suggesting at least some separation of work and domestic life. Builder's premises were often little more than a shed in a tenement back-court containing perishable goods, and yard-space allowing for storage of larger items. Proximity to the workplace was crucial. Plant and materials were usually stored on site, although the nature of the industry tended to dictate that there was little buying ahead of materials, and thus little need for extensive storage space.

As we have seen many of the firms in the dataset claimed a number of trades. In order to classify them more closely a crude method was adopted of taking the first or main trade entry as representing the major activity of the firm.[17] An analysis of these is presented in Figure 12.1. General builders dominated the industry, accounting for nearly 23 per cent of all firms, with wrights and joiners accounting for 18 per cent. Clearly these simple classifications hide a wide variety of types and sizes of business, ranging from that of Thomas Binnie (a successful builder with substantial property interests, and the centre of a family network of building and property professionals) or Alexander Eadie (who despite a sequestration (bankruptcy) in 1879 recovered to be a leading builder and property owner, with a rental from residential property in the city by 1881 of nearly £3,000) to men like the unfortunate William Laught. Laught began business as a wright in 1865 (his first Directory entry was in 1867-68, listed as a joined and cabinetmaker) with a capital of £50, turning to tenement building in 1873 with an accrued stock of £150. His ventures were uniformly unsuccessful, and he was sequestrated in 1878.[18] If men like Laught and Binnie were streets apart in terms of scale of enterprise, capital and business respectability, then similar divisions can be anticipated in all those major areas of activity measured so precisely in Figure 12.1.

The simple analysis by activity of the 1206 firms identified in the 1875

Figure 12.1

Companies in the building industry in Glasgow, 1875, by major activity (source: Glasgow Post Office Directories).

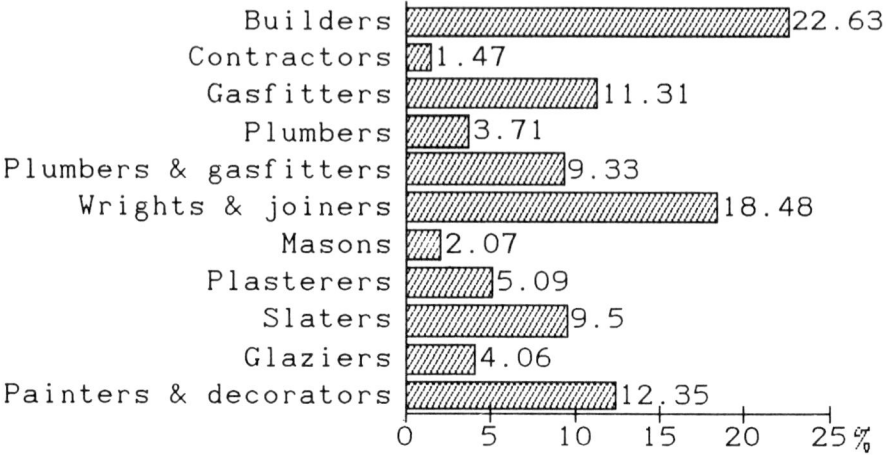

Directory takes us little further in an examination of the lifecycle of building firms. In order to give a dynamic view to the data the Directories were used to trace dates of birth of the firms listed as still active in 1875. The painstaking and time consuming task of tracing the foundation date of each firm[19] has produced data for all but 56 firms, where some ambiguities remain to be resolved. The certain identification of an individual firm is complicated by changes of address and job description. Even firms with relatively short lives were found to have changed address several times. For example, John Duncanson who was in business in Raglan Street in 1875, had moved twice since he started his enterprise in 1859. Since the dataset also included home address, which rarely changed at the same time as the business address, it was possible to achieve a high degree of correlation over time.[20] In seeking the origin of an enterprise, it was assumed that if & Son or & Co was added to the name, it was the same firm, but if a new partner was introduced by name, then it was a new firm. For example, Shirra & Black, blacksmiths in Main Street and Hope Street in 1875, began trading under that name in 1869, although John Shirra had previously been trading at the same address. It is conceivable that John Shirra was financially embarrassed in 1869 and had to take a partner to remain in business, or, on the other hand, Mr. Black could have been his son-in-law, or a trusted manager coming into the firm to assist an ageing principal. Nonetheless for the purpose of the present pilot study the birth of Shirra & Black was recorded as 1869, rather than the earlier date

Figure 12.2

Companies in the building industry in Glasgow, 1875, by year of foundation and major area of activity
(source: Glasgow Post Office Directories).

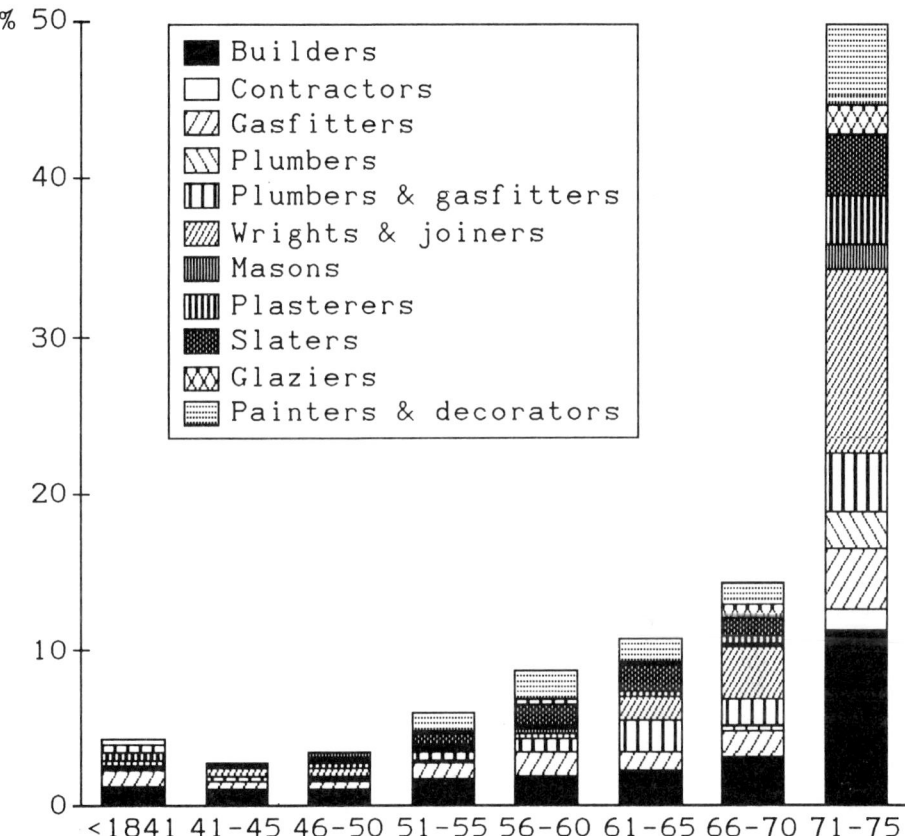

of John Shirra's entry to business. The exclusion of such firms was an arbitrary decision designed in part to compensate for changes in the ownership of a firm (either by outright sale or the introduction of new partners) without any alteration in name.[21] As we have seen from the case of William Laught, cited above, the Directory may (through no fault of its own) lag slightly behind company formation; it remains however the only source for this type of detailed research.

The dates of foundation of those companies active in 1875 is shown in Figure 12.2. Marginally less than 50 per cent. of all companies had been

Figure 12.3

Companies in the building industry in Glasgow, 1875, by age (source: Glasgow Post Office Directories).

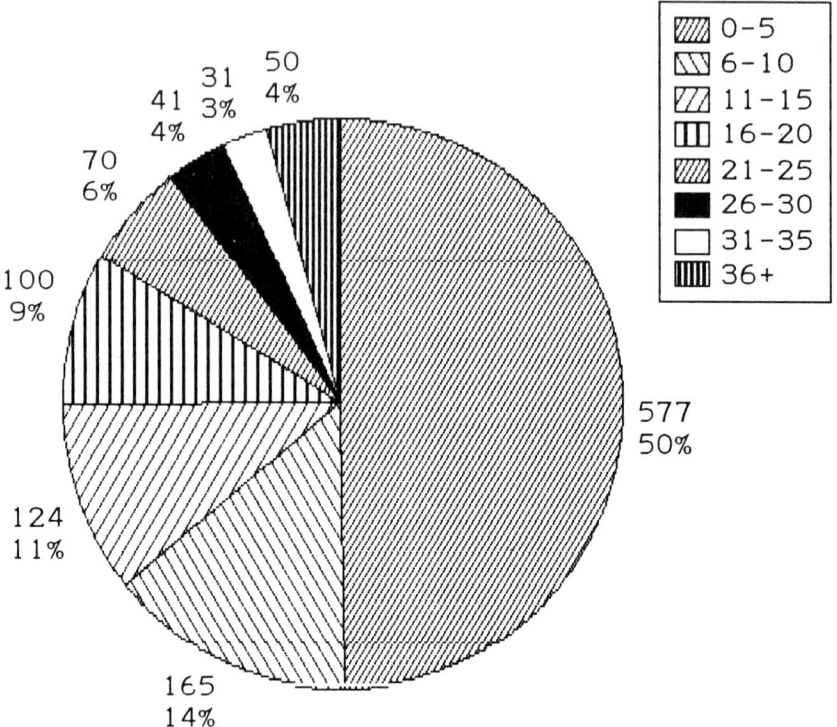

established in the years 1871-75. Prominent among these young firms were builders (49 per cent of whom were five years old or less), plasterers (59 per cent) plumbers (62 per cent) wrights and joiners (63 per cent) and masons (75 per cent). Areas of activity exhibiting some degree of longevity were plumbers and gasfitters, gasfitters, slaters and paperhangers and painters. Slightly over 10 per cent of the firms had been formed before 1850, and were thus more than 25 years old (a breakdown of age cohorts is provided in Figure 12.3). The mean age of all firms active in 1875 was 10.2 years, considerably less than the 16 years identified for dissolved Scottish limited liability firms by Peter Payne.[22] Of the individual areas of activity gasfitters were the longest lived of the live population in 1875, at 14.9 years, glaziers at 11.8 and builders at 10.7. Perhaps surprisingly give the masonic tradition the shortest lived of all companies were masons, with a mean age of 4.6.

Clearly the ages so far discussed do not approximate to lives. In order to gain a clear insight into the lifecycle of firms end dates are currently being amassed from the Directories for the 1875 population, to match the birth dates already obtained. As a starting point for this work the population for 1875 was compared with the population for 1879-80, the year after 'two thirds of Glasgow's builders went to the wall'[23] following the depression of 1877 and the crash of the City of Glasgow Bank in 1878, and the year in which the Directory's editor complained of so many 'removals'. In addition the names of all those firms in the 1875 population were checked against names held in the Glasgow University Sequestrations database, which has now been expanded to included the names addresses and dates of bankruptcy of all those involved in sequestration processes or cessio petitions between 1875 and 1885.[24] In all 337 companies were missing from the 1879 cohort, representing 28 per cent of the 1875 population, but significantly less than the two-thirds cited by Rodger on the basis of contemporary hearsay. In addition a further 116 firms in the population were listed as having been sequestrated or subject to *cessio* proceedings since 1875; some had gone bankrupt prior to 1878, others had done so and nonetheless continued in business, others became bankrupt much later in the century. However only 40 of the 337 missing companies in 1878-79 were accounted for by bankruptcy proceedings, making up only 11 per cent of the failures since 1875. Although a time lag might account for premature removal from the Directory prior to the notification of bankruptcy proceedings in the *Edinburgh Gazette* (which argues for an astonishingly accurate Directory), it seems safe to assume from this that formal bankruptcy was negligible in its impact on business failure in this sector.

Under the old common law in Scotland, a person who failed to pay his debts was treated as a criminal if he allowed letters of diligence against him to expire without meeting his creditors' claims; he was deprived of all civil rights and subject to perpetual imprisonment unless the creditor relented or friends came to his relief.[25] The chief remedy available to an honest debtor under common law, known as *cessio bonorum*, allowed the debtor to obtain personal protection from imprisonment by surrendering his estate to his creditors. The main disadvantage was that it was not binding on creditors who were not cited in the process and it was impossible for the debtor to be discharged from his debts. In 1772 the Bankruptcy Act provided that, upon petition of any creditor of a bankrupt debtor, the Court of Session (Scotland's central court in Edinburgh) would award a general sequestration on arrestment of the bankrupt's moveable estate which would be conveyed to a factor chosen by the creditors for management and recovery on behalf of all the creditors. This Act was amended in 1782 and restricted to merchants, traders and manufacturers. Notices of sequestration and cessio processes were published in the *Edinburgh Gazette* from 1795. It has been assumed that these provide a complete list of all processes.[26] Recent referencing of sequestration processes by the Scottish Record Office has revealed that there is a disparity between the *Gazette* listings and the number of actual processes, accounting for some five per cent. The legislation was improved in 1814 allowing for the discharge of bankrupts.

Under the Bankruptcy (Scotland) Act 1856 sequestration was applicable to all debtors, whether engaged in trade or not and concurrent jurisdiction to award it was conferred on the Sheriffs (responsible for the administration of local courts in Scotland) in the case of all debtors domiciled or carrying on business for certain periods within their respective Sheriffdoms. Provision was also made for annulling of a sequestration and winding up a bankrupt's estate by deed of arrangement on the resolution of a certain majority of creditors, either at the meeting for the election of the trustee (factor) to administer the bankrupt's estate or at any subsequent meeting called for the purpose. By making sequestration available in Sheriff Courts, this Act rendered the old *cessio bonorum* provision practically obsolete. The process had been remodelled by the Cessio Act of 1836 (amended by the Sheriff Courts Act of 1876) enabling creditors to compel a bankrupt debtor to grant a disposition of his whole estate. Although it provided a cheap means of winding up small estates, there continued to be no provision for the discharge of a bankrupt under the *cessio* procedure until the passing of the Bankruptcy and Cessio Act in 1881. Under this Act, in either a *cessio* or a sequestration process, a bankrupt could only obtain a discharge if a dividend of five shillings in the pound had been paid on his debts or the Court was satisfied that failure to pay arose from circumstances beyond his control. R G Rodger, attributed the higher rate of *cessio* to sequestrations in the building trade in the decade 1879-1889 to the 'adverse financial climate in Scotland', ignoring completely this fundamental reform of the legislative framework.[27] The *cessio* statistics for Glasgow in the years prior to 1880 which have been used to measure the 'incidence of failure amongst small building firms', suggest that the frequency was falling. The disappearance of one-third of the firms in existence in 1875 from the directory by 1879, raises questions about this conclusion.

Recourse to the courts was the final, and often reluctant, act of hard-pressed creditors or the debtor himself. In the majority of cases, a private settlement or composition was reached, usually designed to allow the debtor to continue in business. After 1859 it was possible for such compositions to be made at the first meeting of creditors, providing a majority representing three-quarters of the liabilities voted in favour. The process was then aborted. No doubt many of these compositions can be traced through locating started processes, but many others were 'confidential' agreements, designed to avoid embarrassment and loss of business reputation for creditors as well as debtors. This point is illustrated by the case of William Neilson, a builder in Glasgow with extensive interests in the City's fashionable West End, who was sequestrated in 1857. However, during his formal interrogation before his trustees Neilson confessed that 'in the year 1854, and about the beginning of October, I found myself embarrassed and was obliged to suspend payments . . . I arranged a private settlement with my creditors by agreeing to pay a composition of 6 shillings in the pound'.[28] In Neilson's case we only know about the 1854 incident because a few creditors were owed so much that it was in their interests to restart his business, leading to the failure of 1857. Apart from financial misfortune the papers reveal that the main reason for the formal sequestration in 1857 was that a number of the creditors believed Neilson had been making partial settlement with selected parties. Had it not been for this it is likely that another 'private agreement' would have ensued. In a business environment that depended on complex hierarchies of capital networks bankruptcy in the public mind was akin to an infection moving through the miasma, likely to infect all those with whom it came into contact. This handicap, coupled with changes in the legislative framework, make it almost impossible to compare bankruptcy figures over time in the nineteenth century. However, the very large incidence of sequestrations in 1879 revealed when a database of this source was compiled at Glasgow University Archives, confirms contemporary impressions of the severity of the recession.

An analysis of those firms not active in 1878-9 shows that there were significant differences between those firms that simply disappeared from the Directories without apparent recourse to legal proceedings, and those which were subject to the law. Figure 12.4 shows the firms by year of foundation and reason for exit, Figure 12.5 shows bankrupt and failed companies by main sector of activity. The latter shows that builders dominated bankruptcies, followed by a smaller number of wrights and joiners. These were the firms most involved in the complex credit networks which financed building operations that were disturbed by the recession and shaken (in confidence, if not substance) by the 1878 crash. Whilst builders were also prominent among failure the leading group were wrights and joiners, those trades allegedly most able to shift between paid work in, for example, shipyards, and independent business activity. Painters, plumbers and gasfitters were involved in activities where, unlike large scale building, capital requirements were

Figure 12.4

*Companies in the building industry in Glasgow, 1875,
not active in 1879, by year of foundation
(source: Glasgow Post Office Directories & Sequestrations database).*

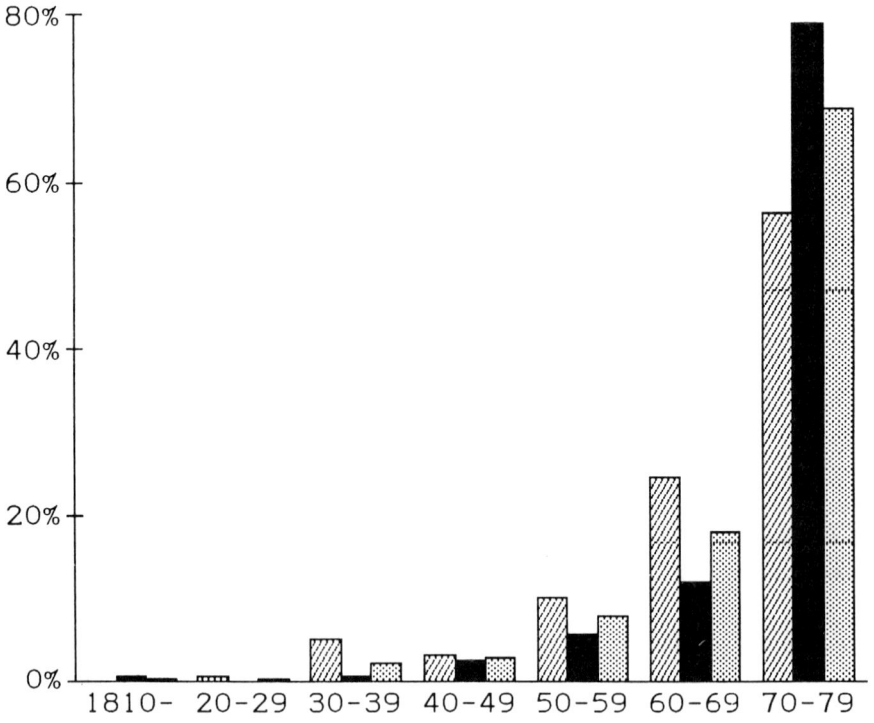

limited, and opportunities for employment in maintenance work during recession considerable.

The birth date of those companies inactive in 1879 are given in Figure 12.4, showing the percentages of all inactive companies, of all bankrupt companies, and all failed companies, by decade of birth. Seventy three per cent of all the firms were formed between 1870 and 1875; 56 per cent of

Figure 12.5

Companies in the building industry in Glasgow, 1875, not active in 1879, by major activity (source: Glasgow Post Office Directories & Sequestrations database).

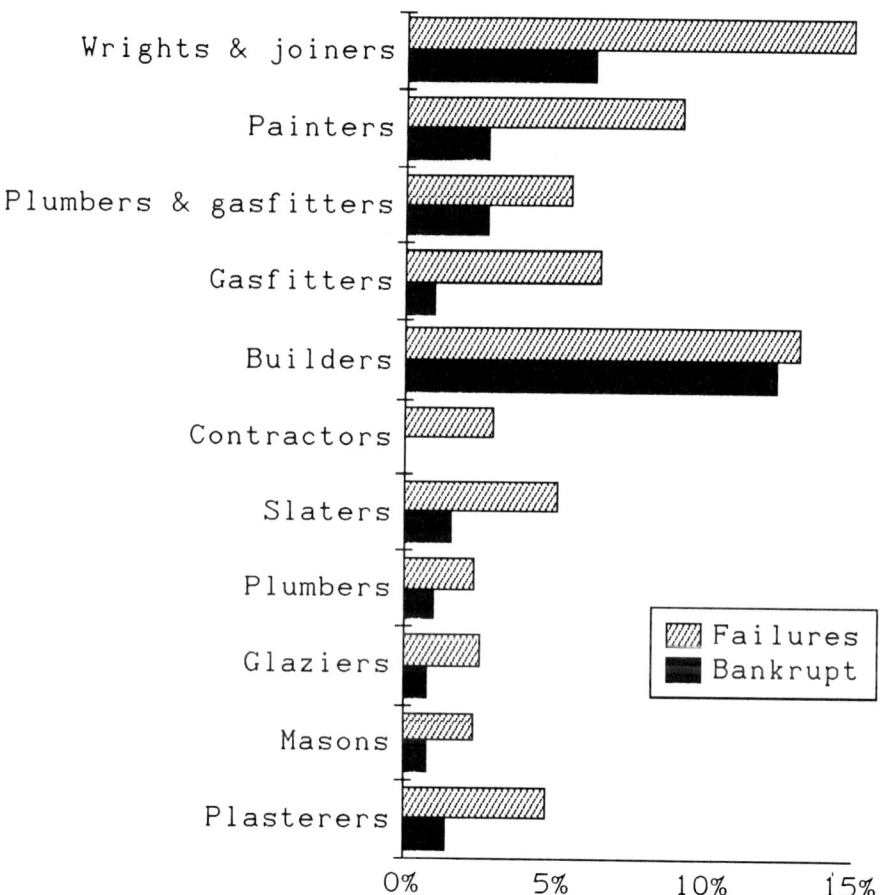

bankrupt companies fell into this category, as opposed to 79 per cent of failed companies. Data for this table (presented in Table 12.1) shows that sequestrated firms had a mean age of 13 years; the failures had an mean age of only 8.7 years (calculated by giving each firm a notional end-date of 1877). Clearly comparisons of mean age at life for the total population (10.2 years) and mean age at death can be misleading, but nonetheless the clear inference on the basis of the data currently collected must be that sequestrated companies were older than the norm; failed or aborted companies younger. This leads to the suggestion that far from being representative bankruptcies (at whatever scale) were not typical of business failures, either in terms of age, numbers, or (as has been suggested elsewhere, for example by Rodger) in terms of the scale or size of the company. Indeed it was probably a consequence of the abnormal size of these enterprises that abnormal methods had to be devised to deal with their demise. Moreover even from our limited survey it is clear that bankruptcy, although an indication perhaps of failed management, does not accurately indicate failed firms: 26 builders who had gone bankrupt between 1875 and 1878 had resumed business by 1879 under their previous titles. Bankruptcies might be regarded as aberrants in a business lifecycle where births and deaths were carried out without the intervention of skilled practitioners, and where recourse to drastic surgery was rare, and frequently (but not always) fatal. Their use as an indicator of typical business activity in the nineteenth century, and more so of the typical lifecycle of the typical nineteenth century firm, is negligible.

Conclusions

The results so far obtained from this pilot study confirm that Directories can provide a reliable source for the reconstruction of entire business populations in specified sectors. We have demonstrated that from this it is further possible to examine the births, deaths, and lifecycles of firms at a level of detail sometimes claimed as impossible in the United Kingdom. It appears that within the building trades at least individual firms were likely to have a lifespan of around ten years, confirming the generally high rate of turnover supposed for this sector, but also suggesting greater longevity than had previously been assumed. Although failed firms had a mean life of eight years the crucial time for survival appears to have been the first five. One area for future research is to examine Valuation Rolls (property registers) and the Register of Sasines (which details land transfers and mortgages)[29] to discover what distinctive strategies (if any) were adopted by long-lived firms to ensure survival. Bankruptcies accounted for only a small proportion of failed firms in the total population; their relative insignificance, the distinctive characteristics of bankrupt firms, and the fact that bankruptcy did not equate with company death, leads to the suggestion that their usefulness as a source for examining the lifecycles of companies must be questioned.

Footnotes

1. See for example Peter L Payne, 'The emergence of the large-scale company

in Great Britain 1870-1914', *Economic History Review*, 20, (1967), and C Shaw, 'The large manufacturing employers of 1907', *Business History*, 25, (1983); Peter Wardley, 'Big business in the twentieth century', Cologne Computer Conference, *Volume of abstracts*, Cologne, 1988, A5-9.

2. For example, Neston Evans, *The East Anglia Linen Industry – Rural Industry and Local Economy 1500-1850*, Gower, Aldershot, 1985.

3. Julian Hoppit, *Risk and Failure in English Business 1700-1800*, Cambridge University Press, 1987.

4. H A Shannon, 'The first five thousand limited companies and their duration', *Economic History*, II (1932), A Essex-Crosby, *Joint Stock Companies in Great Britain 1890-1930*, (University of London: unpublished M Comm Thesis, 1937), and Peter L. Payne, *The Early Scottish Limited Companies 1856-1895*, Edinburgh 1980.

5. For example returns of licensed or entered distilleries in the United Kingdom were regularly made to Parliament, see Michael S Moss and John R Hume, *The Making of Scotch Whisky – A History of the Scotch Whisky Distilling Industry*, Edinburgh, 1981.

6. Julian Hoppit, *op cit*, pp.64-65, 81-82, made calculations from these sources for business populations in Liverpool and Manchester from the 1760s to 1800.

7. The veracity of local directories as a source is discussed in G Shaw, 'The context and reliability of nineteenth century trade directories', *Local Historian*, 13 (1979), and P J Corfield and S M Kelly, '.Giving directions to the towns", the early town directorys', *Urban History Yearbook* (1984).

8. Although Julian Hoppit *op.cit.* counted business populations, he did not seek to link cohorts of bankrupts to entries in directories, because his study was confined to bankruptcy legally defined.

9. The Court was responsible for approving all building operations within the city; a substantial archive of building applications and plans submitted to the Court for the second half of the nineteenth century is held in the Strathclyde Regional Archives, Glasgow. A unique survival of Scottish medieval burgh courts, the Dean of Guild Courts have been described as 'the precursors of modern town planning': R G Rodger, 'The evolution of Scottish town planning' in George Gordon and Brian Dicks (ed), *Scottish Urban History*, Aberdeen, 1983, p.87. See also Andrew Jackson, *Glasgow Dean of Guild Court: a history*, Glasgow, 1983.

10. William Fraser, 'Fluctuations of the building trade and Glasgow's house accommodation', *Proceedings of the Royal Philosophical Society of Glasgow*, 39(1908), pp.30-31, table 4; Nicholas J Morgan, 'Property-ownership in Victorian and Edwardian Glasgow' (ESRC report *D00232126*).

11. Glasgow Municipal Commission on the Housing of the Poor, *Minutes of Evidence*, (Glasgow 1906), qq.6458, 6631, 6962.
12. This work was painstakingly carried out by James Carroll, a volunteer researcher in the Department of Scottish History and University Archives.
13. The Glasgow Post Office Directory Association Limited, *Glasgow a hundred years ago: an illustrated souvenir of the one hundredth issue of the Post Office Glasgow Directory*, (Glasgow 1927): *Glasgow Herald*, 16 May 1828, 23 June 1828; *Glasgow Post Office Directory*, Prefaces, 1850-51, 1852-53, 1854-55, 1877-78, 1878-79.
14. At this time there were only 444 limited liability companies registered in Scotland. The number did not exceed 1,300 until 1892; Peter L Payne, *Early Scottish limited liability companies*, p.32. Payne appears to have discovered no construction companies in his survey, although a number of development and property investment companies with a tangential involvement in building are included.
15. M J Daunton, *House and home in the Victorian city*, London, 1983, p.91.
16. It should be possible to trace partnerships in the Register of Deeds, for which see John Imrie, 'National archive sources for business history' in P L Payne (ed), *Studies in Scottish business history*, London, 1967, p.8.
17. This method of classification was used by Richard Rodger in his study of bankruptcies in the Scottish building industry: Richard G Rodger, 'Business failure in Scotland 1839-1913', *Business History*, 27 (1985), p.78.
18. Scottish Record Office, CS 318/24/219, Sequestration papers of William Laught.
19. This work was carried out by Eilean Malden, an expert in the use of Post Office directories, to whom we are deeply indebted.
20. The authors are sceptical that change of address can be used as surrogate for business expansion. Moving could just as well reflect movement to areas of building activity or displacement within the city during what was, as we have seen, a period of extensive redevelopment.
21. It is possible to trace such changes in partnership from the *Edinburgh Gazette* but the printed notices provide no details as to the reasons or the division of the capital. The causes can sometimes be deduced from concurrent sequestrations or *cessio bonorum* processes. See, for example, I F Russell, *Sir Robert McAlpine & Son*, Carnforth, 1988, p.4-43.
22. Peter L Payne, *Early Scottish limited liability companies*, p.101, table 23.
23. Richard G Rodger, 'Business failure . . . 1913', *op cit*, p.91.
24. We have used the term bankruptcy here simply to denote a business failure that resulted in some form of legal process. The database is described in

M S Moss and J R Hume, 'Business failure in Scotland, 1839-1913: a research note', *Business History*, 25 (1983).

25. This section is based on John McLintock, *An Introduction to the law of bankruptcy relating to Sequestrations,* available from the Scottish Record Office, HM General Register House, Edinburgh EH1 3YY, where the processes relating to sequestrations are held. John McLintock helped in the compilation of the sequestration database 1795-1914 at Glasgow University Archives and has continued to work on this source at the Scottish Record Office. See also William Wallace, *The Law of Bankruptcy in Scotland,* Edinburgh, 2nd ed, 1914, and Henry Goudy (fourth edition by T A Fyfe), *A Treatise on the Law of Bankruptcy in Scotland,* Edinburgh, 1914.

26. Richard G Rodger, 'Business failure . . . 1913', *op.cit.,* p.78.

27. Richard G Rodger, 'Business failure . . . 1913', *op.cit.,* p.91. This argument is nicely borne out, and the technical process illustrated, in the following letter to William Macdonald, dated Glasgow, 7th February 1882 'I regret that owing to your unexpected departure without communicating with your creditors & in order to prevent certain of them from selling off your effects, sequestration of your estates had to be applied for. This is a very expensive mode of winding up an estate, and, had you remained here, the matter could best have been settled under a Trust Deed. Now that I am able to communicate with you, it has occurred to me that this course should yet be adopted in order to save unnecessary expense. Under a Trust Deed the goods will be disposed of, the debits collected, and your creditors paid out of the proceeds, just as in the sequestration; but without heavy expense attending the latter mode of procedure. Some of the creditors have been saying, I believe, that they consider my late father, of whose death you have no doubt heard, to have been liable as a sleeping partner in the business. My Father's Trustees, however, while making no admission of liability, are willing, if you sign this Trust Deed, in order to save expense, further trouble and possible litigation, to come forward & arrange as best they can with your trade creditors for any balances that may remain due to them after the estate has been realised and a dividend paid. The effect of this will be that you will be fully discharged of these debts & they cannot again come up against you. As this seems to me to be clearly the best arrangement for you, I have had a Trust Deed made out in favour of Mr. Hector Ross of the Commercial Bank, Alness, & I send it herewith that you may sign it before two witnesses, & in terms of the accompanying printed directions. Please return the Deed to me signed, with the particulars required by the printed slip filled in, in course of post, so that I may have time to stop the sequestration. You may rely upon it that you can communicate with me with perfect freedom, & that the course I have asked you to take is the best for your interests. University of Glasgow Archives, UGD 224/12/3, p.18.

28. Scottish Record Office, CS 318/3/230, Sequestration papers of William Neilson.
29. Richard G Rodger & Jennifer Newman, 'Property transfers and the Register of Sasines', *Urban History Yearbook*, (1988).

13

Formation and Transformation of Sociétés:

The case of the French public works industry 1914–1939

Dominique Barjot

Since the beginning of the 1980s when the group 'Demography of Enterprises in France in the nineteenth century,[1] was formed, our knowledge of the pattern of formation and closure of firms has progressed a good deal; witness the recent article by Philippe Jobert and Jean-Claude Chevailler on this topic.[2] Because of the available sources, research has been conducted either into the French economy in its entirety[3] or, and more frequently, into one region,[4] such is the case for the principal research programme currently in progress.[5]

However, it does not seem altogether impossible to approach the problem from a sectoral perspective as in the example of the French public works industry.⁶ During the First World War, but also for nearly all the inter-war years, the industry encountered grave difficulties, posing the question, what effects did such circumstances have on the development of the legal status adopted by public firms. To provide an answer, two approaches have to be combined: the first, at a meso-economic level, with the object of producing a rough evaluation of the formation of *sociétés;* the second at a micro-economic level limited to an examination of the firms which played a dominant role.⁷

The Meso-economic approach, An Overview of the whole

The meso-economic approach is based on the use of the directories of the *Syndicat professional das entrepreneurs de travaux publics de France* (professional association of public works' contractors). These list between 1914 and 1938 all the *sociétés* in public works and associated trades formed each year. Even after eliminating firms engaged in related industries (building, the supply of building materials, and the production and distribution of electricity), there are problems in using the data derived from this source. Since the years 1914 and 1915 are characterised by a manifest lack of registrations, the study only really begins in 1916. Until the year 1920 inclusive, the directories do not record previously the form of the *société* other than for the *sociétés anonymes*: differentiation by individual category of *société* is then only possible from the beginning of 1921.

Moreover, no information survives for 1939, the outbreak of the Second World War having prevented the Syndicate from undertaking the work of compiling the directory. This deficiency is all the more regrettable because, for public works contractors, 1939 marks a net recovery in the expansion of formations. This gap can be partially filled as data only survives for *sociétés*. If there are widespread difficulties in studying the birth of all firms, they become more acute in an investigation of public works contractors, a sector which was little capitalized and where it is relatively easy as a single man to launch into business. The sources used in this study pose one final difficulty: they only indicate the declared (nominal) capital and not the capital actually subscribed. The analysis, as a result, reflects more the intentions of the founders or the economic climate in which they acted than real movements in investments.

These imperfections do not detract from the interest of the data abstracted from the directories. Indeed, the *Syndicat des entrepreneurs de France* represented in the inter-war years around 25 per cent of the total strength of the sector, and in the neighbourhood of 45 per cent of related businesses.⁸ Professional researchers have been aware for at least the last twenty years that the directories contain useful information about the provenance of firms,

providing the following indicators:
1) The objects of the business
2) The address of the registered office
3) Capital
4) Duration of the articles of association
5) predominant technical speciality
6) Articles of association
   - date
   - an indication of the terms of the eventual deed
7) In the case of *Société Anonyme*, names, forenames addresses of the administrators distinguished by those who are directors in enterprises with *SARL* status and those who were partners in an unlimited partnerships
8) Date of publication of the articles of association

Fluctuations in the pattern of formations

The pattern of formations can be viewed in three distinct phases. Between 1916 and 1922 there was a veritable explosion: although it is true the number of *sociétés* fell heavily during the conflict – in the seven years as a whole the total multiplied by more than twenty. This is explained not only by a simple phenomena of recovery but also because of optimism deriving from the excellent prospects in the reconstruction in the North East region of France. Furthermore, the amount of capital (expressed in francs of 1913) invested each year by the founders of new *sociétés* tripled in the course of this first period. In examining the very important growth in the number of *sociétés*, the average size of these *sociétés* measured by capital decreased, largely because the boom persuaded many single partnerships to adopt *société* status. From 1923 to 1932 the number of sociétés established each year, subsided fairly rapidly, stabilizing around a mean of 120 to 150. By contrast, from the beginning of 1932 until 1938, the number collapsed spectacularly.[9]

This pattern of development mirrors in an imperfect manner that of the demand from public works in the metropolis.[10] Measured in constant francs, only a slight positive correlation can be discerned between the number of *sociétés* formed each year and the number of public projects in the metropolis. The correlation becomes even worse if one compares the market for public works with the registered capital of the *sociétés*.[11] Financial conditions play a predominant role. There is an excellent correlation between the number of formations of *sociétés* and the amount of capital invested.[12] During the first period registrations were more numerous because promoters of *sociétés* found it relatively easy to lay their hands on the funds they required. The available finance fell rapidly during the 1930s, particularly from the end of the

Reconstruction. Although the total capital raised was very significant from 1930 to 1933, it never recovered when measured in constant francs to the mean of the years 1918-1924. From the beginning of 1934 there was a dramatic collapse: between that date and 1938 the total registered capital of new *sociétés* was slashed by a factor of a hundred measured in constant francs. Consequently, public works contracting can be numbered as one of the most precarious trades of the inter-war depression.

Irresistible increase in the capital of *sociétés*

Worsening financial conditions favoured the development of limited liability.[13] Between the two wars, in public works contracting, *sociétés de capitaux* were definitely preferred to *sociétés de personnes*. From 1921 to 1938 these represent an average scarcely more than a quarter of *sociétés* formed and only a small proportion of the total capital invested. This decline was due entirely to financial causes. In fact, the percentage of *commandites simples* and *sociétés en nom collectif* out of all *sociétés* formed each year remained more or less the same, but the relative proportion of capital fell sharply from 9 per cent to 5.5 per cent between 1921 and 1933. During the second half of the 1930s they did better, only because the formation of SA fell to a very low level. These *sociétés de personnes* did not yield much profit seeing that between 1921 and 1938 the average level of capital raised fell to a fortieth of its level at the beginning of the period.

The decline in *sociétés de personnes* benefited *sociétés anonymes* – (SA). These experienced a remarkable increase from the First World War; between 1916 and 1918 they represented roughly half all new *sociétés* and accounted for four-fifths of the capital invested. The movement persisted during the Reconstruction despite a recovery in interest in *commandite par actions* evident between 1921 and 1924. Even during these years the SA continued to mop up nearly three-quarters of all the funds invested in new *sociétés*. From the outset of 1925 by comparison, the situation changed appreciably to the advantage of the *commandite par actions*, which, until 1929, remained the most popular form of *société* in terms of numbers but not of capital. The period 1930-1933 witnessed the SA asserting itself definitely over the *commandite par actions* which were marginalised in the years 1934 to 1938. Between 1930 and 1938 SAs represented between a third and a quarter of creations and accounted for a little less than two-thirds of investments either in kind or in cash.

The excellent correlation between the number of annual creations of SAs and the amount of corresponding capital measured in current francs testifies to the prime importance of financial factors.[14] Bearing in mind the size of the Paris stock market, it is tempting to think that the *sociétés* of public works contractors were in demand. This was nothing of the kind. The volume of shares issued with variable income in the building – public works – construction materials sector, has been calculated by Françoise Marnata.[15] His figures show that new issues cannot have been sufficient for the needs of the new firms of public works contractors. On average each year the total for the whole sector was only a little more than twice the total capital raised by the new firms of public works contractors alone. Moreover, in the stock market new firms of public works contractors would have to compete with not only their rivals already listed, but also more generally *sociétés* of construction materials, particularly the great concrete companies.

The principal beneficiary of the difficulties of raising finance for enterprise was the *SARL – société à responsibilité limitée* – instituted by the law of 7 March 1925. The new statute ideally suited a sector as marginal as public works contracting. From 1925 to 1929 this form of *société* was adopted in preference to *société de personnes* and *société par actions*. It was still a question of a *SARL* being of sufficient size. From the beginning to the end of the 1930s, the regime of limited liability allowed the formation of *sociétés* which drew on only reduced capital. This development made for the resilience of the SARL during the second half of the 1930s; they represented nearly half of all *sociétés* established between 1934 and 1938 and attracted more than a quarter of all registered capital.

Two predominant technical specialties

Between the two wars, the public works sector already brought together a number of special techniques. The more important were to be found in construction work and civil engineering projects, particularly the building of barrages and the use of reinforced concrete – for example, in bridges and heavy load bearing structures. Specialists in such techniques represented on average 40 per cent of the new *sociétés* established and half of the registered capital. They required more and more investment as construction work became bigger and more complex. In second place came industrial works builders, about a quarter of *sociétés* that came into being were engaged in this speciality, but only represented an eighth of the registered capital. Indeed, the attraction of this speciality declined with time. During the First World War, the sector provided a loophole for shareholders, because it was necessary urgently to build several arms factories. The pace of creations remained constant during the 1920s. On the other hand, the depression put off would-be founders of such businesses.

The creations were fairly numerous in two other specialities. Harbour and waterway works attracted a fairly continual flow of new firms, even increasing their relative share in the course of the 1930s. Of a little below average importance, not so much from the point of view of the number of formations but from the amount of capital collected, roads and aerodromes were making larger and larger claims on available funds, offering entrepreneurs attractive opportunities for profit and expansion. Other specialties experienced a very different development. Despite a relative setback during the 1930s, three specialties featured in the growth in new *sociétés* as well as in capital invested: foundation builders specialising in boring and piling; underground contractors; and sewerage and public health contractors. Electrical contractors were squeezed never representing more than a tiny proportion of creations. Of concern to potential investors was the market for electrical works, which was geared towards the larger undertakings with a high degree of integration with the large electricity companies. This imposed considerable barriers to entry, made more of an obstacle by the depression. In the case of railway contractors, and above all of steelwork constructors, there was a marked decline.

Dominance of the Parisian Region

The new *sociétés* were created principally in the Parisian region. This noticeable preponderance was due in part to a statistical bias, the *Syndicat professionnel des entrepreneurs* was much better represented there than in the rest of France. Nevertheless, the Parisian market was undeniably the strongest. An establishment in Paris had many advantages: the capital contained the leading capital market in France, the vital central services of government ministries as well as the registered offices of the large *sociétés*. At the heart of the region, central Paris itself, provided the greatest attraction, with a total of 60 per cent of new *sociétés* formed between 1916 and 1938, and an equivalent percentage of total registered capital. In the suburbs, roughly one in two of the new foundations was directed solely toward the regional market, unlike the Parisian houses. During the period from 1914 to 1938, there was a perceptible change with the suburbs prospering at the expense of central Paris.

Outside the Parisian region, some *sociétés* were formed of rather greater size than the average. This fact, at first surprising, can be explained without doubt by the success of these firms in attracting more than their fair share of investments in less dynamic markets. This feature was reinforced during the period, until between 1930 and 1938, when provincial *sociétés* accounted for nearly 40 per cent of the total registered capital against just 20 per cent during the previous decade. In terms of formations of enterprises, the region Rhônes-Alpes was ranked second in front of Nord-Pas-de-Calais which benefited from the opportunities provided by the Reconstruction. Amongst other reasons Rhônes-Alpes owed its success to the extensive opportunities offered by the Alpine hydro-electric schemes. Equally it fared better than the Parisian region in the crisis years of the 1930s. Aquitaine profited from a lack of penetration by Parisian enterprises, whereas Burgundy had the advantage of a long established fabric of competitive firms that the difficulties of the inter-war years persuaded to adopt *SA* or *SARL* status. The French Empire gave birth to a limited number of new firms. Most of these concerns working overseas were based in the metropolis. However, Morocco had a share of such enterprises as a result of their unexpected arrival during the First World War, whereas, like French Occidental Africa and Indo-China, it suffered greatly during the depression which affected Tunisia less.

The search for the underlying mechanism

The sources provided by the *Syndicat professional* does not allow a distinction to be made between the transformation of old firms and the creation of entirely new enterprises. For all that, it seems possible to overcome this difficulty at least in part.

The large enterprises born before the war: almost universal conversion to *Société Anonyme*

On tracing the history of a first sample of fifty great public works contractors all established before the First World War, it emerged that 40 per cent had by the outbreak of war adopted the status of *SA* and that of a further 2 per cent opted for this form during the conflict. During the 1920s the shift to *société anonyme* status grew rapidly with a further 40 per cent adopting this form. The Great War had only interrupted the movement which had been under way since the beginning of the century and been particularly intense in the period from 1910 to 1914 immediately before the outbreak of hostilities. It continued until 1929. Between 1919 and 1929 the extensive opportunities provided by the Reconstruction persuaded firms to look for outside capital. Until the beginning of 1925 switch to *SA* status was an acknowledgement of the inadequacy of self-finance. The process was held up in the 1930s because of the considerable difficulties firms encountered in raising external capital. From 1914 to 1939 the majority of transfers to SA status were individual firms, most commonly *sociétés en nom collectif;* in contrast there were few conversions of *sociétés en commandite simple,* as this form of business organization was not much used by large enterprises.

Of all the causes for changing to *SA* status, the most significant undoubtedly (in 55 per cent of the cases) was the necessity of enlarging the investment base of a firm to meet financial needs. Nonetheless, nearly a quarter of enterprises which adopted *SA* status, did so to enter or to master new markets. Nearly as important a motive were questions of succession: absence of an heir willing to take over the business or, more often, the need to effect a division between the claimants.

Alongside the great firms, the *SARL* did not enjoy the same popularity, although it did develop between 1925 and 1929 at the expense of individual enterprises for which it furnished a sort of protective shield. Many individual businessmen used the SARL to protect their independence. By 1939 12 per cent of firms still retained an individual form of enterprise, of *commandites simples* or, more frequently, of *sociétés en nom collectif*.

The formation of new firms: principally in the 1920s

The formation of *sociétés* corresponded usually to the creation of entirely new entities. For this reason a second cohort of fifty firms founded after the declaration of the Great War has been examined. Nearly three-quarters of them adopted the form of *SA*. The First World War in part encouraged this development, the *société anonyme* provided protection from deficiency of capital which affected enterprises engaged in defence contracts, the construction of dams and hydro-electric power stations. These creations were few and far between when compared with the dramatic increase which characterised the period of Reconstruction. Altogether 50 per cent of new firms in the sample saw the light of day during this period of which two-thirds chose the form of SA. Although the rate fell to half the level of the years 1919 to 1924, the pace of creations remained buoyant until 1929. Thereafter it fell away rapidly.

The other forms of *sociétés* did not enjoy the same popularity as SA. Amongst these there was a clear preference for *commandites par actions*. The SARL were no more favoured than in the previous sample, with less than one in ten firms created using this form. As for *sociétés de personnes*, they had a certain attraction until the middle of the 1930s; around a sixth of the firms in the sample adopted this form. If the status of *commandite simple* was not adopted by any new entity, the *entreprises individuelles* and the *sociétés en nom collectif* experienced some popularity especially between 1919 and 1924.

The motive for creation was evidently governed chiefly by technical considerations in 78 per cent of cases. It was a matter of taking advantage of new opportunities, in the first place construction of highways and electrical equipment – especially dams and power stations, but also plant and electricity lines; less important, but significant was the role of markets such as reinforced concrete works, the construction of the Paris Metro, or military engineering projects. On the other hand, only one in ten firms were established because the founders wished to gain a foothold in the colonies. Making obvious the difficulties encountered by French firms in the export trade, none of the firms were formed with the prime motive of working outside France or in the Empire.

The methods of constitution varied greatly. In 58 per cent of cases it was a matter of a formation *ex nihilo* by one or more profession businessmen. The most frequent formula was for an individual to establish a *société* by himself with the help of friendly shareholders. It therefore hardly seems surprising that the *SA* was the form most frequently adopted by new *sociétés*. Nearly a third of shareholders were, at least at the beginning, familial. More often than not these came to hold shares because a pre-existing grouping was converted into a *société autonome*. Very rarely were families persuaded to invest *ex nihilo*. Other than the two main methods of formation already described, there were two other ways; the enlargement of the business by the admission of one or more new partners, and more frequently, amalgamation between two or more *sociétés*.

Three conclusions:

1. Between 1916 and 1939 the movement for the creation of *sociétés* reflected by and large considerations beyond the metropolitan market. An overview of the sector suggests strong growth during the brief years of the Reconstruction which provided the impetus for new creations, returning to normal levels until around about 1932/33, then collapsing as a result of the gravity of the economic crisis which left little opportunity for making a success of the establishment of new enterprises. These cycles were without doubt governed more by the condition of the capital market than strictly by the demand for construction works. Moreover they disguised important differences between the patterns of development in different regions. Central Paris probably benefited most from new creations until the beginning of the 1930s, whereas thereafter the suburbs and the provinces, notably Rhône Alpes – suffered probably less than the capital itself from the sharp decline in the birth of new firms.
2. The period witnessed the victory of *sociétés capitaux* over *sociétés de personnes* above all those with *SA* and *SARL* status. *SAs* were greatly preferred during the period of the Reconstruction, not only because of the size of the demand, but also because of inflationary pressures which made the appeal to outside capital inexpensive while existing corporate funds were devalued quickly. *SA* status regained favour with the business community right at the

beginning of the 1930s, supplanting from now on very definitely the *commandite par actions*. SA status was particularly attractive for the great enterprises, the majority of which, from the end of the 1920s adopted this form. For its part, the *SARL* thrived beyond all question, but did not challenge really the *société anonyme*, except perhaps during the second half of the 1920s. The *SARL* advanced largely at the expense of the *société de personnes*, it became the preferred form of creation of small enterprises in a sector characterised by its durability, with a strong group of large firms opposing a majority of small size, usually engaged in repair work or subcontracting.
3. There was a distinction between the formation of new *sociétés* and the simple transformation of existing businesses into company form. The second, very numerous during the 1920s, were entirely justified by financial considerations. As regards the first, at least in the case of large enterprises, they were in response to the necessity of grasping technical opportunities provided by the market. It was a matter of installing in France and overseas an infrastructure of modern highways, of equipping the home country with power stations and electric lines, of endowing the Empire with bridges, ports and dams, which favoured the formation of *sociétés* with identifiable shareholdings. It is therefore easy to understand that one of the chief reasons for the decline in new formations beginning in 1933/34 was due to the drying up of these opportunities apparent, if not during the First World War – occasionally even before – but at least since the beginning of the 1920s. In stimulating much more severe competition, in reducing the marginal benefits, in favouring firms that were well established, conditions in the 1930s made it much more difficult to launch a new firm onto the market than it had been before. Has not this been the case from the second half of the 1930s until the opening of the 1980s of this century?

Footnotes

1. With F Caron (Paris IV), P Deyon and J Hirsch (Lille III), P Cayez Grenoble II), P Jobert (Dijon).
2. P Jobert, J C Chevailler, 'La démographie des entreprises en France au XIXe siècle. Quelques pistes', *Histoire, Economie, Société*, n° 2, 1986, pp 233-264.
3. P Lévêque, La patente, indicateur de croissance économique differentielle au XIXe siècle?', *Entreprises et entrepreneurs XIXe-XXe siècles* (dir. F Caron), 4e Congrès de l'Association française de historiens économistes. AFHE-03/1980, Presses de l'Université de Paris-Sorbonne – Paris IV, Paris 1984, pp 49-73. L Marco, *Le flux économique des faillites en France, 1820- 1983. Essai sur la*

mortalité des entreprises, thèse de sciences économiques Université de Paris 1, 1984.

4. P Deyon, J P Hirsch, 'Entreprise et association dans l'arrondissement de Lille: 1830-1862', *Entreprises et entrepreneurs,* op.cit., pp 5-21. J C Chevailler, 'En passant par la Franche-Comté, La démographie des entreprises française au XIXe siécle, *Document de travail n° 8801,* Université de Franche-Comté, Besançon, 01/1988, p 46.

5. Thus F Caron on sociétés in Paris during the Monarchie de Juillet or the researches of J P Allinne, M Lescure, and of A Straus and P Verley.

6. D Barjot, *La grande entreprise française de travaux publics (1883-1974); contraintes et stratégies,* Thése de Doctorat d'Etat, Dir. F Caron, Université de Paris IV, Sorbonne, 1989, 4271 p, 7 vol dactyl.

7. For lack of space, I can not show here quantitative results of my researches; these results are available by writing to me at the University of Caen, France.

8. The percentage of firms which were members of the association were 23.4 per cent during the period 1921-24 (average : 814 on about 3500) and 25.4 per cent in 1934-39 (1015 on about 4500). These members enterprises secured 46.2 per cent of the market for public works during the 1921-31 period and 44.1 per cent in the period from 1931 to 1939.

9. Ratio $\frac{\text{annual sociétés creations average number}}{\text{annual enterprises average number}}$
   This ratio reveals the depth of the crisis:
   1921-24 5.5 per cent
   1934-38 1.8 per cent

10. Correlation average rate 1921 and 1938:
    + 0.33 (civil engineering only)
    + 0.18 (civil engineering and military engineering)

11. Correlation average rate 1921-31:
    + 0.12 (civil engineering only)
    - 0.07 (civil engineering and military engineering)

12. Correlation average rate 1916-38: +0.62

13. F Caron et J Bouvier, 'Structure des firmes; emprise de l'Etat', F Baudel et E Labrousse, *Histoire économique et sociale de la France,* tome IV, Vol 2, PUF, Paris, 1980, pp 769-820. G Ripert, *Aspects juridiques du capitalisme moderne,* LGDJ, Paris, 1946, p 348.

14. Correlation average rate between the two series for 1916-38: +0.81

15. F Marnata, *La Bourse et le financement des investissements,* Série Economie française, Travaux de recherches de Sciences économiques, FNSP, Paris, 1973, p 130.

14

Bouchayer-Viallet of Grenoble: the rise and fall of a French metalworking firm, 1870–1972

Robert J Smith

The family firm as an ideal construct has figured in discussions of French economic development for over forty years, but comparatively few studies of individual firms examine in any detail the way their history and character were shaped by the family's proto-industrial origins.[1] This chapter suggests the tension in a family enterprise between an inherited rural proto-industrial mentality and a modern capitalist outlook, or in other words between the family's instinct to retain its unity, control, and authority and the firm's evolving need for new capital, management, and ideas. Descendants of rural artisan nailmakers, the Bouchayer family unconsciously attempted to preserve a family ethos that was conservative, endogamous, and rooted in a particular company and real estate. At the same time, they displayed a more modern entrepreneurial mentality as they built a formidable enterprise.[2] If this case is typical in its broad outlines, then to understand the rise and fall of family firms in France, usually within three or four generations, we should pay particular attention to whether and to what degree the family loosens its attachment to a traditional or proto-industrial mentality stressing family unity, cooperation, caution, and investments in a single factory or land, or, on the other hand, embraces such bourgeois values and goals as individualism, competition, and liquid assets.

1. The First Generation: Joseph Bouchayer (1835-1898)

According to oral tradition, in 1847 twelve-year-old Joseph Bouchayer left home in La Motte d'Aveillans, a village south of Grenoble, after he overheard his illiterate father despair of feeding everyone in a household that included ten children and assorted relatives. His father, relatives, and ancestors lived in a rural mountain environment, where they made nails and raised goats, but competition from new machines in the factories of St. Etienne in the 1840s had forced the elder Bouchayer to take work in the coal mines of La Mure at low wages, and the family's financial crisis ensued. In Grenoble, an uncle sent Joseph to a technical school (later to become the Ecole Vaucanson) for three years, after which he began work in 1852 at the firm of Hippolyte Bouvier, where over the next fifteen years he learned to make and install metal framework, boilers, heating and ventilating equipment, and other fixtures. Following this brief education and longer apprenticeship, Joseph's rise as an industrial entrepreneur began in 1861, when he married his employer's niece and became director of the shop for 25 per cent of the profits in addition to salary.

Throughout his life Joseph remained silent about his family's heritage of artisanal nailmaking, in part, perhaps, because his father never forgave him for leaving the family.[3] But like his father, he became the head of a large family, and he took up an occupation that resembled the one his father was forced to abandon. His father's failure as an independent businessman may indeed have been an incentive to build a successful enterprise for his own family. Joseph groomed his eldest son to take over his business, arranged marriages for his children that were likely to align business and family interests, and generally sought to create a durable family institution rather than merely amass a personal fortune. Unconsciously he may have fostered an endogamous family in Grenoble precisely because his father reproached him for leaving his own family in La Motte d'Aveillans.

Upon Bouvier's death in 1868, Joseph left the firm to set up his own shop in the bankrupt Tallin foundry, which he bought with savings amounting to about 40,000 francs.[4] Then in June 1870 he and Félix Viallet formed a partnership to which each contributed 40,000 francs. The purpose of their business, according to the legal agreement, remained heating and ventilation, construction and operation of gas factories, and operation of an iron foundry.[5] Not mentioned was the hydraulic conduit business that would bring the company fame by the end of the century.

The son of an entrepreneur from Grenoble, Viallet was a brilliant literary student but earned his engineering degree at the Ecole Centrale des Arts et Manufactures of Paris.[6] His education, eloquence, and urbanity complemented Joseph's remarkable practical virtues. Not only did Viallet have the formal training of an engineer, but he possessed a breadth of vision and grasp of strategy that helped propel the small enterprise forward. For instance, he initiated a policy of investment in power companies that gave his own firm influence and leverage that generated orders for construction projects, and he shrewdly anticipated expanding business by investing in capital improvements that exceeded current needs. On the other hand, although he was an equal partner at the beginning, he did not produce a family that could equal the Bouchayers in sheer numbers or talent; nor did his descendants bring fresh leadership to the firm through their marriages.[7] Thus the Viallet influence was critical only at the beginning of the story, when it decisively set the company on an engineering path that made possible the complex technological development necessary for the hydraulic conduit business.

Bouchayer and Viallet built a thriving enterprise over the next three decades. They expanded from the original Tallin property and constructed new shops for boilers, steel framework, and large conduits and pylons for electric transmission lines. During the 1880s the firm averaged 536,000 francs in sales and 56,000 francs in net profit. At the end of the century sales had reached a million francs, with net profit still somewhat higher than ten percent.[8] In the mid-1880s, the company began to install *conduites forcées*, or 'penstocks', for paper mills in the Grenoble area, and toward the end of the century these projects multiplied as the company received orders from municipalities as well as other firms to supply water to electric generating plants. From 1895 to 1900 the company's yearly output in terms of horsepower furnished to hydraulic installations rose from 20,000 to 77,000, and five years later to 158,000 HP.[9] Another indication of the firm's prosperity was the balance sheet of 1883, which attributed capital of 330,153 francs to Joseph Bouchayer, 41,938 francs to his brother Eugène, and 293,158 francs to Félix Viallet, or a total of 665,249 francs – an 832 per cent increase in capital in thirteen years.[10]

Meanwhile, Joseph brought members of his family into the business. In addition to his brother Eugène, whom he sent to the Ecole Vaucanson and who became a partner in 1885, two sons-in-law were important in the company's development. Marius Vollaire, an engineer from the Ecole des Arts et Métiers, married Joseph's second daughter, Marie, and became an effective director of operations. Joseph Prat, a graduate of the Ecole Vaucanson, joined the firm in 1884 at 18. In 1885 he joined Eugène in the sales office in Lyon, and eight years later he married Joseph's youngest daughter, Thérèse. In these marriages and associations with sons-in-law, Joseph replicated the ties that gave him his own start in a family firm. In addition to his sons-in-law, Joseph could count on his eldest son Aimé to succeed him and three other sons to assist in the business. The firm had sufficient capital and human resources to continue into the next generation as a family enterprise. Socially the Bouchayer family was not yet secure enough, perhaps, to celebrate its pre-bourgeois origins, but this heritage marked the clan all the same. The family's size and endogamous character contrasted sharply with that of Félix Viallet.

2. The Second Generation: Aimé Bouchayer (1867-1928)

After Joseph's death in 1898, initially his brother Eugène took control, but within two years, with Viallet's support, Aimé replaced him and rapidly became the leading industrialist of Grenoble and the champion of industrial growth for the entire region.[11] But for Aimé's generation, the company remained essentially a family enterprise in terms of its management as well as the control of its capital, for his three brothers and two of four brothers-in-law associated themselves with the firm in some way.

From 1898 to 1912, the company's gross sales more than tripled, rising to 3.7 million francs.[12] The firm's various shops now spread over 4.5 hectares along the Drac river, whereas in 1878 they occupied only half a hectare; the workforce rose from about 180 in 1902 to 700-800 on the eve of the First World War, or closer to 1000 if one includes the staff in Lyon and Paris and the teams on job sites; and the firm achieved a strong reputation for its engineering. Two of Aimé's brothers earned their degrees in engineering from the Ecole Centrale. Auguste joined the company and acquired a distinguished reputation for defining the standards for the fabrication of penstocks and inventing new welding techniques and other processes.[13] Meanwhile Hippolyte recognized that there was little room for him to advance within the enterprise, and so he became an independent financier, a founder of Péchiney, and a director of numerous companies. But many of these companies became clients of Bouchayer-Viallet, and during the First World War Hippolyte joined the Board of Directors of the family firm. He alone among Aimé's family colleagues constructed a life that implied rejection of the traditional family paradigm-the family centered around a single enterprise that it managed as well as owned. He built a personal fortune that was not identified with a single institution.

By 1912 Aimé Bouchayer recognized that his company required fresh capital to meet rising demand, and so he and his partners transformed the partnership into a *société anonyme*. This required finding twenty more stockholders to raise the capital from 3.2 million francs to 4 million. The sale of 4 million francs worth of bonds completed the financial manoeuvre to form the 'Etablissements Bouchayer et Viallet' (EBV).[14] Although some contemporaries believed that the investors were taking an enormous risk, even in the short run Aimé's bold move bore out his confidence. The first year showed 442,000 francs in net profit, of which 180,000 francs went to the stockholders, and the new capital permitted purchase of heavy machinery that opened up new markets.[15] Furthermore, the reorganization had no effect upon the administration of the enterprise, which the Bouchayer family continued to dominate.

The First World War created new opportunity as well as risk for a firm such as EBV, and it also served to broaden Aimé's perspective beyond the Dauphiné.[16] He came to perceive the Dauphiné in a national context, as fulfilling a special mission during the nation's crisis:

> Aside from our satisfaction to be useful to France, we will have restored to our country an industry that it had lost, for you all understand that with a force of a million horsepower, we have every right to hope that in our Dauphiné, a day will come when we will be able to create a *new metallurgy* based not on coal and ore, but on ore and White Coal [la Houille Blanche].[17]

During the war EBV manufactured bombs, shells for the famous 75s, and other war materiel as it continued some of its hydraulic projects. Many of the trained workers were drafted, but the workforce slowly rose from about 600 to 3,000 with the addition of women and prisoners of war. Aimé's appointment books reveal feverish activity that included visits to factories in the region and repeated trips to Paris, where he dined with his friend Louis Loucheur, a stockholder in EBV who became Under Secretary of State at the Ministry of Munitions in 1916.[18] For the distribution of military contracts in his region, Aimé became a central figure in discussions between Loucheur, other industrialists, and military officials.[19] In addition, he founded Grenoble's *Association des Producteurs des Alpes françaises* in 1918 and was active in many other civic groups that reflected interests transcending the Dauphiné.

Distributed profits (dividends and bonuses) as a percentage of capital increased from 7.16 per cent in 1913 to 8.36 per cent in 1916.[20] The company obtained an additional two million francs in fresh capital in 1916 to finance expansion by offering stock exclusively to the small group of old shareholders. Still in 1917 profits reached 19.09 per cent of capital. The firm's strong results continued through 1918 and 1919, with distributed profits of 16.10 per cent and 12.59 per cent of capital. In 1917 Aimé used part of the profits from these years to acquire a huge tract of land on the outskirts of the city that brought the company's holdings to over 300 hectares – a cushion for the firm in difficult times, a source of security for the stockholders.[21]

Immediately after the war Aimé committed the firm to several new ventures. The first was a factory to manufacture steel pipe by an electrolytic process developed by his brother Auguste. Unfortunately the engineering was faulty and the project was abandonned in 1926 due to a lack of clients and heavy losses. To obtain electric power for Auguste's plant, Aimé had invested heavily in an expensive but ultimately successful hydro-electric project at the confluence of the Drac and Romanche rivers (Pont-de-Claix); however, in 1927 he was forced to use these shares to repurchase some of EBV's own bonds on the open market.[22] Aimé also made EBV a major stockholder (16 per cent) in Les Chaudronneries des Pyrénées, a factory built at Tarbes in 1919 to supply *conduites forcées* to the Pyrénées, assist in the electrification of southwestern France, and furnish current to the railroad.[23] But this project too proved to be expensive, and during the entire inter-war period it drained EBV's resources without generating profits. The Chaudronnerie of Tarbes finally went out of business in 1956 during another slack period.

One creation of EBV, however, consistently showed a profit and offset losses between the wars. In 1917 Aimé set up an affiliate, the Société Dauphinoise d'Etudes et de Montages (SDEM), to carry out engineering studies and install *conduites forcées* and other equipment for hydraulic projects: EBV itself henceforth confined itself to manufacturing. Although the Bouchayer family retained most of the stock, Georges Ferrand, an outsider who had learned the business from Auguste Bouchayer, directed SDEM and was chiefly responsible for its high reputation and financial success. Ferrand's patents for lighter, more resistant, and less expensive conduits (*tuyaux auto-frettés*) placed EBV as well as SDEM in the forefront of their field.

Nevertheless, during the 1920s the market for huge conduits, floodgates for dams, and pylons deteriorated compared with the pre-war era, and thus the company's substantial fixed capital investments were far less productive than in the past.[24] Furthermore, taxes were thirty times higher than in 1913, costs of material, labour, and transportation had risen, and stagnation in savings led to a scarcity of long term capital. The firm's investments in land and stock provided some diversification, but they could not restore profitability in the hydraulic field, which had become the firms major focus. And so after presiding over two decades of dynamic growth, Aimé could achieve only mixed results in the uncertain economy of the 1920s. Nevertheless, he had built a great enterprise and refrained from allowing it to expand beyond the capacity of the extended families to control and direct it. He died suddenly of pneumonia in 1928 and left a void both at the company and in the region. Mayor of his village (Seyssinet) since 1910 and a champion of cultural and social welfare projects, he had become as much a patron of the city and the region as he was its foremost industrialist.[25] But whereas he had been one of eight children, he and his wife raised only three: Jean, Madeleine, and Maurice.[26] Like his father, however, he was determined that eventually his eldest son should succeed him.[27]

3. The Third Generation: Jean Bouchayer (1893-1988)

Under Aimé's successor, EBV faced the world economic crisis of 1930-1945 and began its decline. The company owed its survival during this period to its reputation for quality in a highly technical field that required a large amount of fixed capital for entry, to its investments in real estate, and to the strength of SDEM under Georges Ferrand.[28] At first Jean Bouchayer and his brother-in-law, Louis Le Chatelier, divided the tasks of leadership, but Jean soon emerged as the *patron* of the enterprise. Jean finished his studies at lycée Louis-le-Grand in Paris without taking the examination for Polytechnique, worked for Bouchayer-Viallet briefly in 1912-1913, and then during six years with the alpine troops learned to command.[29] Yet this authoritative presence concealed a lack of commitment to the family enterprise that contrasted sharply with his two predecessors. By nature Jean had a literary and philosophical turn of mind, and he was distracted by hobbies – genealogical studies, stamps, and books. Years later (1960) he acknowledged that he gave less of his time to the enterprise than his father had.[30]

From 1928 to 1954, the period of Jean Bouchayers effective control of the firm, the irregular shifts in net profit reflected the political and economic environment rather than any drastic reorganization or initiative on his part. The days of expansion such as Aimé Bouchayer experienced had passed.[31] Assets sold during these years remained higher than dividends in re-evaluated francs;[32] the company survived the Depression and the ensuing war because of its past accomplishments and especially because of the presence of SDEM's Georges Ferrand in the shops of EBV.

As World War II came to an end, the firm received more orders, and productive hours increased, but inflation, slow payment by clients, and a rapid increase in salaries undermined the recovery and led to rising debt. There followed a highly prosperous period from 1948 to 1952, when the Marshall and Monnet plans produced favorable conditions: in 1950, for instance, return on equity reached 12.6 per cent. But even in this period profit margins were lower than they were in similarly favorable periods before the war.[33] Throughout the lean years, EBV had maintained its reputation for quality and could respond to renewed demand for hydroelectric facilities. But there were signs that international as well as domestic competition had become severe and would pose problems in the future, especially since Jean Bouchayer failed to anticipate changing markets or changing business conditions.

4. The Fourth Generation: Robert Bouchayer (1919-)

Jean Bouchayer remained President until 1963, but in 1954 he yielded effective leadership of the company to his son Robert, the eldest of four children. Because of the German occupation of Paris, Robert took an engineering degree in Grenoble rather than attending the Ecole Centrale. He then worked for Peugeot before joining SDEM in January 1946, where he profited from the tutelage of Georges Ferrand. He and his father, however, differed sharply in mentality, style, and perception of the industrial situation. Jean gave the impression that the ancestral enterprise was basically sound, that once the economic climate improved, the company would regain its former prosperity.[34] He issued no orders for restructuring and maintained the traditional paternalistic tone with respect to the workforce. Robert, on the other hand, identified weaknesses and proposed sweeping changes in the company's procedures and organization. Having become Adjunct Director General of SDEM as well as Vice-President of EBV, in 1956 he delivered an impassioned report to the *Conseil* in which he seized upon a large deficit to criticize the governing structure of EBV, the 'older generation,' and implicitly his father.[35] His reports demonstrated a grasp of the company's history and financial situation and conveyed his determination to bring about a change in philosophy and a departure from the paternalistic 'family firm' model.

He directed a new *Bureau de Méthodes* to analyze work, to 'Taylorize' the manufacturing process, and to institute 'planning'; he instituted a programme of investment in new machines and sought to make better use of those on hand; and finally he pointed out that autofinancing, the method of the past, was inadequate for current capital requirements: land should be sold and new stock and bonds should be issued.[36] His leadership affected employees immediately, for he instituted cost accounting and insisted upon the accountability of personnel.[37]

Despite reforms with respect to the personnel, by 1959 the company's prospects had not markedly improved. From 1950 through 1957 – a period of recession, price freeze, and intense competition – there was a net loss of 10 million francs. Although the company distributed 25 million in dividends, it also sold off over 150 million of its capital (land to Péchiney).[38] The company remained unprofitable in large part because Electricité de France, the principal customer, placed few orders for penstocks and floodgates, the products best suited to the company's investment in machinery and engineering.

Thus, early in the 1960s, Robert began to explore alliances with other firms so that his own company might survive.[39] Undeveloped land, however, comprised an important part of capital assets that stockholders feared jeopardizing in a failing industrial enterprise; this land also, by inflating the company's assets, proved to be an impediment to long term government financing or combination with another company. So Robert divided EBV into several smaller firms, created an industrial holding company, and made the original EBV into a super holding company that controlled both industrial assets and real estate. The objective was to permit these smaller and more homogeneous firms to form alliances with outside companies that would bring capital, expertise, and markets. Robert had concluded, in short, that in the current economic climate, EBV produced too great a variety of products for its size: because of its overall structure, including high fixed costs, none of its products were competitive. In 1964 the most significant joint venture – Bouchayer-Viallet-Schneider (BVS) – transferred the manufacturing of conduits and other large steel equipment for hydraulic projects (about 90 per cent of the business) to the Société des Forges et Ateliers du Creusot (Schneider) or SFAC, thus achieving vertical integration that produced a far more profitable enterprise than the two companies had achieved separately.[40] EBV retained only 45 per cent of this company and thus lost control; Robert became its Vice-President. Next in importance, SDEM, after having been absorbed by EBV, in 1959, regained its independence and continued to prosper while remaining under the control of the Bouchayer group. Other enterprises spun off or created on paper proved to be less successful.[41] In 1967 only BVS made a profit, and this was not sufficient to counterbalance the losses suffered by the others.[42]

Meanwhile the holding company, Société anonyme d'Etudes de Gestion et de Participations Bouchayer et Viallet (SABV), could not invest in other industrial enterprises since the super holding – the new role of EBV – encountered delays in developing its land.[43] All of this highly complex manoeuvring, of course, represented a radical departure for this family firm and generated opposition among stockholders who failed to grasp the incongruity between the requirements of the times and the traditional institution that they had inherited. Hence Robert's decision to gain time for one of the industrial affiliates to pay its debts by declaring bankruptcy gave a coterie of stockholders the occasion to oppose him. Shocked by the bankruptcy and supported by Jean Bouchayer, they were able to remove Robert from the Presidency and proceed to sell the remaining industrial capital rather than risk it in new ventures. As an industrial enterprise the history of Bouchayer-Viallet came to an end. Some stockholders retained shares in SDEM, which now is an affiliate of Neyrpic and Alsthom, part of CGE (Compagnie Générale d'Electricité); and some retained shares in BVS, which fell entirely under the control of SFAC. Of the old heritage only a real estate enterprise, Omnium, remained in Grenoble to dispose of land that had long been a mixed blessing.

5. Conclusion

The rise and fall of Bouchayer-Viallet depended in part upon economic factors over which the Bouchayer family had little control and in part upon the family itself. In the minds of the principal actors, conservative instincts vied with modern ones acquired through experience in a growing industrial economy. The purpose of this paper has been to present the family as a central theme reflecting the tension between past and present. Ultimately, the firm's survival hinged upon the family's capacity to adapt to changing circumstances.

In some respects there was little change over four generations. The family remained socially endogamous in that marriages brought only engineers, industrialists, or merchants into the clan. Although this homogeneity may have been a source of strength, it also suggested a certain narrowness that circumscribed the growth of individuals and limited the horizons of the family as a whole. The men were expected to study engineering if they continued their education beyond the lycée. Jean Bouchayer, a gifted student of letters who abandoned his studies rather than face examinations for the Ecole Polytechnique, may have suffered from the unacknowledged psychological burden of such a tradition . Similarly, a traditional view of family structure and authority underlay the rigid succession of eldest sons from Joseph to Robert.

Some family traditions changed as the firm prospered. Although Joseph's wife Joséphine participated in the firm as its accountant and paymaster even as she raised eight children, the women in succeeding generations were not involved directly in the enterprise but ran their households and engaged in social activities. The size of families also changed. Joseph had nine siblings, and he and Joséphine raised eight children of their own, but in the next two generations the eldest sons raised families of three and four. As the Bouchayers rose into Grenoble's upper bourgeoisie, their demographic pattern and the role of the women changed. As a result the pool of potential managers and engineers for the business diminished.

During the first generation, when there was a favorable economic climate for metal goods, Joseph's conservative mentality proved to be no impediment to the firm's growth. Under his patriarchal authority the family and the business became prosperous as a single institution. His son Aimé was also a stern patriarch, but in other respects he was the antithesis of the traditionally conservative head of a family firm. He invested aggressively in plant capacity, land, and other operations, transformed the partnership into a joint stock company, and established an affiliate under the direction of a talented engineer from outside the family. Moreover, his interests transcended family and firm to include social and cultural projects in Grenoble and the Dauphiné.

Aimé himself had little time to write history, but an address during the First World War about metallurgy in the Dauphiné revealed that he understood the history of his industry.[44] His knowledge of region may well have come in large part from his brother Auguste, who became well established as a man of letters. Not only did Auguste write histories of the Drac river and the iron industry of the Chartreuse, but he produced studies of his own family history as well that linked the metallurgists of Bouchayer-Viallet with his ancestors of La Motte d'Aveillans.[45] For the first time, members of this generation acquired and began to express in literary form a sense of their history and place.

Aimé's son Jean also possessed an impressive grasp of general and family history, but it did not serve as a key to the future. As if to turn his back on pressing problems of his time, he spent countless hours tracing his own ancestry to demonstrate that he had descended from Roman emperors via Charles Martel, Pepin the Short, and Charlemagne. He was erudite, but unable to draw on his sense of history to infuse his enterprise with a sense of purpose, as his father had done. Long before the rupture with his son Robert, Jean demonstrated by his genealogical interests (not confined to his own family), that the richest treasures lay in the past, not the future. In this case the family, according to its traditions, had assigned the role of leadership to an heir unsuited for it.

Jean's son Robert resembled his grandfather in that he saw the firm in a particular geographical and historical context. For Aimé that context was the Dauphiné, which provided attractive industrial opportunities, and for Robert it was the new Europe, which created severe challenges in terms of markets, competition, and reorganization. Robert's reports to the Board of Directors frequently included long historical introductions that put the current crisis in perspective and sketched alternatives for the future. Since it was not feasible for Bouchayer-Viallet to become vertically integrated and efficient in the Chandlerian sense, Robert sought to develop strategies of reorganization that were appropriate at that historical moment. Not lacking a sense of time and place, Robert failed to revive the company for other reasons.

He was thwarted in part by an unfortunate combination of business circumstances – poor management of one of the affiliates, a decline in the market for housing, the construction of a highway exit that undermined a comprehensive plan to develop land, and, perhaps most fundamentally, the company's inevitable loss of a privileged position in a field that it had dominated technologically for decades. Jean Bouchayer had done no planning to anticipate the time when the company would have to enter new fields in order to survive. His genealogical studies reflected his preoccupation with continuity, with maintaining a business that he had inherited. Robert, however, understood that to survive, the ancestral enterprise had to transform itself drastically, but he was pushed aside when many of the more conservative stockholders remained loyal to his father. Over a decade earlier, Robert alluded to the gulf between the generations in a speech before Grenoble's Rotary Club entitled 'Le Chef d'Entreprise':

> We are different from our fathers, and sometimes they reproach us for it, saying that a gulf separates us, but we answer that we do not find, frankly, that they have always been right. Our childhood and adolescence were filled with crises and war. We heard our leaders criticized one after another: everything went wrong in France. So who is there to admire, what great men to imitate? . . . but with tact and heart on both sides, fathers and sons can constitute a team. Sons should receive from their fathers something inestimable, *confidence,* but in exchange they will give them a gift of a *second youth,* if they really want it.[46]

The reconciliation that Robert sought never occurred, and the final drama of Bouchayer-Viallet that ensued was implicitly a conflict between Robert and his father over the nature of the firm.

This is a case history of two institutions that were intertwined – the family and the firm. They proved to be eminently compatible for two generations: indeed the loyalty, aspirations, and energy of the family members were largely responsible for the firms existence and success. Eventually, however, the firm outgrew the family as economic conditions changed: it required capital and leadership from a far broader pool than any family was likely to sustain over several generations. During the first half of its existence, the firm prospered from a rich local and regional market, but later it had to face stiff competition in national and international markets. All of the options for survival – combinations with other firms, vertical integration, or large infusions of capital – involved the family's loss of control. Since family and firm remained inextricably linked, it is remarkable that Bouchayer-Viallet survived so long in a treacherous economic climate.

Footnotes

1. See in particular: Alain Baudant, *Pont-à-Mousson (1918-1939): stratégies industrielles d'une dynastie lorraine* (Paris: Publications de la Sorbonne, 1980); Jean-Pierre Daviet, *Un destin international: la Compagnie de Saint-Gobain de 1830 à 1939* (Paris: Editions des Archives Contemporaines, 1988); Catherine Omnès, *De l'atelier au groupe industriel: Vallourec, 1882-1978* (Paris: Editions de la Maison des Sciences de l'Homme, 1980).
2. I am grateful to Robert Bouchayer for sharing his knowledge of the firm and the family, from which much of this account is derived, and for permitting me access to private family archives (hereafter ARB). This collection includes his own writings about the family, notably: *Bouchayer: Livre I* and *Mémoire pour servir à l'histoire des Etablissements Bouchayer et Viallet*.
3. Robert Bouchayer, 'Chronique des Bouchayer: le fondateur des EBV et ses trois fils..
4. Robert Bouchayer, *Bouchayer*, op.cit., p.48.
5. ARB: 'Convention de société', 20 June 1870.
6. I am grateful to Pierre Viallet for interviews in which he supplied information about his grandfather and the firm.
7. In each revision of the company's charter, Viallet's share of the enterprise declined and the Bouchayer family share increased as relatives invested in it: ARB: 'Conventions de Société'.
8. Aimé Bouchayer's account book: ARB
9. Bouchayer & Viallet, *Conduites d'eau sous pression pour usines hydrauliques* (np: nd), p.17.
10. Photocopies of balance sheets: ARB. Louis Bergeron, in his *Les Capitalistes en France (1780-1914)* (Paris: Editions Gallimard, 1978), p.60, notes: 'La

construction mécanique a été pendant plus d'un siècle un secteur particuliérement ouvert aux ascensions individuelles, du temps des premiéres machines textiles à celui des premières automobiles. Il valorise en effet au plus haut point l'esprit d'invention, ou simplement l'ingéniosité et' habileté d'exécution, et se prête avec une grande souplesse aux agrandissements successifs à partir du petit atelier où s'est élaboré le prototype qui, en cas de succès, fait affluer les commandes et allèche les capitaux'.

11. Concerning the growth of the idea of an alpine region and Aimé Bouchayer's role as president of the Association des Producteurs des Alpes Françaises (APAF), see: Philippe Veitl, 'De Nice au Léman, l'impossible 'invention'de la région des Alpes françaises', *Le Monde alpin et rhodanien* (1987), 133-144; and 'Le Sol ou l'usine: la création des régions Clémentel et l'invention de la région des Alpes françaises', *Revue internationale d'action communautaire* (Autumn, 1989).

12. 'Historique', a company document of 1912 to announce its change of statute and offer of stock and bonds: ARB.

13. See: Jean Linossier, 'Un siècle de conduite forcée en France', *Des entreprises pour produire de l'électricité* (Paris: Association pour l'histoire de l'électricité en France, 1988), 307-309.

14. 'Procès verbaux des Assemblées Générales' (hereafter AG), 31 October 1912: Archives Départementales de l'Isère (hereafter ADI), 73 J 4.

15. Ibid., 28 March 1914, p. 5.

16. Entries in Aimé Bouchayer's daily agenda books reveal the intensity of his patriotism: he followed the course of the war closely and expressed elation or sadness as the war progressed, always vowing that the struggle should continue to ultimate victory: ARB.

17. 'Métallurgie en France et en Dauphiné, son passé, son avenir', reported in *Le Petit Dauphinois,* 16, 17, and 18 Feb., 1917.

18. 'Procés Verbaux, Conseil d'Administraion' (hereafter CA), 21 December 1916, ADI 73 J I, p. 118.

19. This is clear from his agenda book: ARB. In 1917 Aimé was named President of the 'XIXe Groupement des Industriels de l'Armement', an organization charged with distributing coal and raw materials to factories working for national defense in the five departments of Dauphiné and Savoie. CA, 27 June 1917, ADI 73 J 1, p. 146.

20. Figures for total sales for the war years have not yet been located, and so we have used dividends as a percentage of par value of capital stock as a measure of profitability.

21. Recalling that his father 'liked to invest in land', Jean Bouchayer recounted

that during the war, for example, he bought land cheaply at Pont-de-Claix and then resold it to Gillet of Lyon, who created Chlore Liquide. Jean Bouchayer insisted, however, that his father did not buy land simply as a speculation, but much more as an investment in companies like Chlore Liquide that brought something useful to the region. Interview, 22 July 1987.

22. CA, 16 Sept. 1926, 18 April 1930, 25 Oct. 1930, ADI 73 J 2.
23. CA, 30 January 1920, ADI 73 J 1, p. 248.
24. AG, 20 Sept. 1927, ADI 73 J 4, pp. 113-113b. G. Tochon, 'L'aménagement des chutes d'eau et la crise actuelle', *Les alpes économiques,* May 1927, 133-145.
25. For his political and social ideas, such as support of welfare for workers controlled locally by the *patronat*, see his speeches at meetings of the APAF: *Les Alpes économiques,* May 1919, 4-7; July 1923, 120-122; November 1923, 217-218; June-July 1926, 88-90; November-December 1926, 154-160. In the list of his honors and affiliations, there were 56 items, of which 25 pertained to educational, scientific, social, or civic organizations that conferred no remuneration. *Aimé Bouchayer, 1867-1928: Discours prononcés à ses funérailles le 4 mai 1928 (n.p.: n.d.).*
26. Only three of his siblings raised families: Hippolyte, 5 children; Auguste 4; and Thérèse Prat 3.
27. Letters to Jean during the war: ARB. Interview with Jacques Bouchayer, 11 July 1989.
28. On Ferrand and SDEM, see: Jean Linossier, *La Dauphinoise: histoire d'une entreprise au pays de la houille blanche* (Grenoble: Presses Universitaires de Grenoble, 1989).
29. In 1923 he was decorated with the Légion d'honneur on the basis of his war record. Robert Bouchayer, *Bouchayer,* op.cit., p.83.
30. 'J'aurais dû . . . m'efforcer de mériter ma place par un labeur et un dévouement total à mon industrie. Or je me suis laissé entraîner à une quarantaine de fonctions annexes qui ont dispersé mes efforts'. From an address given in 1960 on his award of a rosette of the Légion d'honneur, cited in: Robert Bouchayer, *Bouchayer,* p. 85.
31. See Robert Bouchayer's report: 'Note d'information sur la politique générale des EBV; fusion EBV – Joya – SDEM, 1 July 1959', p. 2, ADI 73 J 2032.
32. *Ibid.*, p. 2.
33. AG [Annual Reports], ADI 73 J 4, 5; In a report dated 27 April 1954, Robert Bouchayer noted (p. 2) that by 1951 the total sales curve dipped *below* the tonnage curve, whereas in a 'normal' year the two were together. He concluded that from this point E.B.V. was incurring regular losses. ADI 73 J 2031.

34. Jean Bouchayer: interview, 22 July 1987. CA, *passim*, ADI 73 J 2-3.
35. Report to CA, 25 May 1956, ADI 73 J 2031.
36. Report to CA, 6 September 1955, ADI 73 J 2031.
37. Report to CA, 23 June 1955, ADI 73 J 203.
38. A Report by Robert Bouchayer: 'Eclatement de la Société-Coût de l'Opération', ADI 73 J 2032.
39. 'Recherche aux Partenaires: Procés Verbaux de la Réunion du Comité du 17 Oct. 1962', ADI 73 J 2033.
40. Two earlier attempts to combine with foreign firms proved unprofitable: in 1949, the formation of Condotte Forzate (COFOR) with the Italian company Terni; in 1963, Bouchayer-Viallet Espanola with the Spanish firm Zabala.
41. These included: Alpes-Rhône (boilers), Générale d'Equipment (milk tanks), DITECHNIC (housing construction), and RIBSAN (faucets).
42. AG, 10 May 1967, ADI 73 J 2035.
43. Undated draft report to the *Conseil d'Administration* [1968], ADI 73 J 2035.
44. See n.17.
45. See, for example: *Les Chartreux, maitres de forges* (Grenoble: Edition Didier et Richard, 1927); 'Batteurs de vergettes: une famille de cloutiers, les Bouchayer du mandement de la Motte', (unpublished); and 'A mes cent neveux' (privately printed). I am grateful to Robert Bouchayer for these works.
46. From text of Robert Bouchayer's address (22 January 1957), ADI 73 J 2193.